Planning Futures

THE UN

SYDNEY JON

Please return or renew, on or before
fine is payable on late returned items.
recalled after one week for the use of anothe.
may be renewed by telephone:- 0151 794 - 267

S.J
2 6 SE

For conditi

Planning Futures

New Directions for Planning Theory

edited by Philip Allmendinger and
Mark Tewdwr-Jones

London and New York

First published 2002
by Routledge
11 New Fetter Lane, London EC4P 4EE

Simultaneously published in the USA and Canada
by Routledge
29 West 35th Street, New York, NY 10001

Routledge is an imprint of the Taylor & Francis Group

Typeset in Akzidenz Grotesk by Wearset Ltd, Boldon, Tyne and Wear
Printed and bound in Great Britain by Biddles Ltd, Guildford and King's Lynn

British Library Cataloguing in Publication Data
A catalogue record for this book is available from the British Library

Library of Congress Cataloging in Publication Data
Planning futures : new directions for planning theory / edited by Philip Allmendinger and Mark Tewdwr-Jones.
   p. cm.
  Includes bibliographical references.
  ISBN 0-415-27003-0 – ISBN 0-415-27004-9 (pbk.)
  1. Policy sciences. 2. Planning. 3. Social planning. I. Allmendinger, Philip, 1968– II. Tewdwr-Jones, Mark.

H97 .P59 2001
320'.6–dc21

2001041852

Contents

List of illustrations

FIGURES

TABLES

List of contributors

Philip Allmendinger is Senior Lecturer in the Department of Land Economy, University of Aberdeen and the Director of the European Urban and Regional Research Centre, Scotland. His previous publications include *Urban Planning and the British New Right* (with Huw Thomas, Routledge, 1998), *Planning Beyond 2000* (with Mike Chapman, John Wiley, 1999), *Planning in Postmodern Times* (Routledge, 2001) and *Planning Theory* (Macmillan, 2001). He is currently undertaking research on Scottish planning after devolution.

Heather Campbell is Professor of Town and Regional Planning at the University of Sheffield, UK. Her research interests include planning theory and its interaction with practice, the interrelationships between the state, society and the development industry and technological change and innovation. In the case of the former she is currently working with Robert Marshall to explore the ethical dimensions of theory and practice in planning.

Bent Flyvbjerg is Professor of Planning at the Department of Development and Planning at Aalborg University, Denmark. He is the author of numerous publications in twelve languages, and his most recent books include *Rationality and Power* (University of Chicago Press, 1998) and *Making Social Science Matter* (Cambridge University Press, 2000).

Neil Harris is Lecturer in Statutory Planning at the Department of City and Regional Planning at Cardiff University, Wales. Neil is interested in questions concerning the utilisation of theoretical frames, in this case communicative planning theory, to assess planning practices. He has published on issues of both planning theory and practice in a series of journals, including the *Environment and Planning* series, *Planning Practice and Research*, *Journal of Planning and Environment Law* and the *Journal of Planning Education and Research*. In addition to his theoretical interests, Neil has undertaken contract research for a range of public sector and charitable organisations in the UK on various aspects of planning policy and development control.

Philip Harrison is Professor of Town and Regional Planning at the University of the Witwatersrand, Johannesburg, South Africa. He was previously an Associate Professor at the University of Natal, Durban, and has worked as a planner in both the public and private sectors. He has served as an adviser to national, provincial and local governments in areas such as integrated development planning and regional policy. His research interests and publications relate to the fields of planning history, planning theory, and local economic development. He also serves on various profession-related bodies and is on the editorial board of two journals.

Jean Hillier is Professor of Urban and Regional Studies at Curtin University in Perth, Western Australia. Her research enquiries into the politics of local planning decision-making and the role of communication and power-plays in planning decisions have resulted in the publication of an extensive range of articles and chapters in edited collections. She is the author of a forthcoming book, *Shadows of Power* (Routledge, 2002) and an edited volume, *Habitus: A Sense of Place* (Ashgate, 2002).

Margo Huxley is an expert in public policy and urban and regional planning and has taught at a number of Australian universities, and has most recently been employed as Associate Professor in Urban Policy at RMIT University, Melbourne. She is currently undertaking a doctoral thesis in Geography at the Open University, UK, developing a Foucauldian approach to urban planning as a spatial technology of governmentality. She has researched and published widely in the fields of critical and feminist urban studies and planning, as well as contributing to the work of community action groups. Her recent publications include work published in the *Journal of Planning Education and Research*, in addition to various book chapter contributions.

Robert Marshall is Senior Lecturer in the Department of Town and Regional Planning at the University of Sheffield, UK. His research interests are in planning history, environmental policy and values, ethics and planning practice. His recent work has focused on the latter, a project he has pursued jointly with Professor Heather Campbell. This has resulted in several journal articles and he is currently preparing with Heather Campbell a book with the provisional title of *Public Values and Private Interests: Moral Action and Planning*.

Mark Oranje is Associate Professor in the Department of Town and Regional Planning at the University of Pretoria, South Africa. His primary research interests are planning theory, policy and history. One area to which he has devoted considerable attention has been the rationale, role and methodology of planning under postmodern conditions.

Mark Pennington is Lecturer in Public Policy at Queen Mary College, University of London, UK. He has written widely on the political economy of planning and environmental policy and has published *Planning and the Political Market: Public Choice and the Politics of Government Failure* (Athlone, 2000), the first book-length attempt to analyse the UK planning system from a public choice perspective. More recently, he has written a series of papers with Yvonne Rydin examining the role of 'social capital' in local environmental policy. At present, he is looking at the hermeneutic elements in Hayek's economics and the implications of these for green politics and the theory of deliberative democracy.

Tim Richardson is Lecturer in Town and Regional Planning at the University of Sheffield, UK. His research interests include using Foucauldian discourse analytic approaches to explore transport and environmental policy-making, European spatial policy, and public participation in planning. He has worked on environmental and planning issues with a range of organisations including the Council for the Protection of Rural England.

Mark Tewdwr-Jones is Reader in Spatial Planning and Governance at the Bartlett School of Planning, University College London, UK. He has published many books and papers devoted to planning theory, the politics of urban planning and development, housing and planning policy, planning professionalism, governance, regionalism and devolution, and the relationship between regulatory processes and regional economic development. He is the author of *The European Dimension of British Planning* (with Richard H. Williams, Spon, 2001), *Rural Second Homes in Europe* (with Nick Gallent, Ashgate, 2000), and is the editor of *British Planning Policy in Transition* (UCL Press, 1996). He is currently completing work on planning, government and the policy process, spatial planning and peripherality, and housing in the European countryside.

Preface

Planning theory is currently in a confused state as a consequence of a number of changes over the last ten years. The demise of Marxism, the rise of new theoretical ideas in the social sciences, the assertion of interests based on gender, ethnicity and regionalism, the narrow scope of planning as a professional practice as opposed to an academic subject, and the rise of pragmatic reformism as a response to the dominance of capitalist processes, have all clouded the planning theory landscape. Even prior to these events, planning theory was an uncertain discipline, reflecting planning's precarious position between and resting upon a range of professional subject areas and philosophical roots. We believe it is time to attempt to pin down the constantly evolving landscape of planning theory and to chart a path through this fast-changing field.

The book intentionally takes collaborative planning as a focus from which other theoretical strands can be considered and which are currently the subject of academic interest. Our intention here is not to reduce collaborative planning's status as a valid and valued area of academic study; it is rather to explore related theories, issues and concerns within the planning field which have emerged from or reacted to collaborative theory's dominant position as one of the main paradigms of and for twenty-first century planning. As a consequence, we see this volume as a review of the current state of planning theory combined with critiques of the practical concerns of professional planning discussed within a strong theoretical context.

We hope the book is viewed as an up-to-date reader on planning theory, but we would also like the work to be seen as one that adds something more to the subject area than merely a textbook since we have explicitly required contributors to attempt to bridge theory and practice while putting forward new theoretical ideas. Many of the chapters draw upon examples from planning practice and case study scenarios to enrich the discussion; this is intended to ensure that the work discusses planning theory within the context of present planning practice. We have also been concerned that the book does not become a rehash of existing social theories within a planning discourse and have therefore encouraged contributors to illuminate professional practice by presenting a series of theorisations of actual planning cases. Nevertheless, the case studies that are presented are drawn from professional planning practice as it exists in not only the UK and other European countries but also in Australia and South Africa, and all have relevance for the form and practice of planning – and academic studies of planning – internationally.

The book is structured into three parts. Following the Introduction, Part I introduces the reader to Planning Thoughts and Perspectives and current debates on collaborative planning and carefully positions these against an alternative Foucauldian perspective of planning. This sets the debate for the chapters that follow. Part II then turns attention to Planning Praxis and Interfaces by exploring professional practice issues within the theoretical discussion outlined in Part I; this covers framing, ethics, values and gender in planning decision-making. Finally, Part III debates Planning Movements and Trajectories by considering some alternative perspectives of planning and planning theory, including pragmatism, postmodernism, and neo-liberalism. The final chapter makes an attempt to draw themes together by offering some brief conclusions.

On the whole, we hope the book proves to be a useful contribution to planning theory debates generally, and for both the development of new planning theorising and informed professional practice in particular. We intend the book to be used not only by undergraduate and postgraduate students of planning, urban studies, geography and political science, but also by theorists and practitioners, all of whom are searching for their own ways to pin down the post-positivist landscape of planning.

Philip Allmendinger
Aberdeen
Mark Tewdwr-Jones
London
April 2001

Acknowledgements

The editors are grateful to a number of individuals for their support and encouragement in aiding the progress of this book. Tentative ideas for an edited planning theory book originated as a possibility over coffee at the 'Once Upon a Planner's Day' planning theory conference in Pretoria in January 1998, and so we are particularly grateful to our hosts Mark Oranje, Phil Harrison and others for their initial enthusiasm. We would also wish to take this opportunity to express our thanks to a number of other individuals who have helped develop our theoretical thoughts over the last ten years, including Ernest Alexander, Mike Batty, Philip Cooke, Michael Dear, John Forester, Patsy Healey, Judy Innes, Ted Kitchen, Gordon MacLeod, Jon Murdoch, Nick Phelps, Yvonne Rydin, Huw Thomas, Nigel Thrift, Geoff Vigar, Chris Webster, and Chris Yewlett. Some of these were kind enough to read initial drafts of the manuscript and we are grateful for their suggested amendments and additions. Finally, and not least, we would like to express our thanks to Susan Dunsmore, our copy-editor, and Routledge for being prepared to run with this project and for all the assistance provided by the editorial and marketing team in progressing the manuscript so smoothly from first draft to publication.

Introduction

THE AIMS AND STRUCTURE OF THE BOOK

The current landscape of planning theory is a mixture of theoretical perspectives dominated by post-positivist understandings and heavily orientated towards the communicative or collaborative planning approach. The future of planning theory is being set without, it would seem, a critical engagement with the thrust of communicative and collaborative planning. This book aims to provide such a critique from a number of different perspectives. First, it will seek to engage with the collaborative planning approach in relation to a number of important issues:

- Power. How does planning theory seek to expose and neutralise powerful interests and is it realistic to expect planning to achieve this?
- Rationality. Will planning theory provide forms of rationality that can challenge powerful interests and provide a basis for collective action and understanding?
- Ethics and professionalism. What are the implications of new developments in planning theory for questions of ethics and professional practice? What new roles, if any, will planners be expected to fill?
- Practice and participation. How can planning theory be used as a basis for planning practice and what kinds of 'participatory stance' on the planners' part does it suggest?

Second, planning theory will be analysed from the perspective of a number of existing schools of planning thought:

- neo-pragmatism
- the postmodern turn
- neo-liberalism.

The result, we think, is a needed critical engagement with collaborative planning theory from a variety of perspectives that adds to our understanding of the current landscape of planning theory. The book is divided into three Parts: Part I Planning

Thoughts and Perspectives considers some of the current and emerging schools of planning thought centred around Habermasian and Foucauldian theories. Part II Planning Praxis and Interfaces considers issues relating to professionalism, values, ethics, participation and gender within the planning arena and debates the extent to which theory is useful in dissecting these issues. Part III Planning Movements and Trajectories considers planning from neo-liberal, pragmatic and postmodern perspectives against the Habermasian communicative and collaborative planning and Foucauldian discussions developed in Part I.

1

The Post-Positivist Landscape of Planning Theory
Philip Allmendinger

INTRODUCTION

The *leitmotif* of planning and social theory over the past two decades or so has been *post*: postmodern, post-structuralist and post-positivist. Whether one argues that planning theory has developed within this spirit (e.g. postmodernism) or in constructive opposition to it (e.g. communicative planning) its influence cannot be denied or ignored. Here, the term 'post', as in the debates over 'post'-modern, does not necessarily follow the strict definition of 'after'. 'Post' is just as likely to mean a *development of* that is significantly different from the original. In this respect, the 'post' of planning theory discussed above (under a wide definition) has been part of and has been heavily influenced by wider shifts in understanding and sensibilities in social theory and the philosophy of science. Planning theory is deeply embedded within social theory generally – communicative planning and critical theory are an example of how both normative and empirical/positive theories have been fused into planning thought. This shift in social theory has involved a questioning of the logic of positivism and the basis to scientific knowledge generally, which sought the discovery of a set of general methodological rules or forms of inference that would be the same in all sciences:

> 'Post-empiricism' signifies a loss of faith in this essentialist epistemology as the proper guide in the philosophy of science, and calls into question the very idea of such a 'logic', as well as all those distinctions – hermeneutic or positivist – which rested upon it.
>
> (Bohman, 1991: 17)

While debates between, for example, positivists and materialists in planning theory naturally continue (see, for example, Farthing, 2000), there have been new developments in old thinking and the emergence of new paradigms, as Muller (1998) has termed them, that have been heavily influenced by such a shift. Like the definition of 'post', whether this amounts to a new paradigm or not is open to question (Taylor, 1999).

In addition to the problems of using the term 'post', one must also be cautious in being too deterministic and remember that shifts in theory may be and often are unrelated to the practice of planning. The feeling that we are living in New Times, as critics of postmodernism point out, has been omnipresent for at least a thousand years. I have argued elsewhere (Allmendinger, 1998) that it is too simplistic to present planning as being either modern or postmodern. The terms themselves do not help in understanding planning practice and miss the rich context within which planning operates. Is a search for consensus 'terroristic' in Lyotard's (1984) terms or a true reflection of genuine sameness or agreement?

With the caveats regarding the meaning of 'post' in mind, three questions arise: *why* has this shift to 'post' come about, *what* does the 'post' shift mean, and *how* can planning practice adapt to meet these new ways of thinking?

WHY 'POST'?

The history of social theory generally has been characterised by debates concerning the differences between the natural and human sciences and distinctions: in method, explanation and understanding; in domain, objects and subjects or nature and culture; and in purpose, technical control and increased understanding (Baert, 1998). The naturalists and positivists, on the one hand, and the hermeneutic or 'interpretative sociologies' understandings, on the other, both existed in isolation. Both broad schools were convinced that they offered a privileged insight into knowledge of society.

Planning has a history of practices and thinking that relates to philosophies, epistemologies and theories broadly associated with modernism and positivism (Goodchild, 1990: 128–129; Low, 1991: 234; Healey, 1993b: 234). One consequence of this, as Sandercock points out, is that this association has crowded out other approaches:

> The social sciences have been dominated by a positivist epistemology which privileges scientific and technical knowledge over an array of equally important alternatives – experiential, intuitive, local knowledges; knowledges based on practices of talking, listening, seeing, contemplating, sharing; knowledges expressed in visual and other symbolic, ritual and artistic ways rather than in quantitative or analytical modes based on technical jargons that by definition exclude those without professional training.
>
> (1998c: 5)

Such approaches became hegemonic and, according to Taylor (1998), few planners or social thinkers queried the plans or the character of knowledge with which they dealt particularly if they emulated the methods of natural science – naturalism, or the unity of method between the natural and social sciences, was accepted as given. As Beiner points out, 'Hobbes saw classical mechanics as supplying the proper "abstractive" method, while Durkheim preferred the holistic features of biology'. Nevertheless, such naturalism, which dominated the social sciences and planning for most of the nineteenth century, began to breakdown in the 1960s and 1970s.

Two reasons can be identified for the shift in thinking away from positivist epistemologies. First, under the new insights provided by philosophers of science such as Kuhn, Hesse and Feyerabend, the positivist understandings of the universalisation of conditions of knowledge, the neutrality of observation, the givenness of experience and the independence of data from theoretical interpretation began to be questioned as did, consequently, the distinctions between the natural and social sciences (Bernstein, 1983; Baert, 1998). In its place, data, theories and disciplines themselves began to be understood as belonging to larger social and historical contexts in which they were applied, changed and developed while social reality came to be understood as a social construction. Such changes in thinking have broadly led social theory to what could be termed a post-positivist position.

A second and additional motivation for planners and others to turn away from naturalism and naïve empiricism emerged because they found techniques and methodologies had not 'improved' practice including the ability to predict behaviour (Hemmens and Stiftel, 1980). The 1960s had been the 'high water mark' of modernist optimism and methodologies typified by rational planning methodologies and reinforced by the quantitative emphasis of comprehensive planning and computer modelling (Taylor, 1998). Such attitudes not only led to a disenfranchised populace but physical, social and economic legacies as great as those that planning had sought to address:

> Evidence of this seemed to be everywhere, from the disaster of high-rise towers for the poor to the dominance of economic criteria justifying road building and the functional categorisation of activity zones, which worked for large industrial companies and those working in them, but not for women (with their necessarily complex life-styles), the elderly, the disabled, and the many ethnic groups forced to discover ways of surviving on the edge of established economic practices.
>
> (Healey, 1993b: 235)

Future directions began to be explored though 'further digging among the social sciences or returning to planning's design origins seemed less likely to bear fruit than exploring other domains especially in the humanities' (Moore-Milroy, 1991: 182). Attention both in the social sciences and planning began to turn to context, practices and histories to explain what counts as knowledge, thereby questioning universalising assumptions, naïve realism and the correspondence theory of truth (Hesse, 1980: vii).

One such focus of attention involved questioning Enlightenment or modern ideals and positivist epistemologies through new *post*modern understandings (Best and Kellner, 1991).

> Postmodern's principal target has been the rationality of the modern movement, espe-
> cially its foundational character, its search for universal truth ... The postmodern posi-
> tion is that all meta-narratives are suspect; that the authority claimed by any single
> explanation is ill-founded, and by extension, that any such attempts to forge intellectual
> consensus should be resisted.
>
> (Dear, 1995a: 28)

Another post-positivist route related to the postmodern attack on totality and struc-turalism has been termed post-structuralism. Post-structuralists emphasise the variant and fluid relationship that exists between objects (signified) and words (signifiers). Meaning is not stable but is changing and incapable of being pinned down. Truth, in the post-structuralist sense, is replaced by interpretation, objectivity with subjectivity.

So the plethora of 'posts' – post-positivism, postmodernism and post-struc-turalism – have questioned and in some cases undermined accepted notions of society and theory often displacing conventional understandings that derived from modernism. As I mentioned at the beginning of this chapter, the term 'post' usually implies something 'after', but it would be more accurate in the sense that it is used here to emphasise development or evolution rather than 'break'. Post-positivism does not mean turning away from experience but it does mean a more contextu-alised and historic appreciation of how that experience is interpreted.

WHAT 'POST'?

Notwithstanding the postmodern and post-structuralist challenges Thomas Kuhn's *Structure of Scientific Revolutions* (1970) set the bearings for post-positivism approaches to social theory (Hesse, 1980). In place of positivist and Popperian perspectives that emphasised rigorous scientific method in the search for 'truth', Kuhn sought to place scientific activity within a social and historical context domin-ated by paradigms of accepted knowledge.

Kuhn and others who have taken up broadly similar positions (e.g. Feyer-abend, Lakatos, etc.) were specifically making reference to the natural sciences. However, the idea of paradigms has been taken up by planning theorists (e.g.

Alexander and Faludi, 1996) and the relevance of the idea of paradigmatic development in planning theory has been broadly accepted (Taylor, 1998). Not only has the idea of paradigms been accepted, Kuhn's analysis has been highly influential in encouraging new directions in social and planning theory. In keeping with the post-positivist emphasis upon social and historical contexts, Healey argues that:

> Every field of endeavour has its history of ideas and practices and its traditions of debate. These act as a store of experience, of myths, metaphors and arguments, which those within the field can draw upon in developing their own contributions, either through what they do, or through reflecting on the field. This 'store' provides advice, proverbs, recipes and techniques for understanding and acting, and inspiration for ideas to play with and develop.
>
> (1997a: 7)

This position is in strong contradistinction to the more positivist, instrumentally rational perspectives of planning theory characterised by the approach of, among others, Faludi, for whom planning was 'the application of scientific method – however crude – to policy making' (1973: 1).

Post-positivism is characterised by:

- a rejection of positivist understandings and methodologies (including naturalism) and an embracing instead of approaches that contextualise theories and disciplines in larger social and historical contexts;
- normative criteria for deciding between competing theories;
- the ubiquity of variance in explanations and theories;
- an understanding of individuals as self-interpreting, autonomous subjects.

Postmodernism is a more diffuse phenomenon and in many ways is linked to tenets of post-structuralism. Post-structuralism seeks to problematise 'truth' by exposing it to scrutiny and by being aware of the role of power in influencing forms of social control. Postmodernism as social theory seeks similar objectives. Though broad and contradictory in places, a general characterisation of what postmodernism as social theory is could be organised around five principles:

1   the break-down of transcendental meaning;
2   the discursively created subject;
3   the role of cultural influences in ordering society;
4   fragmentation and dispersal;
5   Foucault and Baudrillard's power.

The break-down of transcendental meaning

This is not a new or particularly postmodern theme as it goes back at least as far as Nietzsche. However, Lyotard (1984), Baudrillard (1968, 1970, 1975, 1976) and Foucault (1965, 1970, 1972, 1973) all built on the post-structuralist rejection of stable signifiers and emphasise instead the infinity of meaning. But in Lyotard's case this lack of transcendental meaning also manifests itself in what he terms an 'incredulity towards meta-narratives' or grand theories. For Lyotard, reductionist theories no longer (if they ever did) represent the world. Grand narratives of science, reason and progress have been replaced by a plethora of goals, styles and methods. However, Foucault is more open-minded on this, preferring 'suspicion' to an obituary he still seeks to 'problematise' rather than dismiss them entirely. Fredric Jameson's (1984) postmodernism still has a place for the grand narratives though he accepts the need for a more pluralistic and flexible interpretation. For all this suspicion, there is still no convincing theory of why such narratives have lost their meaning and force. This is compounded by the ease and comfort with which they rush to fill the vacuum created by the death of such over-arching theories with ones of their own.

The discursively created subject

Foucault's brilliant exegesis of madness (1965) exposed its lack of a pre-social essence. In doing so, he questioned scientific rationality and Enlightenment 'truths'. History and the self are more likely to lie outside linear and teleological perspectives of the self and history that favour rational, autonomous individuals. Laclau and Mouffe (1985) base their own radical politics on a similar basis though add other more structural influences to make up for Foucault's failure to see the influences of the non-discursive such as the state or economy. The influence of non-discursive spheres is one of the main weaknesses in the discursive perspective on history and the self. One way Foucault and Baudrillard try to explain it is through the existence of an amorphous cultural map labelled the 'code', 'episteme' or 'archive'. However, Jameson (1984) plumps instead for old-fashioned economic determinism and thereby denies the discursive–non-discursive link.

The role of cultural influences in ordering society

Baudrillard's code and Foucault's episteme are tools to help explain why, in such a fragmented and discursively created world, there are still common threads and values. The episteme is a set of discursively created rules that explain why one way of thinking or saying has been chosen over another. The influences upon these rules vary and can (and have) changed over time. But their main role is to limit possibilities and maintain discipline. These two functions were developed in Baudrillard's *code* that he argued created stability within an increasingly unstable world. These sets of rules look uncomfortably like the kind of reductionist logic and meta-narrative they all seek to question. The influence upon such codes is predominantly cultural and media driven which leads to the development of a symbiotic relationship emerging: society created the media and through the predominance of signs the media is increasingly influencing and creating society. Less and less connection and engagement with a world outside of media images is made, as external reality, according to Baudrillard, is lost.

Fragmentation and dispersal

Postmodern thinkers point to an increasingly fragmented and dispersed world where the 'old rules' no longer apply. This is linked in many ways to the New Times theses though less specifically. Lyotard's new times are based heavily on the 'information society' ideas of Daniel Bell (1973). But the theory of fragmentation is most forcefully advanced by Baudrillard to the point of a 'hyper-real' leading to the development of new ethics and values. 'We can no longer make sense of the pieces' seems to be both Baudrillard's and Jameson's interpretations. But Jameson advances a far more hopeful and less nihilistic counter-strategy that is based on his belief in fragmentation being both a threat and an opportunity. For Laclau and Mouffe (1985), fragmentation leads to different political alignments that undermine the emphasis on class.

Foucault and Baudrillard's power

Closely linked in some ways to the fragmentation of society is Foucault's concept of dispersal and disciplining power. Challenging the uni-directional characteristics of economic determinism, Foucault analyses power as 'flowing' at every level of society, thereby focusing his attention upon more micro-political rather than structural constraints. But there is an element of 'structural' control in this in the form of his normalising and disciplining role for power through institutional and discursive practices, for example. Baudrillard's view at first accorded with this but his later radical postmodernism based on extreme fragmentation rejected Foucault's perspective as being too simplistic: power is more dispersed than even he realises and there is no hope of tracing it.

HOW 'POST'?

It has now become common to characterise land use planning *per se* as 'modern' or at least as part of the project of modernity (see, for example, Goodchild, 1990: 128–129; Low, 1991: 234; Healey, 1993b; Sandercock, 1998c: 2) and to similarly characterise the period within which planning now finds itself and operates as 'post-modern' (e.g. Filion, 1996). The implication is of a potential and real mismatch between planning as a modern project and the needs and demands of postmodern or new times that, according to its proponents, explains the lack of participation and democratic content, failed and unrealised results and expectations, urban decay and a host of other outcomes intended or not that characterise 'planning':

> Planners claim that their advanced degrees in relevant disciplines and professional fields give them privileged access to scientific knowledge and know-how. They also claim that this knowledge is generally superior to knowledge gained in other ways (from practical experience, for example). In this respect they speak as true heirs of the Enlightenment.
>
> (Friedmann, 1989: 40)

Post-positivism, postmodernism and post-structuralism have provided both critiques and alternatives for planning theory and practice. Twenty years ago Hemmens and Stiftel (1980) tried to map the routes that different planning theorists were following in the post-empirical landscape. Ten years later the directions were still unclear. Moore-Milroy concluded that 'the hunt is on for a new foundation for planning theory. Many paths are being pursued' (1991: 182).

Baum (1996) makes a convincing case for rejecting the more extreme postmodern 'anything goes' attitude and argues (from his neo-pragmatic perspective) that planning practitioners and others still work within 'frames', constructing theories and reflecting upon power and domination in society. Nevertheless, the postmodern (as opposed to postmodern) search (generally known as the 'paradigm breakdown', Hudson, 1979) or 'theoretical pluralism' (Healey et al., 1982: 5) has a number of implications as planners and theorists tried to grapple with the idea of social reality as a social construction. The most obvious outcome was the problematising of the idea of theory itself. The traditional view of planning saw it based upon 'the neutrality of observation and the givenness of experience; the ideal of unequivocal language and the independence of data from theoretical interpretation; the belief in the universality of conditions of knowledge and criteria for theory choice' (Bohman, 1991: 2). In place of this we have a post-positivist recognition of indeterminacy, incommensurability, variance, diversity, complexity and intentionality in some routes of theoretical development – traits that question the very notion of 'planning'. A post-positivist approach requires 'shifting from causal reasoning as a basis for plan-making to discovering and confirming meaning' (Moore-Milroy, 1991: 182). In short, the post-positivist perspective emphasises that there is no theory-neutral way of understanding theory in planning.

I would also add another implication that seems to have followed from a more post-positivist planning theory: the final nail in the coffin of the distinction between procedure and substance in planning theory and the idea of a theory–practice gap. Although long recognised as an analytical rather than practical or real distinction (Paris, 1982), the idea of planning theory being divided this way has reached hegemonic status thanks to the work of Faludi and subsequent interpretations. According to Faludi, substantive theory 'helps planners understand whatever their area of concern may be' while procedural theory is about 'planners understanding themselves and the ways in which they operate' (1973: 3):

> It is useful to separate between two types (substantive and procedural), mainly because (a) procedural theories are mostly prescriptive whereas analytical theories are explanatory, and (b) the two types *do not*, in the main, relate to the same phenomenon.
>
> (Faludi, 1987: 29, emphasis added)

The thrust of post-positivism implies that there is no ethical neutrality in the framing, interpretation and application of knowledge which means that normative issues (which are the realm of substantive theory) cannot be kept from pervading procedural issues (Taylor, 1980; Cooke, 1983) – procedural theory also reflects beliefs, values and expectations. Previous criticisms of the substantive–procedural distinction have tended to focus on its apolitical or 'content-less' basis (e.g. Thomas, 1982) and its ignorance of the highly political nature of planning. This political nature of planning is a perpetual characteristic as a plethora of studies have demonstrated (e.g. Meyerson and Banfield, 1955; Davies, 1972; Dennis, 1972; Friedmann, 1987; Forester, 1989; Sandercock, 1998c; Flyvbjerg, 1998b). Grant (1994a, 1994b), for example, demonstrates how both procedural and substantive theories are underpinned by normative factors making procedural theories merely a sub-set or element of the substantive. Theories are simply tools to legitimise or achieve existing positions. As Grant concludes:

> As participants frame the discourse of their argument they package their values into theories that explain the nature of the community and to entail particular outcomes. Thus disputants link factual and rhetorical claims together in propositions they hope will persuade decision makers. To enhance the persuasiveness of the theory, participants call on various experts to legitimise positions taken.
>
> (1994a: 67)

Regardless of such evidence, the substantive–procedural distinction persists. This conflation of the substantive–procedural distinction does not mean that we cannot attempt to clarify or understand planning theory from a more analytical perspective, only that our frame(s) needs changing. One way forward through a more post-positivist perspective would be to recognise the different origins of theory. For example, planners have always drawn upon various theories that, while not being specifically concerned with planning *per se*, have a relevance for space, policy processes or governance. Such *exogenous* theories (in that they originate from fields outside planning) include, for example, theories of democracy, cognitive psychology, regime and regulation theory, implementation theory, central-local relations, nationalism and a host of other 'meso-level' theoretical constructs. In contrast, *indigenous* planning theory is more planning specific. Most books on planning theory list various perspectives including the usual suspects of, *inter alia*, Marxism, neo-liberal, advocacy, systems, rational comprehensive, design, communicative and neo-pragmatic theories. Such theories did not originate from within planning discourse but were interpreted, mediated and used to prescribe and understand planning theory and practice.

Two issues emerge that the post-positivist perspectives generally must address and each 'branch' or school of theory outlined below does this in its own way. First is the problem of incommensurability. There is a danger if not inevitability that contextualising, and relativising understanding can make judgements and theories merely *ad hoc* and localised. The role of social theory and planning theory is to systematically abstract and reflect upon the workings of the social world. Does the shift to a post-positivist approach mean that general theorising is replaced by incremental understanding? Second, the introduction of a more relativist form of planning theory in terms of its localised and contextualised approach raises the issues of normative and ethical judgements: can we now judge theories or opinions as 'better' or 'worse'? As Bernstein rightly acknowledges, there is a danger of fragmentation becoming the dominant sensibility and thereby missing any order or cohesion that may exist:

> Everything appears to be 'up for grabs'. There is little or no consensus – except by members of the same school or sub-school – about what are well established results, the proper research procedures, the important problems, or even the most promising theoretical approaches to the study of society and politics. There are claims and counter-claims, a virtual babble of voices demanding our attention.
>
> (1983: xii)

Appeals to methodological rigour, empirical proof or deductive reasoning cannot be counted on. In the post-world such appeals have been diluted. How current planning theories handle questions such as those above is increasingly coming down to normative questions – the spirit of post-positivism.

THE POST-POSITIVIST LANDSCAPE OF PLANNING THEORY

A number of different schools of planning theories have shadowed the broad trajectory of post-positivism, postmodernism and post-structuralism. Here I am using the term 'schools of theory' as shorthand for systematic, self-contained, analytical and prescriptive sets of ideas on the purpose and practice of planning. Under my interpretation of this definition critiques such as feminism are not schools of theory though they may form part of a larger school such as postmodernism. However, the current landscape of planning theory is not exclusively post-positivist. In addition to the broad movements that embrace more historically and socially embedded understandings are schools of theory that reject such shifts such as neo-liberal and project-led planning (e.g. Evans, 1988, 1991; Pennington, 1996, 1999; Lewis, 1992; Ehrman, 1990) and political economy approaches (e.g. Ambrose, 1994).

Although there are difficulties in ascribing labels, the broad post-positivist theoretical landscape is comprised of postmodern planning, neo-pragmatism and collaborative or communicative planning. Postmodern planning theory has been explored by, among others, Dear (1995a), Beauregard (1996), Sandercock (1998c), Boyer (1983), Soja (1997), Moore-Milroy (1991), Allmendinger (2001) and Filion (1996). Postmodern planning works can be broadly divided into two: those concerned with critiques of existing planning practice and those which are more prescriptive. Although the former (e.g. Yiftachel, 1995b, 1998) provide useful insights into the practices of planning, they form part of a much wider critique of planning as a modern enterprise as discussed earlier. The work of Beauregard (1996), Soja (1989, 1997), Sandercock (1998c) and Allmendinger (2001) among others fall into this latter category. For Beauregard postmodern planning follows the tenets of postmodernism generally: 'The texts of a postmodern planner, in fact, should be consciously fragmented and contingent, nonlinear, without aspiration to comprehensiveness, singularity or even compelling authority' (1996: 192).

Similarly, Sandercock is aiming for a 'broader and more politicised definition of planning's domains and practices' (1998c: 204). This new form of planning involves an eclectic approach including 'mobilisation, protests, strikes, acts of civil disobedience, community organisation, professional advocacy and research, publicity as well as the proposing and drafting of laws and new programmes of social intervention' (ibid.: 200).

Criticisms of postmodern planning are built upon firm normative foundations. For example, Taylor dismisses the postmodern turn in social theory generally and planning theory in particular as 'intellectually hopeless' and 'self defeating' (1998: 165). He also criticises the target of postmodern planning thinking: the modernist comprehensive approach. Planning is practised in a multitude of ways and styles, some of which are more postmodern in the sense of being methodologically more fluid while also putting less emphasis upon an agreed end state of what a city or place should be. Harper and Stein have probably been the most forceful in their criticism of postmodern planning theory as a basis for practice. Though admitting that there is no agreement upon what postmodern theory is and what it might mean for practice they nevertheless opine that:

> the uncritical adoption of postmodernist assumptions would bring us to the brink of an abyss of indeterminacy, impairing our ability to maintain social continuity through change, to treat each other in a just and fully human way, and to justify public planning.
>
> (Harper and Stein, 1995a: 233)

Other routes of post-positivist planning theory have followed a renewed interest in pragmatism (e.g. Hoch, 1984, 1996, 1997a; Harrison, 1998). Although pragmatism has a long lineage that can be traced back to the nineteenth-century American philosopher Charles Peirce, the pragmatist understanding that 'emphasises praxis and the application of critical intelligence to concrete problems, rather than a priori theorising' (Festenstein, 1997: 24) became popular in planning through the work of Richard Rorty. Like postmodernism there are disputes about the nature of pragmatism and like the relativist nature of postmodern thinking pragmatists eschew absolutes, consensus or transcendental truth. There is also some overlap with the collaborative concern with conversation as a medium through which disagreements can be overcome. But the pragmatic point of departure concerns the role of liberalism and the individual (including planners) as *ironist* who are charged with constantly questioning and reassessing the processes and institutions of society. The Pragmatist, in William James's view:

> turns his back resolutely and once and for all upon a lot of inveterate habits dear to professional philosophers. He turns away from abstraction and insufficiency, from verbal solutions, from bad *a priori* reasons, from fixed principles, closed systems, and pretended absolutes and origins. He turns towards concreteness and adequacy, towards facts, action and towards power. This means the empiricist temper regnant and the rationalist temper sincerely given up. It means the open air and possibilities of nature, as against dogma, artificiality, and the pretence of finality in truth. At the same time it does not stand for any special results. It is a method only.
>
> (Quoted in Muller, 1998: 296)

Charles Hoch has been foremost in attempting to analyse planning and develop an alternative based upon pragmatic principles particularly from Dewey's interpretation of pragmatism. At the heart of his interpretation are three core themes of Dewey's work. First is the role of experience in providing truth and being the motor of progress. Experience provides the only real test of truth and practicality. Second, following the idea of contingent truth, he focuses on the search for practical answers to real problems. This experimental approach is based on experience as the arbiter of progress:

> When we test plans of action, we try to determine which plan will work best, that is, which plan is right for us. For Dewey, this sort of thinking constitutes the appropriate form of understanding ... truth emerges when an idea (alternative hypothesis or plan) proves successful in solving a problem.
>
> (Hoch, 1984: 336)

Truth is a consequence of what 'works best' in solving a problem or 'making sense' of an issue. Finally, Hoch argues for Dewey's emphasis on practical activity or inquiry through socially shared and agreed means achieved through democratic association. A pluralistic competition of ideas following an experimental method serves freedom best. Like the communicative planners, he also feels that conflict will be overcome through intelligent and reflective discourse.

However, Hoch is also critical of the power-blindness of pragmatism and, drawing on Richard Rorty's later work and elements of Foucault's analysis of power, he comes close to Forester's critical pragmatism (Hoch, 1996). Both Hoch and Forester (1998) argue the need for a plurality of styles to planning and a negotiative attitude which emphasises a communicative or collaborative basis to planning. Planners need to be open about their 'gate keeping' power roles, reflect upon bias and prejudices and be inventive about new processes and aims to stimulate possible new directions for local practice.

Like postmodern approaches, neo-pragmatism has been subject to criticisms. Probably the most relevant criticism has been the conservative nature of such an approach and how it does not address issues of embedded power relations. Hoch argues that 'common sense' will work towards exposing nefarious uses of power – a view criticised by Feldman (1997). Of more concern is the relativism at the heart of the pragmatic approach. There is no 'privileged' position within pragmatism. However, there *are* limits imposed as pragmatism is firmly founded within liberal democracy. Any alternatives in means must conform to the ends of continuing a liberal–democratic system. Nevertheless, this boundary may also be viewed not as a weakness but as a strength particularly as it avoids the extreme postmodern relativism of Baudrillard and others.

Finally, the most significant school of planning theory to emerge in the last two decades is communicative planning (Alexander, 1997). Neil Harris sets out in philosophical and theoretical origins and developments of this school in Chapter 2. It is worth highlighting a few characteristics here to help distinguish it from post-modernism and neo-pragmatism. There are a number of influences upon the communicative approach though one of the most important is the work of Jürgen Habermas. Habermas examines the concept of rationality and its relationship to problems of social action, intersubjective communication and social-historical change drawing heavily on the writings of George Herbert Mead, Émile Durkheim and Aristotle (Dryzek, 1990). Although reaching similar conclusions to the post-positivist thrust of Kuhn and others, Habermas is more influenced by the work of the Frankfurt School in criticising Enlightenment rationality and consequently seeks to finish the 'unfinished' project of modernity rather than abandoning it as some postmodernists would. Consequently, while Habermas embraces the thrust of post-positivism, he also attempts to hang on to Enlightenment ideals and provide an alternative form of rationality with which to expose power relations and avoid the dominant methodologies characteristic of modernity.

'Communicative planning' (Forester, 1989), 'argumentative planning' (Forester, 1993), 'planning through debate' (Healey, 1992a), 'inclusionary discourse' (Healey, 1994), and 'collaborative planning' (Healey, 1997a, 1998) are terms that have been used extensively in planning theory literature over the last decade or so to describe and transform the concepts of Habermasian critical theory into planning. There have been various interpretations of communicative rationality as a basis for planning (e.g. Forester, 1980, 1989, 1993; Healey, 1993b, 1996a, 1997a; Hillier, 1993; Sager, 1994; Innes, 1995; Healey and Hillier, 1996). Three broad categories emerge from these interpretations.

First, there are the micro-political interpretations of planning practice usually based on a combination of Habermasian ideal speech and post-structuralist concern with language (Forester, 1989, 1993; Fischer and Forester, 1993). Following in this tradition are the second category of ethnographic studies comparing this ideal to practice (Healey, 1992a; Hillier, 1993; Healey and Hillier, 1996). Finally, there are the prescriptive (though the authors would deny this label) studies aimed at using communicative rationality as a basis for what has now been termed 'collaborative' or 'deliberative' planning (Healey, 1992a, 1996a, 1996b, 1997a, 1998; Forester, 1999d). In this latter category we find the most developed accounts of communicative planning and the critique of instrumental rationality that aim, in Forester's words, 'to work towards a political democratisation of daily communication' (1989: 21).

Communicative planning differs from postmodern interpretations and overlaps with aspects of neo-pragmatism in its desire to 'hold on' to some absolutes while recognising the social contexts and relativisms of post-positivism. According to Habermas (1984, 1987) instrumental rationality has dominated the world of inter-personal communication which is distorted by power and money. Power is exerted through abstract systems but also through distorting mediums such as professionals including planners. But rather than replacing instrumental rationality Habermas seeks to embed it within phenomenology, action theory and argumentation theory, thereby maintaining a 'core' of positivism.

Communicative planning has not come in for the same degree of criticism as the postmodern or neo-pragmatic approaches although it has been accused of dominating and crowding out other theoretical discourses (Tewdwr-Jones and Allmendinger, 1998), being unconvincing in making the 'argument for argument' (Elster, 1998), being culturally imperialistic (Huxley and Yiftachel, 1998), and being ambiguous in its theoretical origins (Ball, 1998). Such criticisms have been rather muted, however, as planning theorists have sought to embrace the communicative perspective as both a justification and prescription for planning. Yet despite the rich theoretical origins little has been written on the translation into practical approaches and advice.

Perhaps we should not be too surprised that the translation of critical theory at an abstract level has come up against problems when confronted with much more immediate, contextualised and diverse systems and processes. Trying to 'pin down' the problems and interpret communicative planning as a practical basis for planning practice is certainly not easy and this is not helped by the lack of clarity in the relationship between communicative rationality and instrumental rationality.

Part I

Planning Thoughts and Perspectives

2

Collaborative Planning

From Theoretical Foundations to Practice Forms
Neil Harris

INTRODUCTION

The preceding chapter has provided an account of the contemporary landscape of planning theory.[1] The purpose of the present chapter is to provide an introduction to the practice of collaborative planning, including the theoretical bases to collaborative planning practices and the critiques that have developed during the latter part of the 1990s. The chapter outlines several of the key concepts premised by the collaborative planning framework and also presents some of the difficulties that arise in incorporating collaborative planning principles in practice.

Friedmann's account of the development of planning theory suggests that planning theory[2] has developed over a period of two centuries, culminating in a 'virtual explosion in planning literature' in the period since 1945 (Friedmann, 1987: 54). The popularity and fortunes of planning theory varied in the post-war period, although planning theory appeared to have reached an impasse during the 1980s. Considerable effort was devoted to competing conceptions of rationality and establishing an appropriate place for rationality in planning theory (Breheny and Hooper, 1985), often producing extended debates with limited development. Nevertheless, these debates receded to enable sufficient consensus to develop to permit the exploration of new and less-travelled avenues in planning theory during the 1990s. This was almost paradoxical in the sense that what many see as the development of a growing consensus on planning theory has laid the ground for exploration of diversity in planning theories. Consequently, explorations in planning theory continued to provide centre-stage opportunities to theoretical debates that had previously developed on the margins (Mandelbaum et al., 1996). However, consensus had developed around approaches to planning theory based on Habermas's Theory of Communicative Action (1984, 1987a) to the extent that Innes (1995) declared the emergence of planning theory's 'new paradigm'. This claim has since revived debates in planning theory and the demand to search for new directions in planning theory has generated a number of contemporary alternatives. The emergent body of work referred to as 'collaborative planning' that forms the basis of this chapter is one form that derives from this challenge to seek out new directions in both planning theory and planning practices.

DEFINING 'COLLABORATIVE PLANNING'

The term 'collaborative planning' has developed during the 1990s into one of the key phrases in the planning theory vocabulary.[3] The term is used throughout this chapter to refer to the work of Healey (1997a) and other subsequent authors and specifically excludes other uses of the term collaborative planning in urban and regional planning literature, including that used to refer to the application of technology to facilitate group decision-making (Shiffer, 1992). Therefore, although I intend to use the term specifically in relation to planning theory, there is clearly a wider sphere of interest in collaborative forms of planning and decision-making.[4]

Although the term 'collaborative planning' was coined in the late 1990s to refer to a specific body of work deriving from planning theory, it cannot be seen as emerging as an isolated form. Collaborative planning is most suitably interpreted as an element in a longer-term programme of research and theoretical development focused upon a concern with the democratic management and control of urban and regional environments and the design of less oppressive planning mechanisms. The term collaborative planning (and associated theoretical references 'communicative action' and 'communicative rationality') feature as an increasingly prominent part of the vocabulary used in the range of planning literature. The principal difficulty arising from such widespread use of terms and phrases is that popular and ill-defined usage tends to distort understanding of the central aspects of original formulations. It is for this reason that I propose to start with defining a simple definition of collaborative planning using the terms of its principal proponent. In presenting *Collaborative Planning: Shaping Places in Fragmented Societies*, Healey states in the preface to the text: '[Collaborative planning] is about why urban regions are important to social, economic and environmental policy and how political communities may organise to improve the quality of their places' (Healey, 1997a: xii). This is an essentially simple definition, yet it does capture the essence of collaborative planning. One of the first points of interest raised by this simple definition of collaborative planning is that it does not appear to be particularly or expressly concerned with planning theory. Healey's expression of collaborative planning clearly indicates a very practical orientation, illustrated most acutely in the statement that it is about '*how* political communities may *organise* to improve the quality of their places'. As a complementary definition of collaborative planning, it may also be interpreted as a personal statement on how spatial planning should be understood (ibid.: xii). Collaborative planning, therefore, is intended by its proponents to serve as <u>both a framework for understanding</u> and as a <u>framework for practical action.</u>

Healey's (1997a) presentation of a model of collaborative planning is wide-ranging and integrates a series of topics closely related to issues of contemporary concern in the field and discipline of planning. These concerns include: notions of community; relations of power; global economic restructuring and regional impact; environmentalism; cultures and systems of governance; institutional design; technocratic control and the nature of expertise; mediation and conflict resolution; and spatial planning. The identification of this broad range of issues illustrates the ambitious scope of the collaborative planning thesis and it is clear that the successful integration of all of these elements is a considerable and difficult task, as is illustrated below and in subsequent chapters.

THEORY/PRACTICE IN COLLABORATIVE PLANNING

Healey's own definition of collaborative planning has been used above in order to attempt to provide some initial definition to the term. The initial interpretation derived from this has been that collaborative planning revolves around practical concerns relating to understanding and action. Nevertheless, collaborative planning has also been identified as an element in the vocabulary of planning theorists. There is a need to establish, in clear terms, the precise character and nature of the relationship between collaborative planning and planning theory. First, collaborative planning does not rest easily defined as a 'theory'. In addition to the above definition provided by Healey, arguments may be erected against such a definition from a number of standpoints. For example, one argument is that the work is not of an explanatory character and has limited application in wider contexts, a point discussed below. Collaborative planning is conceived of as a 'form' of planning based on certain theoretical foundations and assumptions (Healey, 1997a: 7). These theoretical foundations are discussed in subsequent sections. The essential point to be made is that the advocates of collaborative planning have not advanced it as a theory and that this must shape the parameters within which debate and critique should take place. One consequence of this observation is that forms of planning are recognised as being of greater dependence on contextual factors than are theories. Critics of collaborative forms of planning recognise, in part, the distinction that is emphasised here between planning theories and forms of planning. Critics of collaborative planning, however, have conflated collaborative planning with theory. As an illustration of this, Allmendinger (1999: 8) contends that collaborative planning 'is not simply a theory but a world view'. Elsewhere, references have been made to 'Collaborative planning as a theory of practice' (Tewdwr-Jones and

Allmendinger, 1998: 1987). It is vital to ensure that the relationship between collaborative planning as a form of practice and its underlying theoretical foundations are clearly defined. This clarity of definition is crucial to ensuring that criticisms are appropriate to the form being discussed.

THEORETICAL BASES TO COLLABORATIVE PLANNING

In presenting the model of collaborative planning, Healey constructs a particular history of planning thought and identifies the origins of planning in a 'curious' interaction between evangelism, the generation and application of scientific knowledge and firm basis in the Enlightenment tradition (1997a: 7–8). Continuing within this long-established tradition, collaborative planning theory is a form of practice that, in common with many other forms of planning, is derived from a hybrid of various wider sociological and economic theories. Developing the collaborative planning model, Healey (ibid.: xii) notes that it is very much a product of the complex interweaving together of two distinct bodies of theoretical work, namely the communicative approach to planning theory and institutionalist sociology and regional economic geography. Of these bodies of theory, it is the basis in communicative planning theory that provides the essential foundations and underlying principles to collaborative planning in the sense of devising preferred styles and approaches to planning. The institutionalist and regional dimensions may be regarded as an analytic complement to the normative framework provided by communicative planning theory, drawing heavily on Giddens' structuration thesis (1984, 1990). The two separate bodies of theory are related in a normative/analytic dimension, in which one serves to provide an understanding of the systems and mechanisms of urban and regional planning upon which a normative agenda of democratic and inclusive management may be pursued.

The emergence of any body of theory or conceptual framework (or, indeed hybrid formation) can be assessed as a response to a series of stimuli which may be either internal or external to a discipline. Considered in this way, developments in theory may be interpreted as products of their time and circumstances. Campbell and Fainstein (1996: 149) illustrate the dual response in the case of 'the communicative turn' in planning theory (Healey, 1992a), referring to attempts in planning to 'simultaneously adapt to two crucial changes': 'the resurgence of economic valuation' and 'postmodern critiques of scientific rationalism'. These two strategic changes, allied with a range of other developments in planning theory during the past twenty years, reflect a broader 'crisis' in planning theory related to the decline of the classic rational planning model. This 'crisis' in planning theory has been further enhanced by the failure to develop any convincing alternatives to the classic rational planning model, despite considerable activity in the development of a series of pre-paradigmatic alternatives (Alexander, 1984, 1996).

The 'communicative turn in planning theory' (Healey, 1992a) is a phrase used to identify a change of direction and emphasis in planning theory. The substance of this turn, or change in direction, has been a reorientation towards interactive understandings of planning activity. The communicative turn enshrines 'diverse theoretical impulses' (Tewdwr-Jones and Thomas, 1998: 127) and 'manifests itself in several ways' (Sager, 1990: 544–555). There now exists a wide range of material that may be referred to as communicative planning theory (Healey, 1992a, 1992b, 1993a; Forester, 1993; Hillier, 1993; Sager, 1994; Harper and Stein, 1995; Innes, 1995; Healey and Hillier, 1996). Interest in 'communicative planning theory' remains essentially recent (Campbell and Fainstein, 1996: 11),[5] although, as this body of work has progressed and developed, academics have attended with increasing sensitivity to the variants that combine under the umbrella term of 'communicative planning theory'. It is presently widely recognised that: 'The body of work now labelled under the "communicative" umbrella varies not just in its inspirations. It also has different emphases' (Healey, 1997c: 72). Prior to identifying the key dimensions along which this work is differentiated, it is useful to establish those elements which are common to that material referred to as communicative planning theory. Figure 2.1 illustrates the key dimensions to communicative planning.

The development of planning theory has been characterised historically by the 'claiming' (Friedmann, 1987: 52) of various figures from the disciplines of economics, sociology, social theory, philosophy and the natural sciences. The recent development of communicative planning theory is no exception to this. The principal theoretical resource used in developing communicative planning theory is the theory of communicative action, the thesis presented by the sociologist–philosopher Jürgen Habermas (1984, 1987a). Commentators within the wider social sciences have described Habermas's Theory of Communicative Action as an 'important but inaccessible work' (Brand, 1990: vii), a 'sprawling, uneven work' that is 'unnecessarily long' (Giddens, 1985: 96), and as 'massive and complex' (White, 1988: 1). Within planning theory, reference is also made to Habermas's theory as a 'rather abstract philosophical work' (Taylor, 1998: 123). Friedmann (1987: 267) also remarks upon 'the density of [Habermas's] language' and remarks that 'few bothered to read the fine print' as a result. These characteristics of complexity, abstraction and inaccessibility combine to generate ideal conditions for misinterpretation, simplification and selective appropriation and have also contributed significantly to the 'diverse theoretical impulses' (Tewdwr-Jones and Thomas, 1998: 127) evident in the literature on communicative planning

(a)   Recognition of the social construction of knowledge and the exercise of both practical reason and scientific knowledge.

(b)   Acknowledgement of the different forms for the development and communication of knowledge (analysis, storytelling, expression).

(c)   Internal within social contexts acknowledged as of importance.

(d)   Identification of diverse interests and the subordination of interests through relations of power.

(e)   The concept of stakeholding, spreading ownership and the range of knowledge and reasoning.

(f)   A shift from competitive interest bargaining to collaborative consensus building.

(g)   Recognition of planning activity as being embedded in day-to-day relations; the linking of practice and context.

2.1 Key emphases in communicative planning theory

Source: Derived from Healey, 1997a

theory. These defining characteristics also lead Taylor (1998: 123) to hint at the question as to why planning theorists increasingly engaged in the analysis of planning practices should turn towards a work of such great abstraction.

The direct use of Habermas's Theory of Communicative Action represents one of a series in the turn towards philosophy and social theory for sources of inspiration in planning theory (Harris, 1999). This derives from an ambition to develop in planning a more philosophical notion of reason to compensate for strict utilitarian definitions of rationality (Dalton, 1986: 150). Habermas's work has been identified by planning theorists as part of an attempt to develop an alternative to a 'clean, calculating and homogenizing' instrumental rationality (Dryzek, 1993: 213) that is contended to have crowded out moral and aesthetic discourses. The search for alternative forms or conceptions of rationality follows considerable debate which has addressed the decision over whether to strengthen the rational model or allow it to decline in the face of repeated criticisms (Healey, 1983: 19). Debates continue on the extent to which traditional conceptions of planning define the parameters that frame contemporary debate in planning theory (Alexander, 1984, 1996; Dalton, 1986). For example, some authors question whether communicative action is the 'significant departure from the rational comprehensive model' that is claimed of it (Sandercock, 1998c: 96), while others have concluded that communicative planning theory represents a continuation of the principles and ideals of the classic rational view of planning (Taylor, 1998: 152).

The continuing decline of the classic rational planning model represents one of the principal reasons for directing attention to Habermas's theory. In addition to this largely theoretical agenda of deriving an alternative and improved conception of rationality, practical concerns also contributed towards the 'search' phase in planning theory. Taylor (1998: 122) reveals that material on both implementation (citing Pressman and Wildavsky) and action planning (citing Friedmann) 'drew attention to the importance of interpersonal skills of communication and negotiation for the effective implementation of policies and plans'. Taylor (1998: 122) is right to identify that a concern with communication was not new to town planning, although an emphasis upon interpersonal elements of communication marks the 1990s as distinct from earlier periods. Campbell and Fainstein (1996: 11) also refer to the centrality of the conception within communicative planning theory of 'planners as communicators rather than as autonomous, systematic thinkers'.[6] This is illustrative of the close relationship between planning as communicative action and planning as argumentation (Goldstein, 1984; Dryzek, 1990, 1993; Dunn, 1993; Fischer and Forester, 1993; Lapintie, 1998). A related interest in interpersonal communication has been sustained by the action-focused concerns of those planning theorists that have directed attention towards the micro-sociology and politics of planning practice. These theoretical and practical agendas driving the search for interactive concepts for import into planning theory are not mutually exclusive. For example, the introduction of deliberative concepts into planning theory has been identified as a means of simultaneously reflecting the reality of practice situations and as an attempt to overcome some of the limitations of the classic rational model of decision-making (Alexander, 1992: 51). The theory of communicative action and forms of planning derived from it continue to be represented in the literature as concerned centrally with issues of communication (see Voogd and Woltjer, 1999) although its proponents would argue that this is an overly narrow interpretation.

It is necessary, in the interests of enabling an appreciation of 'the wider picture', to place the theory of communicative action within a historical and intellectual context. Friedmann (1987) provides a competent and strategic account of the development of planning theory from the late eighteenth century through to the 1980s.[7] The account provided by Friedmann identifies Habermas's work as part of the lineage of the Frankfurt School of Critical Theory, characterised by the earlier works of Horkheimer and Adorno. Critical theory takes as its substantive focus systems of domination and alienation, and is in particular oriented towards understanding the complexity of domination (Morrow and Brown, 1994: 10–11). A similar portrayal of the principal concern of critical theory is provided by Friedmann (1987: 55) as 'a radical critique, grounded in Hegelian and Marxist categories, of the multifaceted cultural manifestations of capitalism, including the deification of technical reason itself'. Conceived of as a form of social or cultural criticism, 'critical theory retains its ability to disrupt and challenge the status quo' through the production of 'undeniably dangerous knowledge' (Kincheloe and MacLaren, 1998: 260). Commentators have, however, recently questioned the unification of material sufficient to be considered a distinct school of theory and have stated the degree of homogeneity attributed to the Frankfurt School to be overemphasised (Morrow and Brown, 1994: 19; Kincheloe and MacLaren, 1998: 260–261). In addition to this, the degree of connection between Habermas's works, including the TCA, and the Frankfurt School of Critical Theory are contended to be over-stated (Outhwaite, 1994: 5). Despite such observations, a number of unifying (or common) characteristics can be identified, notably an attempt to ameliorate oppressive social structures and to diagnose the pathologies of modern culture (Chriss, 1995: 546).

Critical theory has been identified as being 'especially important for planning theory' (Friedmann, 1987: 55). Critical theory in the form of Forester's work (1980) was also identified by Alexander (1984) as one of a series of stimulating ideas that presented themselves as pre-paradigmatic alternatives to the classic rational planning model. Forester's (1980, 1993) work, in addition to other authors' early uses of critical theory (Cooke and Kemp, 1980; Kemp, 1982, 1985), has enabled a wide use and interpretation of concepts derived from critical theory.

As Figure 2.2 demonstrates, the critical theory component of planning theory is located by Friedmann (1987) within a broader social mobilisation tradition of intellectual thought in planning. This tradition is itself identified as exhibiting particular contemporary relevance to planning theory. The social mobilisation tradition is characterised by three principal features: the assertion of the primacy of direct collective action; the conception of planning as a form of politics; and the seeking of transformative processes. These characteristics identify the social mobilisation tradition as 'an ideology of the dispossessed' (Friedmann, 1987: 83–84). It is these characteristics that lead to Friedmann's (ibid.: 55) depiction of critical theory in the development of planning theory as located 'midway between utopian anarchism and historical materialism'. The critical theory of the Frankfurt School is, however, distinguished from historical materialism by 'its complete lack of interest in revolutionary practice' (ibid.: 265). This is particularly so in the case of Habermas, who displays tendencies to be led 'into rarified regions of abstract thought, far removed from the pressing concerns of everyday life' (ibid.: 267). Such a degree of abstraction, combined with Habermas's philosophically conservative stance and adherence to basic liberal values in society (Harper and Stein, 1995b:

(a)	Non-manipulative leadership in a democratic frame.
(b)	Encouraging the disinherited to believe that they can effect change.
(c)	Encouraging satisfaction and maintaining commitment from partial victories in an interminable struggle.
(d)	Determination of appropriate strategies for achieving desirable ends (e.g. acceptability of violence?).
(e)	How to define the characteristics of a 'good society'?

2.2 Central questions faced by adherents to the social mobilisation tradition

Source: Derived from Friedmann (1987).

55) has tended to result in a less radical agenda than theoretical lineage would suggest.

CONTEMPORARY CRITIQUES OF COLLABORATIVE PLANNING

The fact that critics have questioned the extent of the distance between traditional conceptions of rationality and those premised in communicative planning theory has allowed many of the well-rehearsed criticisms of rational planning to be 'read across' to communicative planning theory. In addition to these historical criticisms, a range of competitor paradigms have developed that provide a series of alternative positions from which to direct criticism (see Part III in this volume). These alternative theoretical positions vary in the extent to which they engage directly with communicative planning theory. Certain paradigms appear as direct competitors, where there exist close approximations in terms of the relevant object of study or concepts employed. Others have been defined historically as separate traditions[8] and the distinctions have been clearly defined through argument.

Critics have not always been clear on whether criticisms are being levelled at communicative planning theory or collaborative planning as a form of practice derived from that theory. Much of this has arisen through the misdirected conflation of collaborative planning and communicative planning theory. In addition to this, critics have not always made clear whether they are engaged with Habermas's original concepts or their interpretation in the field of planning theory. This tendency is given appropriate expression in Friedmann and Douglass' (1998: 5) reference to the use of Habermas and Foucault as 'surrogate warriors' by planning theorists. The material that follows presents the principal criticisms as they have been expressed by academics aligned with alternative or competitor paradigms. It is true to state that many of the differences and oppositions between these alternative philosophies or competing paradigms are rendered less problematic in the research and analysis of planning practices than in theoretical deliberation (Murdoch et al., 1998: 5). Consequently, many of the criticisms that follow pertain more closely to communicative planning theory than to collaborative planning.

Collaborative planning has been identified as a complex interweaving of two distinct bodies of theory to develop a form or model of practice (Healey, 1997a: xii). The criticisms directed at the theoretical foundations to collaborative planning have, therefore, also tended to separate into two distinct categories related to the bodies of theory used in developing the collaborative planning model. However, the nature and orientation of the criticisms differ between these categories. The first category is directed specifically at the use of communicative planning theory in developing collaborative planning and the basis of criticisms revolves around differences of theoretical position. The second category is not as directly confrontational as the first category, and criticisms relate to weaknesses of interpretation, omissions and theoretical blindspots.

The 'dark side' of planning theory

Contemporary developments in planning theory have witnessed the ascendancy of a body of theoretical material that has been characterised as the 'dark side' of planning theory (Flyvbjerg, 1996, 1998a, 1998b; Flyvbjerg and Richardson, 1998; Yiftachel, 1998; Huxley and Yiftachel, 2000). This material is partly concerned with the illustration of planning as an oppressive mechanism of social control (Yiftachel, 1998) and has developed to become the primary critique of the communicative action paradigm. The critical, analytic character of the 'dark side' of planning theory contrasts sharply with the overt normativism of mainstream planning theory, regarded by critics as responsible for contributing towards an aversion to critical analysis in traditional planning theory (ibid.: 404; see also Poulton, 1991). This contended aversion to critical analysis manifests itself in a concern for how things should be with limited regard to consequences or whether such end-states are achieved or indeed achievable.

Foucauldian concepts have been imported into planning theory as both an alternative and complement to Habermasian communicative rationality (Sager, 1990; Hillier, 1993; Allen, 1996; Richardson, 1996). In particular, a Foucauldian approach to the study of planning is contended by its proponents to account for relations of power, which are considered by such authors to be deficient in forms of planning based on communicative rationality (Hillier, 1993; Feldman, 1995; Richardson, 1996; Reuter, 1997).

> This Foucauldian critique leads to the conclusion that policy making developed from
> communicative theory of planning, contrary to expectations, is likely to be vulnerable to
> the workings of power, allowing manipulation and control, confusion and exclusion, and
> other distortions, to disrupt the process.
>
> (Richardson, 1996: 280)

However, even proponents of a Foucauldian approach concede that the intention is not to dissolve relations of power in a utopia of transparent communication[9] but to play games with a minimum of domination (Flyvbjerg, 1996: 391). Foucauldian analyses are, however, best interpreted as a warning rather than an ultimatum in developing less oppressive forms of planning (Hoch, 1992: 214). Consequently, Foucauldian analyses of planning can have a powerful 'sobering effect' (Flyvbjerg, 1996: 389).

In addition to this explicit challenge to communicative planning theory from theorists advocating Foucauldian approaches, challenges have been presented both to communicative planning theory and planning theory more generally by a series of writings drawing upon postmodern sensibilities (Beauregard, 1989, 1991; Dear, 1986, 1995a; Milroy, 1991; Allmendinger, 1998, 1999). Planning theory has not been an exception to the trend to embrace a variety of forms of relativism across a range of disciplines (Bernstein, 1983: 3). Postmodernism, as it has been developed in planning theory, has been interpreted as deconstructive, anti-foundationalist, non-dualistic and encouraging of plurality (Milroy, 1991: 183). Interpretations of this form have had considerable and discomforting implications for planning theory: 'Postmodernism has created a crisis in planning because it undermines and rejects Modernist bases for planning, yet it provides no substitute rationale' (Harper and Stein, 1995b: 61).

Communicative planning is often referred to as an alternative to postmodern approaches to planning theory (Campbell and Fainstein, 1996: 12). This is primarily a result of the communicative planning theorists use of Habermas, a theoretical resource that proposes universalistic criteria during a period of intense interest in 'relativistic styles' (Giddens, 1985: 97–98). However, it has been recognised within the planning theory literature that certain eras may predispose theorists to exaggerate a sense of disruption and lose sight of continuities (Sandercock, 1997: 90). In re-establishing or reasserting these continuities, one possible interpretation of postmodernism is as an 'appraisal' or internal critique of modernism (Dear, 1986: 370). Such a view reinforces the notion that a state of modernity has not yet been realised and that modernism, appropriately redefined and evaluated, or, indeed (Re)Enlightened (Gleeson, 2000: 131), may still yet act as an appropriate framework for societal action (Bernstein, 1985: 31).

Regulation theory, institutionalist geography and political economy

Communicative planning theory is identified as directing insufficient attention to the dynamics of urban regions (Healey, 1997a: 30) and it is partly for this reason that collaborative planning integrates spatial and political sensibilities from urban political economy and elements of communicative planning theory. Collaborative planning complements a traditional analytic orientation to understanding the complexities of socio-spatial processes and impacts with an explicit normative agenda based on communicative practices. It is this integration of communicative planning theory with institutionalist and regional geography that has attracted a second and separate series of criticisms. This critique has been most clearly expressed by planning theorists adopting positions within a framework of urban political economy and urban regime theory (Fainstein, 1995; Feldman, 1995, 1997; Lauria and Whelan, 1995; Lauria, 1997). Such commentators criticise communicative planning theory for its apparent neglect of issues of structure and for its over-emphasis of the capacity of individual agency. It is a characteristic feature of approaches derived from critical theory to risk advocating individualistic and naïve responses (Kemp, 1982). To account for this, regime theory is proposed as a useful complement to communicative planning theory that locates planners in their institutional context (Lauria and Whelan, 1995). The contextual deficiency levelled as a criticism of communicative planning theory arises in part from a selective reading of the past. The critique of communicative planning theory provided from the quarters of regime theory and political economy illustrates the depth of theoretical roots that are often not acknowledged by communicative planning theorists. Lauria and Whelan (ibid.: 19) contend that Innes (1995), in declaring communicative and interactive practice as planning's new paradigm, exhibits theoretical and historical amnesia in the neglect of a series of political economic approaches to planning, citing the work of Cockburn (1977), Cooke (1983), and Paris (1982) among others. These works are suggested as being able to restore 'the important interconnections between individuals, institutions, and society' that communicative theorists are considered to have lost sight of (Lauria and Whelan, 1995: 19). The loss of these important connections is claimed to direct attention towards the actions of individuals to the neglect of wider relations, leading to 'incomplete, perhaps balkanized and dislocated interpretations' (Lauria, 1997: 40). As an interesting counterpoint to these criticisms drawn from the previous category, Tewdwr-Jones and Allmendinger (1998: 1980) criticise research using communicative rationality concepts that focus upon the institutional aspect of power structures to the exclusion of power exerted and expressed by individuals. Critics identifying deficient consideration of structure–agency relations in communicative planning theory share many characteristics with advocates of collaborative planning. Healey

(1997c) has identified that communicative planning theorists have paid insufficient regard to those issues arising from institutionalist and structuration theories of urban regions, and has deliberately attempted to incorporate such issues into the hybrid theoretical framework that acts as the basis for developing collaborative forms of planning. This institutionalist understanding of urban planning activity is not without historical reference, for such frames of understanding have been employed previously and elsewhere (Healey and Barratt, 1990; Healey, 1992c; Ball, 1998).

These criticisms will be developed further and added to in subsequent chapters in this edited volume. It would, therefore, be pre-emptive to conduct an assessment of whether these theoretical criticisms are fatal. The likelihood is that they are not fatal in terms of undermining collaborative planning, given that critics in each category have identified the possibility of different theoretical frameworks acting as useful complements to communicative planning theory. Confrontation and denial between different approaches to planning theories are counterproductive (Lim, 1986: 83). Nevertheless, concerns have been expressed on the artificial syntheses that may be attempted, particularly in developing hybrid Habermasian–Foucauldian frameworks (Richardson, 1996; Flyvbjerg, 1998b).

FROM THEORETICAL FOUNDATIONS TO PRACTICE FORMS

The preceding section has identified the principal theoretical basis of communicative planning theory, which itself acts as the theoretical resource for the development of collaborative forms of planning. Despite the adoption of Habermas's theory of communicative action as a common theoretical basis, the point that there exists considerable theoretical diversity within communicative planning theory has already been made. The key dimensions along which elements of communicative planning theory differ are identified as the treatment of context, treatment of issues of structure, precise focus of interest, and analytic versus normative content (Healey, 1997c: 72). These essentially practical factors enable a considerable diversity of work to be similarly labelled: 'Communicative action is a surprisingly simple, yet immensely difficult concept that when carried into practice can assume virtually unlimited forms' (Friedmann and Lehrer, 1998: 80).

One of the forms that practices derived from communicative action theory can take is that of collaborative planning. Assessed on the basis of the key dimensions identified above, collaborative planning may be identified as intimately concerned with issues of context (the nature of particular places and systems of governance) and structure (institutional organisation). In addition, the model of collaborative planning attends to issues of the manifestation of power relations and, most importantly, adopts an explicitly normative agenda of developing better (read 'more democratic') planning practices (Healey, 1997c: 72).

One deficiency for which planning theory has been criticised is its limited reference to issues of 'place' (Hague, 1991). The place-deficiency characteristic of planning theory displays a number of dimensions. First, planning theories tend to discuss and develop concepts devoid of any historical, cultural or constitutional references. Certainly, a defining characteristic of theory generally is its application outside of any particular set of circumstances. However, a considerable body of planning theory does implicitly presuppose certain factors such as those indicated (i.e. constitutional and institutional settings), yet does not raise these to the level of explicit consideration.[10] Second, planning theory often fails to consider the nature of particular places that provide the context for the application of theoretical frameworks. However, the most serious criticism of planning theory is the perceived lack of concern with space and place as distinct concepts. Planning theory has previously aligned itself so closely with the analysis of decision-making and public administration that the issues of space and place often appear as additional attributes of planning theory rather than central ones.

The development of the collaborative planning framework develops the argument for a reassertion of place-focused concerns in public policy generally, and for an acknowledgement of the importance of geography in public policy matters (Healey, 1998: 3). An attempt to inject an element of spatial awareness and understanding into communicative approaches to planning theory is one of the defining characteristics of collaborative planning. The elevation of issues of space and place to an explicit consideration has also actively drawn communicative planning theory towards the development of practice forms, leading to a process of the spatialisation of normative planning theory.

In a European context, practical and policy agendas related to spatial planning have acted to promote the development of new approaches to planning activity at the regional and sub-regional levels. Indeed, Healey (1996a: 218) draws attention specifically to the resonance of collaborative and strategic planning approaches to contemporary planning issues in Europe (Healey et al., 1997; Committee on Spatial Development, 1999). The concept of 'place' employed in collaborative planning is one of space as a social construct (Healey, 1998: 5). In such a concept of place, places are no longer co-terminous with physical spaces and consequently places become subject to competing definitions between different groups. Places become formed as the product of competing and collaborative groupings in space, and may sustain multiple meanings and references contemporaneously. The increasing importance of spatial issues, combined with the development of revised conceptions of place, highlights the importance of establishing 'a new spatial imagination' and the need 'to reconfigure the time–space vocabulary used in planning practice' (Graham and Healey, 1999: 641).

The concept of stakeholding is a central element in the development of the model of collaborative planning (Healey, 1997a: 69–70, 91). The term is used in a relatively literal interpretation referring to all those who have a stake in a particular place. The nature of these stakes in places are recognised as diverse (ibid.: 69) and collaborative planning exercises call for the complete range of stakeholders to be acknowledged in the process (ibid.: 70). An important consideration in acknowledging the multitude of stakes is how such stakes find their expression through community-level formations (ibid.: 123–124). The concept of community enshrined within the collaborative planning framework is as both a spatially-based and a stake-based concept (Healey, 1996a: 223). A related concept of elevated importance in a collaborative planning framework is that of diversity. The collaborative planning model directly addresses and recognises issues of diversity in relation to planning (Healey, 1997a: 96–112). This recognition of diversity does not extend to the overt celebration of diversity as is evident in Sandercock's multiplicities (Sandercock, 1998c). Criticisms of Habermas's TCA include its denial and suppression of difference in favour of unity, and the suggestion of a perfectly transparent life, and where difference is recognised it is bracketed as a 'generalised other' (Cooke, 1994: 45; Huxley, 1998a; Hillier, 1998a). A collaborative model of planning is inclusive in the sense that access to strategy-making arenas is not restricted, yet this is again not as radical in orientation as the giving of 'voice' to poor and marginalised groups (Hillier and van Looij, 1997) or actively attending to the 'voices from the borderlands' (Sandercock, 1995).

A further key concept at the core of collaborative planning is that of strategy (Healey, 1996a). Strategy-making is proposed as a process of 'deliberative paradigm change' (Healey, 1997a: 244), a means of shifting systems of understanding and frames of reference. Clearly, the collaborative conception of strategy is more far-reaching than is the traditional understanding of strategy in the context of plan-making. One of the practical dilemmas at the core of collaborative planning practices is that between ensuring democratic and open process of participation while also ensuring the possibility of extracting and devising an appropriate (spatial) strategy (ibid.: 276). Strategies, once devised, are not incapable of being revised. Strategies may be altered or undermined by conflicting strategies arising from shifts in the bases of power or may simply be subject to interpretive drift (Healey, 1996a: 230). Indeed, built in to the model of collaborative planning is the need to subject strategic policy discourse to a process of 'continual reflexive critique' (ibid.: 230).

A concern for normative issues has been a long-standing feature of the planning discipline (Healey, 1983: 25), although the challenges presented by postmodern thought in planning have either detracted altogether from normative discussion or have criticised as 'naïve' (Flyvbjerg, 1996: 383) the normative agendas of modernist planning. Collaborative planning, however, is explicitly and intentionally concerned with progressing normative agendas (Healey, 1997a: 69–71; 1997c: 72). It is this characteristic, derived from theoretical foundations[11] and progressed into practice forms, that has provided opportunity for considerable criticism of collaborative planning. Dual criticism is levelled at the concept of collaborative planning in relation to its normative content. These dual criticisms also appear to contradict each other. The first criticism related to the normative dimension of collaborative planning is that it is normative to the point of prescription. The right to modify normative criteria in light of emerging processes is, however, reserved in a model of collaborative planning (Healey, 1997a: 69). The second dimension follows directly on from this statement by Healey and claims that there is insufficient normative content of a substantive nature – that collaborative planning is characterised by procedural normativism.[12] The apparent reluctance to direct normative criteria is illustrative of the tensions evident in the combined attraction to and repulsion from an emancipatory role. The collaborative approach attempts on the one hand to admit alternative methods of knowing and reasoning and to be able to accommodate different cultural standpoints within spatial planning processes. The counterpoint is that in refraining from stipulating elements of the process or of stating desired outcomes (leaving such issues to be determined by participants), the collaborative approach risks enabling narrow instrumental and utilitarian forms to continue to predominate.

The challenge of procedural normativism in collaborative planning has been outlined above. Commentators have developed criticism of collaborative forms of planning further in the sense of illustrating proceduralist tendencies. The contemporary attraction to issues of process derives from the identification of the possibilities that such a route offers of overcoming some of the issues of relativism (Healey, 1992a: 144). Collaborative planning clearly incorporates issues of process, yet it is also proposed as a form of planning that is not exclusively concerned with technique and procedure (Healey, 1997a: 71, 86). This appears to be contradicted by the statement that spatial planning efforts should be judged by their qualities of process (ibid.: 71) which will themselves be locally specific (Healey, 1996a: 231). Such a statement appears to diminish the importance of outcomes in planning activities. Planning academics are noted as having previously developed a preoccupation with procedural issues to the exclusion of the merits of issues of substance (Darke, 1985: 16) and this serves as a clear warning to those advocating collaborative planning practices that such activities do not negate the requirement to formulate some conception of a 'good society'.

PLANNING SYSTEMS, PLAN-MAKING AND PLANNERS

Collaborative planning has been identified as a form of practice, directed towards the transformation of current professional practices. The conception of collaborative planning as a form of planning requires attention to be paid to the manner in which it will be implemented and the precise form that it will take in practice. In the same manner in which many of the criticisms of the rational planning model focused on problems of implementation and the qualities of action as well as decision (Taylor, 1998: 111–118), collaborative planning as a form of planning must also demonstrate its qualities in implementation and action if it is to be deemed an effective model of planning. The preceding sections of this chapter have presented a series of issues related to collaborative forms of planning that present considerable challenges to both the machineries and general conceptions of modern planning systems in Western democracies. As a practical and theoretical concern, attention also needs to be given to the possibility of accommodating collaborative forms of planning. This section attempts to synthesise some of the consideration given to the extent to which present practice forms lie apart from those (ideal) forms proposed by advocates of collaborative planning approaches.

Planning systems
The following extract from Healey's *Collaborative Planning* identifies the strategic agenda for change demanded of planning systems and processes as a result of progressing collaborative forms of planning:

> planning processes need to work in ways which interrelate technical and experiential knowledge and reasoning, which can cope with a rich array of values, penetrating all aspects of the activity, and which involve active collaboration between experts and officials in governance agencies and all those with a claim for attention arising from the experience of co-existence in shared places.
>
> (Healey, 1997a: 87)

These are considerable demands and their achievement is likely to require fundamental change in the philosophies and practices of different planning systems. Consequently, a considerable amount of attention is paid within collaborative planning thesis to the strategic and systemic institutional design of governance and planning systems (ibid.: Chapter 9). The successful implementation of collaborative forms of planning establishes the need for a reassessment and evaluation of both planning systems and planning practices (ibid.: 72–73). There is, in a sense, a high degree of optimism that prevails among the advocates of collaborative planning and consideration of the potential for future change and action have not been circumscribed by existing and prevailing constraints. Collaborative and communicative theorists have been criticised for such optimism and the very real and practical difficulties of accommodating collaborative planning methods within the parameters of existing systems have been restated as a reminder of the factors mitigating against a collaborative approach. Critics are right to remind collaborative planning advocates of these difficulties, yet it is incorrect to state that the positions of those advocates are naïvely optimistic. Calls for widespread and systemic change are accompanied by statements acknowledging both the extent of that called for and the real difficulties in achieving this. In relation to the British planning system, Healey notes that: 'To develop this [collaborative] approach within the British planning system, however, will require a considerable transformation of the parameters of the current system and its practices' (Healey, 1998: 18).[13] The very real difficulties in accommodating collaborative forms of planning within existing planning frameworks and of transforming those frameworks are therefore recognised, although the possibilities of these being overcome are exaggerated.

Plan-making

The need to accommodate collaborative approaches to planning has directed attention towards the forms of plan-making that are appropriate to deliver the new forms of planning advocated within these frameworks (Healey, 1993b). In the United Kingdom, development plan-making (see Davies, 1999) provides 'an already-existing arena' (Healey, 1998: 4) for the development of collaborative planning infrastructures, although the development plan framework is simultaneously noted as placing limitations on the achievement of collaborative planning practices. The extent to which collaborative planning activities are able to make use of 'existing institutional capital' (Healey, 1998: 14) is a key consideration, particularly in the extent to which dominatory practices are perpetuated in making use of existing practices and institutions (Healey, 1996a: 223). Applying the perspective of collaborative and communicative practices to a consultation exercise in plan-making, Tewdwr-Jones and Thomas (1998) identify the dual difficulties arising from relatively open discussion forums in plan-making, as advocated in a collaborative approach. The first of these is, as identified by Healey, the difficulty in developing coherent strategies out of the proceedings of open discussion forums.

The second difficulty is the converse of the first, in that it identifies the difficulty in accommodating discursively produced strategies within the scope of existing frameworks.

Planners' skills and competencies

Collaborative planning is one of a series of recent developments in both planning theory and planning practice that demand new knowledge, skills and competences on the part of planners (Sandercock, 1998c). The fact that advocating new forms of planning demands new skills and competences is not readily translated into the practical achievement of the elements demanded. Indeed, the idea of prescribing new forms of planning for adoption by 'planners' is itself problematic and laden with tensions. The central tension in advocating new forms of practice for planners to engage in is illustrated in the following quotation: 'The figure of "the planner" is both an object of blame and hostility, and the subject of our hopes for effective community regulation' (Healey, 1997a: 3).

The condition is complicated further by the recognition that collaborative forms of planning present a number of challenges that are often more difficult than engaging in traditional and conventional forms. This is a characteristic common to any transformatory practice and is often associated with practices formulated on the basis of material derived from critical theory (Beauregard, 1995: 164). However, in advocating collaborative planning, Healey is careful not to distance such practices from the reach of those engaged in traditional planning practices:

> [Collaborative planning] will require a renewal of the expertise of those locked into the ways of thinking and acting of previous government practices and an enlargement of the fields of attention of the 'new' experts being drawn into the field, to ensure that they are able to relate knowledge about particular areas to the social context of the governance relations within which their expertise is being drawn upon (Albrechts, 1991; Healey, 1991b).
>
> (Healey, 1997a: 309)

These demands and changes are identified as presenting ethical challenges to experts (Campbell and Marshall, 1998, 1999, 2000b), to which planners are stated as already responding to or being transformed by (Healey, 1997a: 309). The impacts of collaborative planning forms upon the character and activities of planners also extend to the very materials with which planners work:

> In this context, the traditional spatial planner is in many cases being transformed into a kind of knowledge mediator and broker, using an understanding of the dynamics of the

governance situation to draw in knowledge resources and work out how to make them available in a digestible fashion to the dialogical processes of policy development.

(ibid.)

This reconceptualisation and transformation of traditional planners into mediators skilled in the management of knowledge do not, however, presuppose the continuation of central roles for planners. In accepting 'the fact that genuine planning means giving up an element of control' (Hillier, 1996b: 294), it follows that planners adopt less central roles in communicative models of practice such as collaborative planning (Van der Valk, 1989: 419, cited in Faludi and Korthals Altes, 1994). The effective integration of new, collaborative forms of planning into the present machinery of planning, along the lines identified above, necessarily poses specific challenges to planning educators (Christensen, 1993; Healey, 1996a: 232). Restoring knowledge of the processes and dynamics of urban and regional change, educating in skills of consensus-building and strategic ability are all areas identified as required skills for practising collaborative forms of planning (Healey, 1996a) with implications for the education of planners.

The preceding paragraphs have illustrated briefly the practical challenges presented in attempting to accommodate collaborative planning, from the practical skills of professional planners and their daily practices, through to the broader conditions and parameters of planning systems. The utilisation of existing frameworks and machinery of planning ultimately means that a theoretical foundation in social mobilisation is modified to become a reformist agenda. Proponents of collaborative planning models have been cautious in devising an agenda for change and have been careful not to propose a radical form of planning that is distanced from the realities of practice. In the same way that Habermas 'allowed [sociologists] to feel radical without actually being so' (Friedmann, 1987: 267), collaborative planning promises a suppressed radical and transformative edge to practice with limited scope for or evidence of delivery. Although 'the provocative contributions of critical theory' within the planning discipline (Briggs, 1998: 1) can be identified, it cannot be said that when translated into practice forms that it has produced the 'undeniably dangerous knowledge' (Kincheloe and MacLaren, 1998: 260) suggested possible within the wider context of critical theory.

CONCLUSION

The recent history of literature in planning theory illustrates the relative frequency with which theorists are called upon to search for 'new directions' in planning theory (Hemmens, 1980; Fainstein, 1999). The past two decades have witnessed the emergence and increasing credibility of different strands of planning theory, which may be interpreted as competitor paradigms in the wake of damaging criticism of the classic rational planning model. These different strands draw to variable extents on the rich history of intellectual thought in planning, where some remain relatively close to predecessor paradigms and others introduce new and radical ideas into planning theory discourse. Inevitably, it has been those ideas that do not deviate radically from traditional concepts in planning theory that have accumulated wide support and academic interest. It is the body of work labelled as communicative planning theory that has attracted such interest and remains as a testimony to the continued practice within planning theory of 'grand theorising' (Taylor, 1998: 152). It is precisely this characteristic that has generated increasing criticism from advocates of alternative theories and, as a result, planning theory discourse remains a vibrant and competitive arena, as illustrated by the selection of materials that are contained in this edited volume.

This chapter has utilised explicitly the concept of collaborative planning as a model or form of planning as opposed to a planning theory, a formulation evident in proponents of collaborative planning although often misinterpreted. I have also argued in this chapter that the development of collaborative planning is itself a response to certain contemporary socio-spatial and institutional trends that are presently developing within European spatial planning systems. If collaborative planning is to be properly regarded as a form of planning, then it must demonstrate its ability to be translated or carried into practice and to be able to shape that practice. Collaborative planning attempts to perform the intricate task of retaining allegiance to the utopian normative principles of the Habermasian project while also striving to gain credibility as a model of planning, a practice that is both capable of being carried out and socially worthwhile to do so. In this context, collaborative planning is proposed as a remedy to past experience in which 'the world of planning theory seemed yet again to have floated away from the world of those interested in planning policies and practices' (Healey, 1997b: 11). A number of issues have been sketched out in this chapter which suggest that there continue to be key areas in which collaborative planning may be criticised and considered deficient in relation to both its theoretical foundations and the forms that its practices adopt as derived from those foundations. The task of reconciling theory and practice is an extremely difficult one that carries with it a high risk of failing to satisfy the audiences and critics on either side. At a practical level, proponents of collaborative planning have conceded that some may find a model of collaborative planning 'too leisurely' or 'too unfocussed and diffuse' (Healey, 1992a: 159). At a theoretical level, critics who promote more fundamental and radical change in present societal relations may find collaborative planning to be a form that is too conservative, reinforcing present relations, and that ultimately belies its foundations in the social mobilisation tradition. In the same sense that Habermas (1984: xli) acknowledged the difficulty of simultaneously satisfying sociologists and philosophers, the model of collaborative planning also appears to risk being unable to reconcile the demands imposed by communicative planning theory with the accomplishment of collaborative forms of planning in practice.

NOTES

1   Both landscape and terrain (see Friedmann, 1987 on the latter) have proven to be popular metaphors in providing accounts of contemporary theorising. This popularity extends to both planning theory and wider geographical and urban studies.

2   Friedmann (1987: 35) uses and defends a general concept of planning rather than a specific urban and regional planning one, thereby enabling the claim of two centuries of planning theory to be broadly substantiated.

3   The author's own experience has also presented instances of use of the term collaborative planning in practice, illustrating (albeit anecdotally) the permeation of the term into professional practice.

4   The interrelationship between collaborative planning forms and technology in the form of urban modelling has been considered recently in the context of urban modelling as communicative action (Guhathakurtu, 1999). This specifically addresses the notion of computer-based collaborative planning (ibid.: 286).

5   As an example, Alexander's (1992: 51) account of different approaches to planning refers only to 'the communicative-interactive part of decision-making' rather than any specific body of communicative planning theory.

6   It is a fiction that any planning theorists ever regarded planners as autonomous thinkers, without expressing the important caveat (often omitted in caricatured forms used by proponents of other paradigms) that it represented an extraction from the realities of planning practice.

7   Interestingly, Friedmann (1987, figure 2) presents an account of the intellectual influences on *American* planning theory. Despite Friedmann's particular reference, his account provides adequately for a wider framework for understanding the development of planning theory, such is 'the discourse of international planning theory' (Healey, 1998: 14, citing Innes, 1995).

8   Friedmann's account (1987: 74–75) is again useful in understanding the extent to which different paradigms may be regarded as competitors or as historically separated traditions.

9   This phrase encapsulates a popular caricature of communicative action theorists' positions.

10   Planning theory as it is discussed here and is typically referred to in literature presupposes an Anglo-American context (Hall, 1983; Taylor, 1999).

11   Healey (1997a: 71) refers directly to Habermas's theory of communicative action as a 'useful normative resource' for constructing a model of collaborative planning.

12   The debate over proceduralism and substantivism is now often regarded as sterile (Graham and Healey, 1999: 623–624). However, it remains a useful principle for analysing and organising the content of different planning theories.

13   The principal barrier to the adoption of collaborative forms of planning within the British planning system is identified as its progressive restriction in the post-war era to a regulatory mode of planning.

3

Planning and Foucault

In Search of the Dark Side of Planning Theory
Bent Flyvbjerg and Tim Richardson

In this chapter we argue that the use of the communicative theory of Jürgen Habermas in planning theory is problematic because it hampers an understanding of how power shapes planning. We posit an alternative approach based on the power analytics of Michel Foucault which focuses on 'what is actually done', as opposed to Habermas's focus on 'what should be done'. We discuss how the Foucauldian stance problematises planning, asking difficult questions about the treatment of legitimacy, rationality, knowledge and spatiality. We conclude that Foucault offers a type of analytic planning theory which offers better prospects than does Habermas for those interested in understanding and bringing about democratic social change through planning.

INTRODUCTION

Power has become an inevitable question for planning theorists. John Friedmann, reflecting on the progress of theory to date, identifies theorists' ambivalence about power as one of the biggest outstanding problems in theorising planning (Friedmann, 1997). He urges theorists to build relations of power into their conceptual frameworks. But to bring power more closely into planning theory, we need to consider carefully what is meant by 'power', a concept which has long been the subject of philosophical discourse. For power cannot be simply bolted on to existing planning theory. What lies ahead is what John Friedmann has called 'the long trek' of integrating discourses on power with the 'still sanitised multiple discourses of planning theory' (ibid.). We believe that along the way, emerging theoretical work will be subjected to difficult challenges about power. Power may become the acid-test of planning theory.

In this chapter we take a few short steps on this long trek, and find our progress blocked by an unresolved difficulty with one such emerging body of theory. We encounter an emerging paradigm which asserts a new, Habermasian communicative rationality for planning (e.g. Innes, 1995), which is just beginning to be subjected to sustained critique on its treatment of power (e.g. Huxley, 1998a;

Huxley and Yiftachel, 1998). Some planning theorists may feel they have already explored this route, and that the obstacles to a Habermasian paradigm have been removed. We disagree. In this chapter, we argue that treatment of power in communicative theory is compromised by the nature of the theory itself.

We suggest that further progress towards the integration of power can benefit from the work of Michel Foucault, an *œuvre* which has been cited already by many planning theorists. We will argue that Foucault's work holds more promise, and is more relevant to planning theory than seems to have been generally recognised. The chapter pursues its arguments by exploring some of the vexed differences between Habermas and Foucault. We attempt to show that Foucauldian theory is not what has been described as a 'single minded preoccupation with the politics of coercion' (Friedmann, 1997), but a sustained analytics of power and rationality which we can use in productive ways to support the empowerment of civil society. This productive interpretation of Foucault's work appears to have been missed, or dismissed, which has facilitated the rejection of his theories in relation to planning. The position we are attempting to establish is that communicative planning theory fails to capture the role of power in planning. As a result, it is a theory which is weak in its capacity to help us understand what happens in the real world; and weak in serving as a basis for effective action and change. Because of these weaknesses, we believe that this approach to theory building is highly problematic for planning.

Some theorists might contend that 'using' Foucault, they have repaired the weaknesses in communicative theory which are exposed by juxtaposition with Foucault's work. We believe, however, that this cannot be done convincingly. More importantly we are concerned that, in spite of regular reference to Foucault in planning theory literature, there has not so far been a cogent exploration of the full import of his work for planning. In turning to Foucault's work, we argue that Foucauldian planning theory addresses exactly the weaknesses in the communicative paradigm, and makes effective understanding (*verità effettuale*, in Machiavelli's words; *wirkliche Historie* in Nietzsche's and Foucault's) and effective action possible, something planners and planning theorists have typically said they want. It requires a turn towards the dark side of planning theory – the domain of power – which has been occasionally explored by planning theorists (e.g. Marcuse, 1976; Roweis, 1983; Yiftachel, 1994; Flyvbjerg, 1996) but has been avoided by many others who see only oppression and coercion where power operates.

THE HABERMASIAN LEAP OF FAITH – A WEAK BASIS FOR PLANNING THEORY

We do not seek to summarise Habermas's work here, or to carry out an exhaustive critique, since that is undertaken elsewhere (see Chapter 2 in this volume). Instead, we engage with the treatment of power in Habermas's theories of discourse ethics and communicative rationality, which provide the theoretical cornerstones to the communicative planning movement. Habermas's utopian world is oriented towards an ideal speech situation where validity claims are based on consensus amongst equal participants, and the negative, distorting effects of power are removed. Friedmann compared this ideal of a 'perfect polity' to a graduate university seminar (1987: 267).

Habermas's definitions of discourse ethics and communicative rationality, and their procedural requirements (Habermas, 1979, 1983, 1985, 1990) are based on a procedural as opposed to substantive rationality: 'Discourse ethics . . . establishes a procedure based on presuppositions and designed to guarantee the impartiality of the process of judging' (Habermas, 1990: 122). Habermas is a universalistic, 'top-down' moralist as concerns process: the rules for correct process are normatively given in advance, in the form of the requirements for the ideal speech situation. Conversely, as regards content, Habermas is a 'bottom-up' situationalist: what is right and true in a given communicative process is determined solely by the participants in that process.

Habermas operates within a perspective of law and sovereignty which contrasts with that of Foucault (1980a: 87–88) who finds this conception of power 'by no means adequate'. Foucault (1980a, 82, 90) says about his own 'analytics of power' that it 'can be constituted only if it frees itself completely from [this] representation of power that I would term . . . "juridico-discursive" . . . a certain image of power-law, of power-sovereignty'. It is in this connection that Foucault (1980a: 89) made his famous argument to 'cut off the head of the king' in political analysis and replace it by a decentred understanding of power. For Habermas the head of the king is still very much on, in the sense that sovereignty is a prerequisite for the regulation of power by law.

The basic weakness of Habermas's project is its lack of agreement between ideal and reality, between intentions and their implementation, and is rooted in an insufficient conception of power. Habermas himself observes that discourse cannot by itself ensure that the conditions for discourse ethics and democracy are met. But discourse about discourse ethics is all Habermas has to offer. This is the fundamental political dilemma in Habermas's thinking: he describes to us the utopia of communicative rationality but not how to get there. Habermas (1990:

209) himself mentions lack of 'crucial institutions', lack of 'crucial socialisation' and 'poverty, abuse, and degradation' as barriers to discursive decision-making. But he has little to say about the relations of power that create these barriers and how power may be changed in order to begin the kinds of institutional and educational change, improvements in welfare, and enforcement of basic human rights that could help lower the barriers. In short, Habermas lacks the kind of concrete understanding of relations of power that is needed for political change.

Habermas (1987a: 322) tells us he is aware that his theory of communicative action opens him to criticism as an idealist: 'It is not so simple to counter the suspicion that with the concept of action oriented to validity claims, the idealism of a pure, nonsituated reason slips in again.' We would argue further that not only is it difficult to counter this suspicion, it is impossible. And this impossibility constitutes a fundamental problem in Habermas's work.

'There is a point in every philosophy,' writes Nietzsche (1966: 15[§8]), 'when the philosopher's "conviction" appears on the stage.' For Habermas that point is the foundation of his ideal speech situation and universal validity claims upon a Kirkegaardian 'leap of faith'. Habermas, as mentioned, states that consensus-seeking and freedom from domination are universally inherent as forces in human conversation, and he emphasises these particular aspects. Other important philosophers and social thinkers have tended to emphasise the exact opposite. Machiavelli (1984: 96) states: 'One can make this generalisation about men: they are ungrateful, fickle, liars, and deceivers.' Less radically, but still in contrast to Habermas, are statements by Nietzsche, Foucault, Derrida and many others that communication is at all times already penetrated by power: 'power is always present,' says Foucault (1988b: 11, 18). It is therefore meaningless, according to these thinkers, to operate with a concept of communication in which power is absent.

For students of power, communication is more typically characterised by non-rational rhetoric and maintenance of interests than by freedom from domination and consensus-seeking. In rhetoric, 'validity' is established via the mode of communication – e.g. eloquence, hidden control, rationalisation, charisma, using dependency relations between participants – rather than through rational arguments concerning the matter at hand. Seen from this perspective, Habermas (1987a: 297–298) seems overly naïve and idealistic when he contrasts 'successful' with 'distorted' utterance in human conversation, because success in rhetoric is associated precisely with distortion.

Whether the communicative or the rhetorical position is 'correct' is not important here. What is decisive, rather, is that a non-idealistic point of departure for planning theory must take account of the fact that both positions are possible, and even simultaneously possible. In an empirical-scientific context, something to which Habermas otherwise takes great pains to define himself, the question of communicative rationality versus rhetoric must therefore remain open. The question must be settled by concrete examination of the case at hand. The researcher must ask how communication takes place, and how politics, planning and democracy operate. Is communication characterised by consensus-seeking and absence of power? Or is communication the exercise of power and rhetoric? How do consensus-seeking and rhetoric, freedom from domination and exercise of power, eventually come together in individual acts of communication?

The basic question being raised here is whether one can meaningfully distinguish rationality and power from each other in communication and whether rationality can be viewed in isolation from power, as does Habermas. To assume an answer to this question *a priori* is just as invalid as presuming that one can ultimately answer the biblical question of whether humans are basically good or basically evil. And to assume either position *ex ante*, to universalise it and build a theory upon it, as Habermas does, makes for problematic philosophy and speculative social science. This is one reason we have to be cautious when using the theory of communicative rationality to understand and act in relation to planning.

Constituting rationality and democracy on a leap of faith is hardly sustainable. Habermas here seems to forget his own axiom that philosophical questions ought to be subject to empirical verification. And it is precisely in this sense that Habermas must be seen as utopian.

Furthermore, by determining validity, truth, justice, etc., as an outcome of 'the better argument', Habermas simply moves the problems of determination from the former concepts to the latter. As Bernstein (1992: 220) correctly points out, 'the better argument', and with it communicative rationality, is an empirically empty concept: 'Abstractly, there is something enormously attractive about Habermas' appeal to the "force of the better argument" until we ask ourselves what this means and presupposes.' The problem here is that in non-trivial situations there are few clear criteria for determining what is considered an argument, how good it is, and how different arguments are to be evaluated against each other. This does not mean that we should not attempt to identify arguments and evaluate them. Yet as Bernstein (1992: 221) states, 'Any society must have some procedures for dealing with conflicts that cannot be resolved by argumentation – even when all parties are committed to rational argumentation.' In real society – as opposed to Habermas's ideal types – it is precisely these kinds of conflicts which are of interest, both empirically and normatively.

In his *Between Facts and Norms* and other recent work, Habermas (1996a, b; 1995) has attempted to deal with power, and he has, at the same time, developed a deeper analysis of civil society (Carleheden and Rene, 1996). Despite these efforts, however, Habermas's approach remains strongly normative and procedural, paying scant attention to the preconditions of actual discourse, to substantive ethical values and to the problem of how communicative rationality gets a foothold in society in the face of massive non-communicative forces. Habermas also continues to disregard the particular problems relating to identity and cultural divisions as well as the non-discursive ways of safeguarding reason that are being developed by so-called minority groups and new social movements.

If Habermas's discourse ethics were to be constituted as reality, this would not signify an end to power, it would be a way to regulate power. And to the extent that actual implementation of discourse ethics would run counter to the interests of social and political actors – which is bound to be the case for societies and decisions of any complexity – discourse ethics will be opposed, whether such opposition can be rationally justified or not. The basic contradiction here is that coercion would be needed to arrive at Habermas's non-coercive communication. Agreement would, in this sense, be forced. So even if one could imagine the existence of what Habermas (1992a: 453) calls 'a political public sphere unsubverted by power', such a sphere could not be said to be free of power since it was established through a claim to power. The Nietzschean insight that historically morality has typically been established by immoral means would hold true for Habermas's morality, too. Power is needed to limit power. Even to understand how publicness can be established we need to think in terms of conflict and power. There is no way around it. It is a basic condition for understanding issues of exclusion and inclusion, and for understanding planning.

Habermas draws on the vocabulary of Enlightenment rationalism which Rorty has argued has become an impediment to the preservation and progress of democratic societies, in part because it has little to offer in understanding power (Rorty, 1989: 44). Habermas's efforts to achieve more rationality and democracy, however laudable, draw attention away from critical relations of power. The neglect of power is unfortunate, because it is precisely by paying attention to power relations that we may achieve more democracy.

If the goal of planning theorists is to create a planning which is closer to Habermas's ideal society – free from domination, more democratic, a strong civil society – then the first task is not to understand the utopia of communicative rationality, but to understand the realities of power. And it is here that the work of Michel Foucault, who has tried to develop such an understanding, becomes relevant.

TOWARDS FOUCAULT

Instead of side-stepping or seeking to remove the traces of power from planning, an alternative approach accepts power as unavoidable, recognising its all perva-sive nature, and emphasising its productive as well as destructive potential. Here, theory engages squarely with policy made on a field of power struggles between different interests, where knowledge and truth are contested, and the rationality of planning is exposed as a focus of conflict. This is what Flyvbjerg has called *Real-rationalität*, or 'real-life' rationality (Flyvbjerg, 1996), where the focus shifts from what *should* be done to what is *actually* done. This analysis embraces the idea that 'rationality is penetrated by power', and the dynamic between the two is critical in understanding what policy is about. It therefore becomes meaningless, or mislead-ing – for politicians, administrators and researchers alike – to operate with a concept of rationality in which power is absent (Flyvbjerg, 1998b: 164–165).

Both Foucault and Habermas are political thinkers. Habermas's thinking is well developed as concerns political ideals, but weak in its understanding of actual political processes. Foucault's thinking, conversely, is weak with reference to gen-eralised ideals – Foucault is a declared opponent of ideals, understood as defini-tive answers to Kant's question, 'What ought I to do?' or Lenin's 'What is to be done?' – but his work reflects a sophisticated understanding of *Realpolitik*. Both Foucault and Habermas agree that in politics one must 'side with reason'. Refer-ring to Habermas and similar thinkers, however, Foucault (1980b) warns that 'to respect rationalism as an ideal should never constitute a blackmail to prevent the analysis of the rationalities really at work' (Rajchman, 1988: 170).

Habermas's main complaint about Foucault is what Habermas sees as Fou-cault's relativism. Thus Habermas (1987a: 276) harshly dismisses Foucault's genealogical historiographies as 'relativistic, cryptonormative illusory science'. Such a critique of relativism is correct, if by relativistic we mean unfounded in norms that can be rationally and universally grounded. Foucault's norms are not foundationalist like Habermas's: they are expressed in a desire to challenge 'every abuse of power, whoever the author, whoever the victims' (Miller, 1993: 316) and in this way 'to give new impetus, as far and wide as possible, to the undefined work of freedom' (Foucault, 1984a: 46). Foucault here is the Nietzschean demo-crat, for whom any form of government – liberal or totalitarian – must be subjected to analysis and critique based on a will not to be dominated, voicing concerns in public and withholding consent about anything that appears to be unacceptable. Such norms cannot be given a universal grounding independent of those people and that context, according to Foucault. Nor would such grounding be desirable, since it would entail an ethical uniformity with the kind of utopian–totalitarian implications that Foucault would warn against in any context, be it that of Marx, Rousseau or Habermas: 'The search for a form of morality acceptable by everyone in the sense that everyone would have to submit to it, seems catastrophic to me' (Foucault, 1984c: 37, quoted in Dreyfus and Rabinow, 1986: 119). In a Foucauldian interpretation, such a morality would endanger freedom, not empower it. Instead, Foucault focuses on the analysis of evils and shows restraint in matters of commitment to ideas and systems of thought about what is good for man, given the historical experience that few things have produced more suffering among humans than strong commitments to implementing utopian visions of the good.

For Foucault the socially and historically conditioned context, and not fictive universals, constitutes the most effective bulwark against relativism and nihilism, and the best basis for action. Our sociality and history, according to Foucault, are the only foundation we have, the only solid ground under our feet. And this socio-historical foundation is fully adequate.

Foucault, perhaps more than any recent philosopher, reminded us of the crucial importance of power in the shaping and control of discourses, the production of knowledge, and the social construction of spaces. His analysis of modern power has often been read by planning theorists as negative institutionalised oppression, expressed most chillingly in his analysis of the disciplinary regime of the prison in *Discipline and Punish* (Foucault, 1979). However, it is Foucault's explanation of power as productive and local, rather than oppressive and hierarchical, that suggests real opportunities for agency and change (McNay, 1994). While Foucault saw discourse as a medium which transmits and produces power, he points out that it is also 'a hindrance, a stumbling-block, a point of resistance and a starting point for an opposing strategy'. So, at the same time as discourse reinforces power, it also 'undermines and exposes it, renders it fragile and makes it possible to thwart it' (Foucault, 1990: 101).

Foucault rarely separated knowledge from power, and the idea of 'power/knowledge' was of crucial importance:

> We should abandon a whole tradition that allows us to imagine that knowledge can exist only where the power relations are suspended and that knowledge can develop only outside its injunctions, its demands and its interests ... we should abandon the belief that power makes mad and that, by the same token, the renunciation of power is one of the conditions of knowledge. We should admit rather that power produced knowledge ... that power and knowledge directly imply one another; that there is no power relation without the correlative constitution of a field of knowledge.
>
> (Foucault, 1979: 27)

For Foucault, then, rationality was contingent, shaped by power relations, rather than context-free and objective.

According to Foucault, Habermas's (undated: 8) 'authorisation of power by law' is inadequate (emphasis deleted). '[The juridical system] is utterly incongruous with the new methods of power,' says Foucault (1980a: 89), 'methods that are employed on all levels and in forms that go beyond the state and its apparatus . . . Our historical gradient carries us further and further away from a reign of law.' The law, institutions – or policies and plans – provide no guarantee of freedom, equality or democracy. Not even entire institutional systems, according to Foucault, can ensure freedom, even though they are established with that purpose. Nor is freedom likely to be achieved by imposing abstract theoretical systems or 'correct' thinking. On the contrary, history has demonstrated – says Foucault – horrifying examples that it is precisely those social systems which have turned freedom into theoretical formulas and treated practice as social engineering, i.e. as an epistemi-cally derived techne, that become most repressive. '[People] reproach me for not presenting an overall theory,' says Foucault (1984b: 375–376), 'I am attempting, to the contrary, apart from any totalisation – which would be at once abstract and limiting – to open up problems that are as concrete and general as possible.'

What Foucault calls his 'political task' is

> to criticise the working of institutions which appear to be both neutral and independent; to criticise them in such a manner that the political violence which has always exer-cised itself obscurely through them will be unmasked, so that one can fight them.
>
> (Chomsky and Foucault, 1974: 171)

This is what, in a Foucauldian interpretation, would be seen as an effective approach to institutional change, including change in the institutions of civil society. With direct reference to Habermas, Foucault (1988b: 18) adds:

> The problem is not of trying to dissolve [relations of power] in the utopia of a perfectly transparent communication, but to give ... the rules of law, the techniques of manage-ment, and also the ethics ... which would allow these games of power to be played with a minimum of domination.

Here Foucault over-estimates his differences with Habermas, for Habermas also believes that the ideal speech situation cannot be established as a conventional reality in actual communication. Both thinkers see the regulation of actual relations of dominance as crucial, but whereas Habermas approaches regulation from a uni-versalistic theory of discourse, Foucault seeks out a genealogical understanding of actual power relations in specific contexts. Foucault is thus oriented towards phronesis, whereas Habermas's orientation is towards episteme. For Foucault praxis and freedom are derived not from universals or theories. Freedom is a practice, and its ideal is not a utopian absence of power. Resistance and struggle, in contrast to consensus, are for Foucault the most solid basis for the practice of freedom.

Whereas Habermas emphasises procedural macro-politics, Foucault stresses substantive micro-politics, though with the important shared feature that neither Foucault nor Habermas venture to define the actual content of political action. This is defined by the participants. Thus, both Habermas and Foucault are 'bottom-up' thinkers as concerns the content of politics, but where Habermas thinks in a 'top-down' moralist fashion as regards procedural rationality – having sketched out the procedures to be followed – Foucault is a 'bottom-up' thinker as regards both process and content. In this interpretation, Habermas would want to tell individuals and groups how to go about their affairs as regards procedure for discourse. He would not want, however, to say anything about the outcome of this procedure. Foucault would prescribe neither process nor outcome; he would only recommend a focus on conflict and power relations as the most effective point of departure for the fight against domination.

It is because of his double 'bottom-up' thinking that Foucault has been described as non-action oriented. Foucault (1981) says about such criticism, in a manner that would be pertinent to those who work in the institutional setting of planning:

> It's true that certain people, such as those who work in the institutional setting of the prison ... are not likely to find advice or instructions in my books to tell them 'what is to be done.' But my project is precisely to bring it about that they 'no longer know what to do,' so that the acts, gestures, discourses that up until then had seemed to go without saying become problematic, difficult, dangerous.
>
> (cited in Miller, 1993: 235)

The depiction of Foucault as non-action oriented is correct to the extent that Foucault hesitates to give directives for action, and he directly distances himself from the kinds of universal 'What is to be done?' formulas which characterise procedure in Habermas's communicative rationality. Foucault believes that 'solutions' of this type are themselves part of the problem. Seeing Foucault as non-action oriented would be misleading, however, insofar as Foucault's genealogical studies are carried out only in order to show how things can be done differently to 'separate out, from the contingency that has made us what we are, the possibility of no longer being, doing, or thinking what we are, do, or think' (Foucault, 1984a: 45–47). Thus Foucault was openly pleased when during a revolt in some of the French prisons the prisoners in their cells read his *Discipline and Punish*. 'They shouted the text to other prisoners,' Foucault told an interviewer. 'I know it's pretentious to say,' Foucault said, 'but that's a proof of a truth – a political and actual truth – which started after the book was written' (Dillon, 1980: 5). This is the type of situated action Foucault would endorse, and as a genealogist, Foucault saw himself as highly action oriented, as 'a dealer in instruments, a recipe maker, an indicator of objectives, a cartographer, a sketcher of plans, a gunsmith' (Ezine, 1985: 14).

The establishment of a concrete genealogy opens possibilities for action by describing the genesis of a given situation and showing that this particular genesis is not connected to absolute historical necessity. Foucault's genealogical studies of prisons, hospitals and sexuality demonstrate that social practices may always take an alternative form, even where there is no basis for voluntarism or idealism. Combined with Foucault's focus on domination, it is easy to understand why this insight has been embraced by feminists and minority groups. Elaborating genealogies of, for instance, gender and race leads to an understanding of how relations of domination between women and men, and between different peoples, can be changed (Benhabib and Cornell, 1987; Fraser, 1989; Bordo and Jaggar, 1990; McNay, 1992).

The value of Foucault's approach is his emphasis on the dynamics of power. Understanding how power works is the first prerequisite for action, because action is the exercise of power. And such an understanding can best be achieved by focusing on the concrete. Foucault can help us with a materialist understanding of *Realpolitik* and *Realrationalität*, and how these might be changed in a specific context. The problem with Foucault is that because understanding and action have their points of departure in the particular and the local, we may come to overlook more generalised conditions concerning, for example, institutions, constitutions and structural issues.

In sum, Foucault and Habermas agree that rationalisation and the misuse of power are among the most important problems of our time. They disagree as to how one can best understand and act in relation to these problems. From the perspective of the history of philosophy and political theory, the difference between Foucault and Habermas lies in the fact that Foucault works within a particularistic and contextualist tradition, with roots in Thucydides via Machiavelli to Nietzsche. Foucault is one of the more important twentieth-century exponents of this tradition. Habermas is the most prominent living exponent of a universalistic and theorising tradition derived from Socrates and Plato, proceeding over Kant. In power terms, we are speaking of 'strategic' versus 'constitution' thinking, about struggle versus control, conflict versus consensus.

EMPOWERING SPACE

A discussion of the full potential of Foucauldian analysis in enhancing our understanding of policy-making would not be complete without considering the spatiality of Foucault's work. This dimension has often been overlooked by theorists who have utilised his theories of discourse and power. Yet it is the spatiality of Foucault's thinking that makes his work particularly relevant to those working in overtly spatial activities such as planning. The importance of Foucault's attempted 'spatialisation of reason' has been discussed elsewhere (e.g. Flynn, 1993; Marks, 1995; Casey, 1996). For the purposes of our argument, it is important to explain here briefly how Foucault links space with the operation of discourses, and hence with power.

Foucault's critique, in *Discipline and Punish*, of Jeremy Bentham's panopticon is perhaps the archetypal example of this linkage (Foucault, 1979). Bentham published his plan for the panopticon in 1791. The object was to create a prison arranged

> [in a] semi-circular pattern with an inspection lodge at the centre and cells around the perimeter. Prisoners ... in individual cells, were clearly open to the gaze of the guards, but the same was not true of the view the other way. By a carefully contrived system of lighting and the use of wooden blinds, officials would be invisible to the inmates. Control was to be maintained by the constant sense that prisoners were watched by unseen eyes. There was nowhere to hide, to be private. Not knowing whether or not they were watched, but obliged to assume that they were, obedience was the prisoners' only rational option.
>
> (Lyon, 1993: 655–656)

Foucault explains the panopticon as a physical space which, through its design, permits physical functions such as surveillance and control of prisoners, and in so doing makes possible the prevailing modern social discourses of punishment, reform, and education (Marks, 1995: 75). The panopticon therefore serves as an axiom for contemporary socio-political conditions, illustrating how surveillance and control are reproduced in the fine grain of daily life, in cities where 'factories resemble schools, barracks, hospitals, which all resemble prisons' (Foucault, 1979: 228).

The construction of the panopticon therefore creates a social 'space-time': it creates or makes possible a particular set of practices and knowledges that are specific in both space and time. In this way, social norms are embedded in daily life, and the individual is 'constructed' to think and act in particular ways. Through this type of analysis, it becomes possible to understand, for example, how different planning policies construct their own 'space-time'. For example, discourses of personal freedom and mobility may require transport policies which produce transport spaces which are dominated, for example, by high speed private transport, at the expense of other types of movement. In this way, the late-modern individual is constructed as increasingly mobile, rejecting barriers to freedom of movement. The pattern of daily life adapts to the opportunities of increased mobility, and land use patterns shift to accommodate the new trends. Conversely, discourses of accessibility, which recognise the mobility needs of those who, for example, do not have access to a car, or wish to travel by other modes, may require policies which intervene to restrict the opportunities of movement by private car. Physical spaces may be characterised by pedestrianisation and traffic calming.

However, if spaces may be constructed, in this way, to allow certain forms of control, they may also be reconstructed by others, to serve different functions. Crush has shown, using Foucauldian analysis, how mining compounds in South Africa, which were designed using panoptic principles, were not simply environments for repression and coercion, but that they 'were also sites for the development and practice of rich oppositional cultures' (Crush, 1994: 320). Spaces, then, may be constructed in different ways by different people, through power struggles and conflicts of interest. This idea that spaces are socially constructed, and that many spaces may co-exist within the same physical space is an important one. It suggests the need to analyse how discourses and strategies of inclusion and exclusion are connected with particular spaces.

Perhaps most importantly in the context of this chapter, exploring power–space relations begins to suggest how we can supplement the preoccupation with language and communication, and develop a distinctively spatial planning theory.

FROM COMMUNICATIVE RATIONALITY TOWARDS POWER ANALYTICS

Many planning theorists have explored Habermas's work, and applied it to planning theory, notably John Forester, Patsy Healey and Judith Innes. Similarly, these theorists recognise the usefulness of aspects of Foucault's work in understanding the micro-politics of power, and how it affects planning in the real world. Indeed, John Forester seems to identify Foucault's genealogical approach – the contingent way he carried out his analyses of power, as opposed to his theories of power – as the type of thing he would like to see planners doing, advocating a Foucauldian 'contingent staged agency' (Forester, 1989: 237). However, Foucault's work has seldom been developed further than this in planning theory or research.

It is understandable why planning theorists have found Habermas a useful ally. He at least offers an alternative form of rationality to the modernist instrumental rationality, which continues to be asserted in, for example, the new technical approaches to environmental planning (Wong, 1997), and in the neo-liberal assertion of the critical role of market forces in shaping policy (Healey, 1997a). Habermas's work supports the attempt to break free from instrumentalism.

In the new paradigm power is acknowledged, but regarded as a negative, distorting influence whose effects can be removed by constructing idealised debate. The normative gaze of communicative theory looks towards an idealised future state of power-free critical debate. However, in the same way that Habermas fails to tell us how this ideal state can be reached, and so raises expectations without the prospect of fulfilling them, planning theorists who talk of Habermasian communicative planning as an actual possibility are constructing a powerful idea, without promise of its achievability.

Perhaps in recognition of this dilemma, another strategy adopted by planning theorists has been to use Habermas's ideals as a reference point, and to work backwards. The Habermasian ideal is accepted by many planning theorists as being out of reach, so the theory is applied in a different way, as a benchmark, a way of recognising the distortion of communications in real-life planning processes, and thereby guiding action to remove some of these distortions. This application of Habermas is shaping a tranche of empirical analysis of discourse in planning, and can be seen for example in the writings of John Forester:

> the responsibility of planning analysts is *not* to work to toward the possibility of 'fully open communications'. It is to work instead toward the correction of *needless* distortions, some systematic and some not, that disable, mystify, distract and mislead others: to work towards a political democratisation of daily communications.
>
> (Forester, 1989: 21)

Habermas does not provide a detailed vocabulary of power, or a theory of its workings, which might facilitate the close understanding of how power shapes policy-making and implementation, and rationality itself. Healey recognises the risk that the focus on the analysis of communicative acts 'could render the researcher myopic to the power relations among planners, municipal councils and clients' (Healey, 1992b: 10). She, like others, addresses the problem by emphasising the permeation of power into communication:

Communicative acts contain assumptions and metaphors, which by conveying meaning, affect what people do. These assumptions and meanings may carry power relationships or structure within them. In turn, the way communicative acts are created and used help sustain or challenge power structures.

(ibid.: 10)

This argument seems to acknowledge the importance of an understanding of power, but then turns away from it, towards a preoccupation with the mechanics and dynamics of communication.

This power blindness is keenly recognised by Hillier, who like Healey seeks to resolve matters by combining Foucauldian power awareness with Habermasian communicative rationality (Hillier, 1993). Her aim is to create the idealised Habermasian planning arena, where 'rational debate and negotiation are possible between proponents of different truths, tellers of different stories . . . The idea is to pre-empt conflict through negotiated agreement rather than entrenching it' (ibid.: 108). It seems that the point of linking Foucault and Habermas is again to remove the effects of negative power on the planning process. Yet Hillier's aim, like Healey's is the empowerment of disadvantaged interests, which surely requires an acknowledgement of power relations, and the possibility of power being used in a 'positive' way. Ultimately, it is not clear how the 'actualisation of Habermasian communicative action' (ibid.), which appears to depend on removing power from the gaze of planners and theorists, is to be achieved.

So Habermas neither provides an achievable model for planning, nor does he explain planning as it is actually done, to the exasperation of many practitioners. He therefore fails to provide guidance for those involved in bringing about change – he does not describe a world they inhabit. We see two dilemmas here for the communicative paradigm. First, why ground a planning paradigm in theory which is in turn grounded in an idealism that even Habermas, together with the proponents of his paradigm, accept as unattainable? Power-free critical debate is set up as the essence of what planning ought to be, when no planner has yet had the good fortune to work in such conditions. Nor are they likely to. Second, how can this theory help planners understand the full richness of what happens in real-life planning, when they are restricted to a vocabulary of communication, which conditions the thoughts of planning analysts?

Nevertheless, the rhetoric of communicative rationality is reproduced in a burgeoning of interest in, variously, communicative, collaborative, consensus-seeking analysis and normative theorising which is beginning to be translated into new models of practice. The outcome of the new consensus-based approaches to planning remains to be seen, particularly when applied to bitterly fought disputes, with which planning is well supplied.

Michel Foucault presents an alternative theoretical approach which deliberately focuses on 'what is actually done' and embraces the centrality of power. Additionally, the spatiality of Foucault's work opens up the possibility of developing a planning theory which understands how power and space are closely bound up in planning. The Foucauldian approach problematises existing planning tools and processes, suggesting the need for a power-sensitised understanding of the nature of knowledge, rationality, spatiality, and inclusivity in planning theory.

Communicative theory, unsurprisingly, tends to focus on communicative elements of planning. This focus risks over-emphasising the importance of key communicative events in planning, such as public meetings, while failing to capture the importance of non-communicative processes and actions. Communication is part of politics, but much of politics takes place outside communication. The reorientation from Habermasian towards Foucauldian planning theory – or planning analytics – would involve detailed genealogies of actual planning in different contexts, of the type we have mentioned above, which would allow a re-imagination of planning in the light of conflict. Foucault takes us towards a different kind of empirical work. Many of the methods are familiar to social researchers, but there are important differences in the overall approach:

- The researcher is equipped with a language and theoretical analysis of power and its techniques and strategies which guides the researcher through the studies.
- Research is based on richly contextualised, detailed case studies.
- The relations between power and rationality are a central focus.
- The focus moves beyond communicative events.
- The language is of conflict rather than communication. Planning processes and events are written as the playing out of strategies and conflicts rather than debates or arguments.
- There is no assumption of the key role of the planner as the facilitator of a rational, communicative process. This can be the role of some planners, but others, clearly, choose to work in other ways.

Even in the analysis of communicative events, a language and analytics of power are required, if the non-communicative effects on communication are to be understood.

Cases in point

More detailed theoretical argument, and detailed analyses of the type we advocate may be found elsewhere (e.g. Flyvbjerg, 1996, 1998b; Richardson, 1996, 1997, forthcoming). Here, we simply highlight what these studies of the '*Realrationalität*' of policy-making can reveal.

Bent Flyvbjerg's study of planning in Aalborg is a case study of planning and policy-making in practice, where rationality is malleable, and where power games are masked as technical rationality. The study focuses on the Aalborg Project, a scheme designed to integrate environmental and social concerns into city planning, including how to control the car in the city – a cause of degradation of the historic core. The planners of Aalborg are found to be real people who, like other actors in the case, engage in deception to achieve their ends, manipulating public debates and technical analyses. Institutions that are supposed to represent what they, themselves, called the 'public interest' are revealed to be deeply embedded in the hidden exercise of power and the protection of special interests. The project is set in Aalborg, but it could be anywhere. Aalborg is to this study what Florence was to Machiavelli's, no other comparison intended: a laboratory for understanding power. The focus is on a classic and endless drama which defines what modern planning and policy-making are and can be: the drama of how rationality is constituted by power, and power by rationality. Drawing on the ideas of Machiavelli, Nietzsche, Habermas and Foucault, the Aalborg case is read as a metaphor of modernity and of modern planning and policy-making. The study shows how power warps deliberation and how modern rationality can only be an ideal when confronted with the real rationalities involved in planning and policy-making. Finally, the study elaborates on how fruitful deliberation and action can occur by following a century-long, and historically proven, tradition of empowering democracy and civil society.

Tim Richardson's research has explored the construction sites of rationality: the critical stages in planning processes where the frameworks and tools are crafted which will shape later decisions. His study of the planning process for the Trans-European Transport Network explores how, in a heated power-play, the deployment of Strategic Environmental Assessment (SEA) became the central instrument for achieving environmental integration. However, SEA techniques were not simply taken off the shelf by policy analysts, and applied objectively in laboratories. They were constructed through contested political processes and were vulnerable to shaping by, and in favour of, particular interests. The political and institutional setting of SEA clearly shaped its scope, timing, methodology, and ultimately its impact. In this case SEA was shaped by the discourses of the single market and political integration, by inter-institutional politics, and by the actions of interest groups. Much of the policy process took place outside the public domain, and through non-discursive events, rendering a purely communicative focus unuseful. Communicative actions, such as the use of advocacy documents, or argumentation in committee, were tactical elements on a much broader canvas of power dynamics.

CONCLUSION: TAKE A WALK ON THE DARK SIDE

Planning theorists (and other modernist thinkers) have tended to disregard Foucault's work as being oppressive. His talk of the all-pervasiveness of power has been seen as crushing the life out of any possibility of empowerment, of change, of hope. Yet this analysis seems to be based on a superficial reading of parts of Foucault's major works, such as *Discipline and Punish*, rather than an attempt to understand his overall project. Foucault's theory of power is exactly not about oppressiveness, of accepting the regimes of domination which condition us, it is about using tools of analysis to understand power, its relations with rationality and knowledge, and using the resulting insights precisely to bring about change.

When it comes to portraying planners and planning, the quest of planning theorists could be called the escape from power. But if there is one thing we should have learned today from students of power, it is that there is no escape from it.

We wish to stress that the modern normative attitude – an attitude that has been dominant in planning theory throughout the history of this discipline – does not serve modernity, or planning theory, well. The ideals of modernity, democracy and planning – ideals that typically are worth fighting for – are better served by understanding *Realrationalität* than normative rationality. Normative rationality may provide an ideal to strive for, but it is a poor guide to the strategies and tactics needed for moving toward to the ideal. This, in our analysis, is the quandary of normative idealists, including the majority of planning theorists: they know where they would like to go but not how to get there.

The focus of modernity and of planning theory is on 'what should be done'. We suggest a reorientation towards 'what is actually done' – towards *verità effettuale*. In this way we may gain a better grasp – less idealistic, more grounded – of what planning is and what the strategies and tactics are that may help change it for the better.

Foucauldian analysis, unlike Habermasian normativism, offers a type of planning theory which is more useful in understanding how planning is actually done, and offers better prospects for those interested in bringing about democratic social change through planning. Habermas, among others, views conflict in society as dangerous, corrosive and potentially destructive of social order, and therefore in need of being contained and resolved. In a Foucauldian interpretation, conversely, suppressing conflict is suppressing freedom, because the privilege to engage in conflict is part of freedom.

The Foucauldian challenge applies to theory too: perhaps social and political theories that ignore or marginalise conflict are potentially oppressive. And if conflict sustains society, there is good reason to caution against an idealism that ignores conflict and power. In real social and political life self-interest and conflict will not give way to some all-embracing communal ideal like Habermas's. Indeed, the more democratic a society, the more it allows groups to define their own specific ways of life and legitimates the inevitable conflicts of interest that arise between them. Political consensus can never be brought to bear in a manner that neutralises particular group obligations, commitments and interests. A more differentiated conception of political culture than Habermas's is needed, one that will be more tolerant of conflict and difference, and more compatible with the pluralisation of interests.

A strong democracy guarantees the existence of conflict. A strong understanding of democracy, and of the role of planning within it, must therefore be based on thought that places conflict and power at its centre, as Foucault does and Habermas does not. We suggest that an understanding of planning that is practical, committed and ready for conflict provides a superior paradigm to planning theory than an understanding that is discursive, detached and consensus-dependent. Exploring the dark side of planning theory offers more than a negative, oppressive confirmation of our inability to make a difference. It suggests that we can do planning in a constructive empowering way, but that we cannot do this by avoiding power relations. Planning is inescapably about conflict: exploring conflicts in planning, and learning to work effectively with conflict can be the basis for a strong planning paradigm.

Part II

Planning Praxis and Interfaces

4
Personal Dynamics, Distinctive Frames and Communicative Planning
Mark Tewdwr-Jones

INTRODUCTION

Planners have long been concerned with the nature of planning as a decision-making process involving a variety of actors communicating, negotiating, bargaining and arguing over the 'right' way forward. The communicative school is the most recent body of literature that has sought to theorise the inter-personal relationships between actors in the planning arena (e.g. Forester, 1989, 1993, 1999c; Healey, 1992b; Sager, 1994). This school has received praise and an enthusiastic reception from the academic community for awarding almost a renaissance to planning theorising (Innes, 1995; Mandelbaum, 1996; Alexander, 1997). Notwithstanding the ongoing difficulties of ensuring that communicative theory is empirically fitting (Tewdwr-Jones and Allmendinger, 1998; Hillier, 2000; Phelps and Tewdwr-Jones, 2000; Tait and Campbell, 2000), in the way Forester (1993) has called for, this literature has opened up some reflective debate about the very purpose of planning theory, its tributary and cadet branches, and ways forward.

For the purposes of my own contribution to this volume, I wish to devote attention to one particular aspect of recent theorising related to politics, professionalism and public participation, and assess – in the context of the communicative debate – the planner's personal behaviour, motivations and dilemmas. These issues remain undeveloped in the emerging paradigms of planning theory although they have, of course, been discussed elsewhere previously by established academic names. More recently, Philip Allmendinger and I have argued (e.g. Allmendinger and Tewdwr-Jones, 1997; Tewdwr-Jones and Allmendinger, 1998) that what is termed 'the personal dynamic' or individualistic dimension of planning has not been thought through sufficiently in the development of recent planning theorising. The personal dynamic, thoroughly debated by the likes of such respected theorists as Friedmann (1973, 1987), Faludi (1987), Schön (1983), and Hoch (1994), remains just as relevant today as it seemed twenty or thirty years ago. Indeed, within the context of communicative planning, the position of the individual planner, with his or her motivations, ways of thinking and styles of acting and communicating, employing personal and professional goals, seems to be pivotal in the adoption of more inter-personal relations between different planning actors. Forester's (1999b, 1999c) call for planners to supplement their reflection-in-action role with a more social and political work of deliberation must be seen within a new untapped challenge: convincing the individual planner that a particular ethical position in the way they approach decisions, reconcile different thoughts and then decide to act is warranted and can be justified. If this ethos is one that planning academe aspires to, more work needs to be undertaken in the world of planning practice concerning the behaviour of individual planners.

Forester has firmly thrown in his lot with the oppressed, possibly power*less* groups, and encourages planners to enhance participatory processes to provide a voice and opportunities for all sections of society. But the question that constantly focuses my mind is, 'Do planners (even public sector planners) actually have a moral obligation and political purpose to enhance community participation?' More fundamentally, what exactly is a 'moral obligation in planning'? This perspective, inherent throughout Forester's work, revolves around the planner being viewed as someone who should continually foster participatory processes to expand democratic rights, and access to those rights, to support citizens' voices, and to redirect resources to the most needy. In many contexts, this is indeed a goal worth pursuing (race, gender, culture and ethnicity) and, in the *parlance* of Forester, worth deliberately acting on. But it is a rather sensitive view when planners (variedly defined as Forester himself admits) work in various political settings, workplaces, economic and environmental conditions, and social contexts, and – more fundamentally – possess varied personal preferences. In our global world, it can be easy to forget that geography, politics and culture vary markedly. In a world of difference (Sandercock, 1998c) issues such as thinking to act in the public interest is often questioned as a feasible goal (Campbell and Marshall, 1999), particularly when so much relies on the individual to achieve implementation. These issues do possess some important implications for the future of planning theory, the direction of the communicative school, and the expectations placed on planners as individuals. In short, this chapter is my own development and use of theories in 'paying attention to the world' (Forester, 1990: 53); my own particular world for theorising concerns the individual planner's abilities to think (not necessarily to act) in an environment of pressure.[1]

The personal dynamic is also an important issue to consider since Forester (1999c) is calling more explicitly for planning schools to subject their students to this type of reflection and learning with the purpose it seems of leaning heavily on 'moral duties'. Ultimately, the decision whether to act deliberatively or not remains the planner's. But it brings into question what goals planners possess, to act in favour of the public, and to foster mutual learning, discourse and collective action.

Both goals may be relevant for some people some of the time, individually or collectively, and possibly should be written onto the hearts of those emerging with planning qualifications. But these goals are not the only reasons why people choose to study planning, why planners exist, or why planning is stretched across various agencies of governance, sectorally, territorially, and substantively.

The individualistic element of planners' thinking, reflecting and learning in the face of collective community need or action is perhaps the crucial aspect of planning academy's precarious role in all this. Forester contends that it is simply not sufficient for planners to identify or rediscover power in practice and makes a passionate plea: 'Let us stop rediscovering that power corrupts, and let's start figuring out what to do about the corruption' (Forester, 1999c: 9). In the face of Holocaust historiography presented both here and elsewhere (Forester, 1999b) (that is intended explicitly to present the argument of the need to rebuff the powerful in society and those with narrow self-interest concerns), to suggest here that not all planners are imbued with liberal notions of democracy (Allmendinger, 1996; Tewdwr-Jones, 1996; Allmendinger and Tewdwr-Jones, 1997) might be viewed in some quarters as, at best, overt individualism, and at worst, support for power-playing groups bent on strategic behaviour to counteract public participatory views. I would suggest there are both institutional and territorial dependencies to 'acting on', let alone varying personal capacities of thinking whether and how to act, that as educators we need to consider further. This is the theme of the chapter.

There is also an alternative view not particularly discussed by Forester of why planners tell each other stories, learn from each other and act in a reflective way and, at times, deliberatively. To put it in the starkest terms, they reflect as autonomous individuals and learn 'how not to get caught out', either in adversarial settings, in politically-charged debates, or at public meetings. Here, under this scenario, it is self-interest, career development, and professional esteem that are the goals at the forefront of planners' minds.[2] The difference is actually one of presentation (Goffman, 1959), or rather between backstage and frontstage deliberations so that there occurs a dressing up dramaturgically in the language of participation generation, fostering open and inclusive dialogues, and mutual learning.[3] This is obviously a less receptive view in planning academe than that propounded by Forester and might even be called 'cynical'.[4] But there is nothing anti-community about this view nor is it necessarily a weak view in the face of a political challenge within planning 'to act'. What is more important for us as planning theorists and educators is to highlight the possibility for these individual types of thought processes to exist or, rather coexist, and to dissect the notion that encouraging collective open action in planning necessarily equates to the correct moral stand of the planner.[5]

In this chapter, I would like to discuss dilemmas of planning practice, using a number of stories from my own period in local government, and to discuss issues revolving around the individual planner's interest in public participation, professionalism, and politics. My use of personal experiences to prove my argument seems to be an obvious, if a rather revealing way to illustrate these issues, but I hope they dovetail with other contemporary theorising. There are some extremely good examples of these debates currently underway by the likes of Heather Campbell and Bob Marshall relating to ethics, morals and dilemmas in British planning practice (see, for example, Campbell and Marshall, 1998, 1999, 2000b; see also Chapter 5 in this volume). This work builds on work undertaken by a variety of British and North American authors over the past twenty years, including Forester (1993), Healey (1992b), Hoch (1984), Howe (1994), Howe and Kaufman (1979, 1981), Thomas and Healey (1991), and Wachs (1985). John Forester has shown to good effect how stories are useful in dissecting planning theory (see, for example, Forester, 1999c) and so I take a cue from him.

In debating these issues, I hope to be able to expand some issues that have been touched upon previously in dialogues with Philip Allmendinger (Tewdwr-Jones, 1995, 1996; Allmendinger, 1996) and Ernest Alexander (Alexander, 1997, 1999a; Allmendinger and Tewdwr-Jones, 1997; Harris, 1997) relating to the relationship between planning theory and planning practice and the opinions of planners themselves towards the apparent 'gap' or translation between the theory and practice sides of the discipline. Although some of this material has been discussed before, I wish to include it in this volume devoted to planning futures since I believe we are closer to finding ways of resolving and understanding the nature of the translation process for individuals from theory (or university) to practice (or professionalism). I hope the chapter will also assist students of planning to understand the sorts of dilemmas I went through during my degree and professional training, many of which are still experienced by students each year both before they enter and during their experience of the real world. I conclude the chapter by debating some theoretical deliberations and suggesting where some branches of planning theory might lead next.

Before we commence, some caveats are necessary. This chapter does not offer a grand prescription for answering the big question, 'What is planning?', but it does provide some clues as to how we can make a better effort in planning education towards theoretical teaching and in preparing students for their professional roles. I do not intend for my work to be allied to non-communicative theories of action. Although links may be drawn to teleological, normatively regulated and dramaturgical actions, I wish to focus on the thought process – 'the art of thought' – that occurs one stage prior to action and determines whether and how the individual acts, that Wallas (1926) classically discussed seventy-five years ago. Finally, although it may be possible to draw links with 'dark side theorists' in the style of Foucault and Nietzsche (e.g. Flyvbjerg, 1998b; Flyvbjerg and Richardson, 1998; Huxley, 1998a; Yiftachel, 1994), I am less interested in the planner who appears to be Machiavellian bent on utilising strategic action to reach a desired pre-determined end. The planners I discuss here are those who perhaps possess no clear idea of where they want particular decisions or plans to lead to. In essence, we need to acknowledge that planners vary and are constantly searching for a role (Underwood, 1980) that they themselves are comfortable with. In relation to the stories from practice, names of the innocent have been protected.

THE INDIVIDUAL PLANNER: RELATIONAL WEBS, MOTIVATION AND THE WILL TO ACT

At the outset, it is worth discussing the communicative approach in relation to one of the main concentrations of power within planning: the individual planner. What are the implications of the communicative turn for planners and professionals? Tewdwr-Jones and Allmendinger consider that:

> A strong theme of the communicative rationalists' theory is to deny a central co-ordinating or expert role for the planner in the discourse arena, as it is the planner who is tarnished with the power and administrative trappings of the administrative elite.
>
> (1998: 1984)

Campbell and Marshall (1999) also highlight the lack of universal principles for planners in communicative planning. This possibly results in a tendency for planners to undertake a procedural role rather than attempt to facilitate discourse and ensure that marginalised interests are heard. Both Forester and Healey have rather ambiguous roles for planners under their communicative turns. Healey (1997a: 309) calls for a 'more interactive relationship between experts and the stakeholder communities they serve' while Forester (1996b) sees planners as performing the role of a 'critical friend'. Healey has also stated her own position on the individual instrumentalities:

> Our sense of ourselves is socially constructed in social relations with others ... We work at this sense throughout our lives, but always spinning around these relations. We are distinctly ourselves, but also a part of others. What we are not are autonomous individuals, with our own little package of preferences ... If planners come with too much pre-packaged, they haven't much option but just to say no. They are saying no as much to the process as the product.
>
> (Healey, 1996b: 4)

Healey (1999a) has recently discussed, after Latour (1987) and Bourdieu (1990), how webs of relationships are important in the development of intellectual, social and political capital, citing Hwang's (1996) discussion of the relationship between knowledge and action and Shotter's (1993) view that social life is 'an active process of continual creating and transforming of identities and social bonds in interaction with others' (Healey, 1999a: 114). Webs develop some meaning and coherence as they become relational worlds in which people construct their being, and some sense of themselves, although these webs tend to differ in different places, spaces and at different levels without, perhaps, interacting (ibid.: 115).

This is where the communicative theorists and I start to disagree. I accept that individuals do develop their own sense of identity and mature their opinions as they become involved, or are affected by, relational webs. Furthermore, these relational webs do need some co-ordinating to ensure some element of compatibility or coherence is provided strategically in order to develop shared understandings. My fundamental problem with this notion rests not with the principle itself, but rather on discovering individuals' thought processes as they exist – perhaps subconsciously – prior to interaction in or with their relational webs, that is, before individuals are subjected to interaction with other planning actors. Or, to place it in the context of webs and planning, how do graduate planners resolve their existing relational webs (developed prior to or outside education and professional practice) with new or emerging relational webs (developed once their planning education commences or once graduates are employed within particular planning organisations)?

I firmly believe that individuals can hold personal preferences, gathered independently from experiences and influences, not only from relations with other contacts but through varying sources, including media, culture, education, and environment, and bring these to bear on their professional planning activities. Alexander (1999b), discussing the relationship between the self as a strategic actor, and the need to foster open inclusionary participation in the style of communicative planning, has stressed that 'Planning never really involves independent, autonomous action.' I would agree with the sentiments of both Healey and Alexander with regard to *action*, but both seem to miss the point that the individual planner will possess autonomous *thought* prior to his or her interactions with others in the planning arena. It is possible that the individual planner will possess dilemmas of how to resolve the pre-professional relational webs with post-education relational webs. These pre-professional webs may yield a particular thinking style or belief that becomes stamped on the heart of the individual; they may even relate to beliefs, values, trust, sincerity, and legitimacy, some of which are features of communicative action. They may, alternatively, possess beliefs to be strategic, competitive, or political. The question for the individual planner once he or she graduates into employment, is 'how do I resolve my possibly conflicting values developed from my different relational webs?', 'For the purpose of my personal thought processes − rather than of the institutions I work within − who is going to advise me on how I should resolve my thoughts?'

Alexander (1999b) calls for academia to consider looking at interdependence as the link between the 'planner-prince' and communicative planning, but this assumes that planners will always possess a desired end once they commence acting. This may be a correct assertion, but planners may not possess a desired end either before they consider how and whether to act or even prior to entering interaction with others. Here lies the dilemma for the individual in his or her own mind, faced with the need to act and the requirement to be strategic to reach an end, on the one hand, and communicative for wider interests and voices, on the other. In essence, and utilising Alexander's (1999b) distinction, it is not only a question of the planner relating strategic action to communicative action, it also involves the planner relating his or her personal dynamic to the two types of action.

Personal preferences are pivotal to the delivery of communicative planning systems. Some of what we know is generated 'implicitly', that is, without our conscious awareness (Underwood and Bright, 1996) and it would be correct to believe that parts of us, and what we believe, are determined by other people, our contacts with them, and the way we react to these representations. But that is only part of the picture. Planners, as professionally trained individuals, are influenced by a whole series of codes and experiences, some of these are 'explicit' and some are 'implicit'. It is notoriously difficult, even for cognitive psychologists (Wilson and Stone, 1985), to identify the way people 'perceive and remember objects and events, store and retrieve knowledge, think, reason and solve problems' (Dorfman et al., 1996). But the pre-packaging that is inherent within individuals does not necessarily cancel out other interests or opportunities when they need to be confronted, as Healey (1996b) seems to think, and certainly it seems inappropriate to generalise that all individuals think in the same way. This broader thesis, that attempts to distinguish between implicit and explicit cognition within individuals and their perceptions towards situations, merely *acknowledges* that the psyche of individuals is a relevant factor in establishing inter-personal relations. If anything, it legitimises the planner and his or her background (and thought processes) even before discussions take place on fostering open communicative action (through the ability to act). Why is this relevant? Put simply, analysis of the thought processes of the planner before considering whether and how to act is one of the fundamental determinants in whether communicative processes are able to be delivered.[6]

With particular regard to planning, there are two problems with a communicative role if, in the style of Forester (1999b, 1999c), planners are to be persuaded to take a more proactive role. First, how do and why should planners think that acting communicatively to counteract incidences of distorted communication within a public arena is an ethically correct position? The 'public' are only one part of a multifarious, conflicting and confusing number of clients in urban planning. Kitchen (1997) identifies ten 'customers' within the planning system that exhibit potentially incommensurable interests, while Campbell and Marshall (1998) in discussion of the various roles expected of planners, rhetorically ask: 'are planners obliged to secure the interests of their political employers, the organisation, personal values, clients, the wider community, future generations or the profession?' (1998: 117).

Forester (1999b, 1999c) has made it clear that he believes planners should act in the interests of the disadvantaged or oppressed. So communicative theory in planning, as it has now been transposed under 'deliberative planning', can hardly be concerned with achieving non-distortion, since the planner under Forester's thesis is expected to enter into the arena with a pre-packaged notion that he or she is there to act for a particular interest or need; in other words, the planner enters with an *a priori* assumption that their role is to facilitate the disadvantaged. This might be seen to be constituting teleological action (Tewdwr-Jones and Allmendinger, 1998), although Habermas has identified the possibility of other pure forms of action co-existing with communicative action (Habermas, 1984: 327–328). To make a link here with the idea of relating the personal dynamic with the requirement to act, would such a role, if adopted by a planner consciously, constitute a particular style of action within the arena of debate that has been *either* conceptually driven by personal preferences, perceptions and memories in advance – the 'pre-packaging' that Healey (1996b) refers to – *or* constructed out of ongoing spinning social relations? Isn't there a possibility for it to be both? If planners determine whether they want to adopt the role of a facilitator of action for the disadvantaged against powerful interests, do they decide in the context of society and the debating arena, or do they decide prior to entering the debating arena as autonomous individuals? In the style of Alexander (1999b), how do planners marry up their existing thought processes with the interactions they are about to experience? This is the crux of the problem.

Second, there is evidence to suggest that some – but maybe not all – planners do not hold thought processes to suggest that they should act in a more open and democratic way (Allmendinger, 1996; Kaufman and Escuin, 1996). In this context, I can well understand Forester's (1999c) frustrations with the planning profession and the will to act. In the UK, attempts at fostering enhanced public participation in planning remain comparatively rare (Thomas, 1996; Tewdwr-Jones and Thomas, 1998). Recent graduates entering the planning profession have been less – rather than more – positive about public participation, preferring instead to view a more technocratic role that emphasises professional competency over consensus building (Tewdwr-Jones, 1995, 1996; Campbell and Marshall, 1998; see Chapter 5 in this volume). This *technocentric* perspective derives from two sources. The first is the realisation by planners of the existence of competing and often irreconcilable interests associated with the growth in recent years of adverse public reaction both against development and the professionals charged with co-ordinating change (Tewdwr-Jones, 1999). This perspective has often coloured the attitude of public sector planners and made them suspicious about increasing the degree of participation that often tends to favour narrow sectional (powerful) interests.

A second reason for the *technocentric* perspective is that planners in the UK have never been encouraged or trained to act in a democratically biased way. The very notion of 'professional' is premised upon the idea of specialist knowledge, something that separates the professional as an elite (rightly or wrongly) from the rest of society. Reade (1987) and Evans (1993, 1995) have followed the socio-logical interpretation of these elites and argued that planning, like other professions, has formed a 'corporatist bargain' with the state, exchanging economic security for compliance in capital accumulation. Planners are consequently caught in a trap: to be a professional requires possessing a specialised area of knowledge for which they are rewarded and this fact rests heavily on their mind. But the communicative turn argues for a more pluralistic and equal relationship between 'the planner' and the planned; it is hardly surprising, therefore, that some planners are reluctant to question their supposed professional status even if they share the values that underpin the communicative turn in planning for fear of losing status or rewards. This provides a good example of the problem of attempting to marry up the personal dynamic with the will to act, and act in a particular way.

If planners are required to ditch their pre-packaged attributes before entering into an arena of debate, one assumes that this includes their education, training, professional status, and even personal views. Disarming planners of their professionalism would seem an obvious move to rid the system of some of the pre-packaging.[7] This is something that has not been discussed in the literature to date but one which certainly could be expected if the theorists advance their theses to their logical conclusions (Alexander, 1999a). The outcome of this, however, might prove to be a weakening of planning. It could also impact on recruitment: enhancing the public's voice in the profession is not the only reason why students choose to study planning or become professional planners.

Overall, then, the personal dynamic or individualistic dimension of planning will prove to be a contributory, although imprecise, factor in determining whether and how the planner acts in the first place and then acts in a particular way. Crudely put, communicative planning seems to be premised on an assumption that planners, faced with 'the truth' and the evidence of the need to act in a more open and inclusionary way for wider interests, will automatically change their allegiances (their pre-packaged thought processes) to this new noble cause. This, after all, is the very purpose of Habermasian communicative theory of action: achieving open inter-personal communication and avoiding the restrictive attributes of the isolated actor (Habermas, 1984). In adopting this wider role, planners would be expected to abandon the trappings of a professional elite, the rewards and status associated with the group, and avoid any discourse or styles of thinking that could give rise to the suggestion that they possess pre-packaged ideas contrary to those they are facilitating in the arena of debate.

ROOTING AROUND IN THE PAST: CONFUSION AND UNCERTAINTIES DURING THE EARLY YEARS

In order to debate these issues further, I wish to change the nature of the discussion at this point and tell some stories. My intention here is to illustrate at first hand the individualistic element in planning, and the implicit and explicit assumptions that exist within individuals as thought processes. These thought processes cause both conceptually driven ideas and views formulated out of spinning social relations and occur (or exist) prior to acting. Since I claim to be no expert in cognitive psychology, either academically or in the undertaking of psychological tests in the laboratory, the nearest position I can advance in order to illustrate my arguments is for me to take examples that I, personally, was involved with during my time in planning practice. If these stories and experiences are not viewed as representative, this merely adds weight to my perspective: individuals *do* possess self-grown dilemmas, goals and preferences that *could* cause impediments to foster either the establishment of open and inclusionary arenas or the determined need to act strategically for a given end.

My experience in practice and my own dilemmas about what planning was supposed to be all about deeply affected me. My uncertainties about planning practice shaped my own pre-packaged views of planning as I eventually entered a period in local government planning practice. Fifteen years on, these crucial questions remain with me, as I have mentioned elsewhere (Tewdwr-Jones, 1996, 1999). They are fundamental to this chapter and, indeed, to this edited collection as a whole. They represent the ongoing search by planning academics for some sort of

Holy Grail of planning theory, the ultimate answers to the big questions that have always been inherent within the individual planner, which can affect the 20-year-old planning student as much as the professor of planning:

- What is planning and who does it operate for?
- What is the distinction between professional duties and personal interests?
- What role should the professional planner take in wider public interests?
- In whose interests should professional planners work?
- What is the relationship between planning theory and planning practice?

I wish to analyse these questions with reference to four stories taken from my planning practice experience. The objective here is to demonstrate, on the one hand, the problems of translation from pre-packaged thoughts to the real political world of planning, and on the other, the difficulties of reconciling personal views with professional duties. This is the subject of the next section.

THE TRANSLATION FROM PRE-PACKAGED IDEAS TO PRACTICE

Here, I wish to reveal some illustrations from my own experience of professional planning practice relating to dilemmas, uncertainties, and ethics that affected me during my immediate post-degree training – examples that basically I had been ill-equipped to deal with. They are drawn from a period in UK local government practice where I was employed, first of all, as a planning control (zoning) officer with responsibility for negotiating with developers and consulting members of the public, and then as a forward planner responsible for drafting planning policies. The examples are routine in nature, and are drawn from well over a decade ago although I have chosen not to reveal the names and geography of the cases referred to.

The stories are revealed in relation to four broad themes relating to my own thought processes and experiences as a junior professional planner: moral dilemmas; acting unprofessionally; public frustrations; and the loyalty card. Each possesses an element of humour,[8] although there are clearly important professional issues at stake in each case, and certainly ones that gave rise to concern or worry on my part at the time. In each example, after setting out the story within its wider conceptual question, I provide a self-reflective discussion of the influences on the decisions and the reasons for them, together with an overview of the implicit and explicit factors at play.

Story 1: Moral dilemmas. What is planning and who does it operate for?

In my fourth week of employment after graduating, I was asked by one of my senior planning colleagues to go out on a site visit to meet a member of the public who had submitted an application for planning permission to place a large neon-lit sign advertising his hairdressing business at the front of his property. His business was located some way back from the main highway and he was concerned that the public were unable to see his present small sign. His business was housed in a Grade II* Georgian listed building in an extremely prominent part of a small market town, recognised by the local authority for its historical and urban townscape attributes. Both the property and this part of the town were designated for conservation purposes. It was my duty to inform the applicant that he would be 'unlikely to receive planning permission from the local authority' to erect this enormous sign (local government-speak for a pending refusal) for conservation reasons, namely that it would detract from the surrounding area. The authority would be willing, however, to consider a smaller, more appropriately designed sign, at the front of his property if he was willing to change the dimensions of his scheme.

I motorcycled down to the town and met the businessman within his hair-dressing premises and explained to him the nature of my visit, adding that it was an issue 'of some delicacy'.[9] He took me to a back room and it was there the conversation progressed, I explaining to him the planning, conservation and urban design problems of his application and he telling me how important the new large sign would be for business purposes. I had some personal sympathies with his predicament although knew that I was there purely for professional planning reasons. His tone increased noticeably as his anger developed over the course of the 5-minute conversation once he started to realise that his current scheme was unacceptable. I stood there, a little nervously to say the least, while the ranting and raving continued. Having been warned in advance by my superiors 'not to react on any count' if matters became difficult, I decided to terminate the meeting there and then since there was clearly no scope for negotiation and the applicant was demonstrating a complete refusal to compromise. As I made my way out of the room, the applicant rounded on me, shut the door I was about to leave through in my face and stood directly in front of me, so close that I felt the breath emanating from his nostrils. He looked me straight in the eye and said quietly, 'OK, I've heard about this sort of thing with planning. How much do you want?'

At this point, I am sure my pupils expanded to enormous proportions. Did I really hear that? Was he suggesting what I thought he was suggesting? 'Pardon?', I stuttered. 'How much do you want?! You planners are all the same. So if it's going to cost me to get the sign through, tell me what it's worth . . . A Thousand? . . . Two thousand? . . . A car? I could get you a second-hand BMW, if you like . . .'. By this time, not only were my eyeballs bulging out of their sockets but my head was in a spin. I could almost hear some harp music in the distance as I pondered – for what seemed like minutes but what was probably seconds – the potential of accepting £2000 to pay off my college debts, of vacationing in Hawaii, or driving around in a BMW. This was quite a bribe and he obviously desperately wanted that sign.[10]

I could not recall receiving any teaching at university about accepting bribes (or rather how to act professionally in the face of an offer of a bribe) but knew that it was an impossible situation. I regained my composure and stated to the applicant that I thought it best if I ignored that last comment and duly left the premises. I walked away and rode through the town with the sound of £2000 in my ears but knew I had acted professionally and correctly. Not only would it have been unethical to accept such an offer, it was also potentially dangerous to be seen to be considering it. There may not have been anything to offer, merely the applicant's way of toying with the planner to see whether a bribe would be acceptable. This would have been sufficient grounds for malpractice in itself and warrant a case of dismissal if the applicant had contacted my superiors.

The pre-packaged notions that I had taken into the meeting were various. Personally, I had sympathies with his cause: he wanted to make a living and advertise his premises more prominently; he viewed the planning system as a block to his personal ambitions; he viewed me as a bureaucrat with no public feelings. I went out of my way to offer and negotiate alternative possibilities but all were unacceptable to him. In this case, planning was acting in the wider interests against individual preferences but was simultaneously being chastised for acting in an noncommunity way. Personally, I wanted to act for him, but felt constrained by my professional duty to present my employer's perspective. I did not seriously consider the bribe, although I was caught unprepared for a moment. Implicitly, I knew that accepting a bribe was wrong but wanted to support him; explicitly, I was a professional charged with performing a straightforward duty. My thought processes evident prior to the meeting were simply to act professionally, although my agenda had been determined by my interpretation of what was politically and organisationally acceptable to my professional peers. The thought processes I possessed relating to this type of meeting before entering practice was to say yes to a member of the public or at least listen to a case with a view to delivering as far as possible what was being required (irrespective of the bribe offer). I learnt quickly that, despite my own thought processes, I was committed – even constrained – into styles of thinking that personally I did not necessarily agree with. In this respect, my pre-packaged implicit thought processes (self-cognition) conflicted with three explicit thoughts: my personal view that I was prepared to support the applicant (listening and public-spirited); the need to act in such a way as to deliver what was expected by my colleagues (strategic); and the retention of some professional credibility in the process (normatively regulated behaviour).

Story 2: Acting unprofessionally. What is the distinction between professional duties and personal interests?

The second theme I wish to address is acting unprofessionally. How one defines unprofessional behaviour is a moot point, since it depends on how one defines professional action and this, with particular regard to planning, is rather problematic as commentators over the years have shown (see, for example, Reade, 1987; Evans, 1993; Evans and Rydin, 1997; Tewdwr-Jones, 1999). In this story, I relate how I acted unprofessionally in a practical setting involving drafting local planning policies for my employing local authority. I was one of four members of a policy formulation team writing the local plan; it was my duty to formulate policies with respect of finding new potential employment sites within the district. The district was primarily rural in character with one major east–west highway running through it. Employment opportunities, in terms of large spaces suitable for new industry, were few and far between, although it was acknowledged professionally and politically that a broad band of land running adjacent to the main district highway would be the most suitable land to identify new sites.

Having established the parameters for site selection and drafted all other sections of the employment chapter of the local plan, all that remained was for the team to identify land. We already possessed a very good knowledge of the whole district and of the environment immediately abutting the major highway; although I had only worked in the section for six months, my three colleagues possessed over thirty years' experience of planning in the district between them. Our first task was to locate sites via a base map. After selecting five sites and considering the agricultural, environmental, transportation and infrastructure problems relating to each, we eventually settled on one principal site. The chosen site was centred around a working farm immediately to the south of an existing interchange on the highway. Although there were a few existing buildings on the land, it was thought these could be swept away in the development scheme. The remainder of the site contained prime agricultural land (it was greenfield) but was ideal in offering the opportunity of good transport access and a level site for development. Although there would be environmental problems, there were no designated environmental protection policies in place for the land and a development located on the site would not detract substantially from the amenity of the surrounding area. The land was further considered by the whole of the local plans team, a policy was drafted and the council – internally – agreed to the chosen site. A formal policy identifying the farm as potential employment development was included in the draft local plan when it was published four months later.

As part of the consultation process for local plan preparation in the UK, draft plans are put out to the public and local communities and the local authority invites comments on the plan as a whole and on the proposals contained within the documents within a strict timescale (see Thomas, 1996). In the instance of our identified major employment site within the draft local plan, the policy and proposal attracted a number of objections from environmentalists and community groups concerned at the loss of agricultural land and the detrimental effect a development proposal would have on the immediate vicinity. This was only to be expected since it was the largest (in size) of all the development policies contained within the plan. As a consequence, the local plans team was not that concerned at the strength of opposition.[11] Since the policy had been confirmed by senior management within the authority and had been legitimised by the political ruling group in advance of public awareness, the chance of it being lost at this stage was going to be remote. And so it came as something of a surprise to the local plans team to receive one letter of objection from a member of the local community, a retired gentleman unconnected to any community or environmental pressure group, asking the planning department how it was proposed the employment development would be carried out when the farm was a Grade II* listed building and the group of farm buildings had been designated a conservation area in its own right.

Needless to say, this was a complete bombshell to the local plans team: all the professional planners had overlooked the conservation designations.[12] The oversight was even more problematic when we discovered that the farm buildings were early eighteenth century, dating from the 1730s. The dilemma the four members of the local plan team were now faced with was thus: nobody other than the team, and of course the gentleman objector, knew the truth, not even senior management or the local politicians. People would find out eventually though. It would only be a matter of time before English Heritage, the government agency responsible for the preservation of conservation designations in England, possibly objected to the scheme, and if the press and media discovered our anomaly, the extent of environmental objections would be significant as would the public ridicule of the expertise of professional planning officers. We therefore possessed a choice: did we own up to the mistake quickly and then discuss internally how to address the subject, by possibly withdrawing the proposal and the site from the plan? Or did we pretend that we always knew about the special protection afforded to the farm and that the special character of the buildings would be integral to the scheme, yielding a high quality environment once the farm buildings were renovated sympathetically for employment use?

At a meeting arranged between the four of us in a local pub, we decided to plump for the latter option. The unprofessional aspect of this example lay not only in the wilful incompetence of four professional planners in site selection in the first place. It was even more serious because to all intents and purposes, the professional planners were now lying – deliberately distorting or obfuscating the facts – to save their professional esteem. The public had been duped, and the obfuscation went so far as to bluff senior management and the authority's politicians. At detailed discussions with conservation interests and other public and community bodies, including the farm owner, grand plans were drawn up for a high quality, sensitively designed hi-tech employment site retaining the conserved features of the eighteenth-century farm buildings. Interest was received from a number of high profile developers; the scheme was eventually developed a couple of years later.

The pre-packaged ideas here centred on the need to identify an employment site. Personally, I held no views on whether the site had to be brownfield or greenfield, or be located in any particular area. I did not even consider acting in a more open communicative way by asking the public first for site selection options; this was, to some extent, our job as professionals and we were, after all, meeting a request from politicians. The dilemmas were more concerned with my reaction once we had discovered about the conservation designations. Implicitly, I wanted to open up the debate to the community, and discuss the problem the department was now faced with, even accepting that that might mean a degree of ridicule, even malpractice accusations. Ethically, this seemed to be the correct course of action. Explicitly, I was part of a team and my allegiances were stretched as much to my colleagues as my employing organisation. My colleagues, with much longer experience than I, were more wary of the possibility for adverse reaction. Professionally, the team considered that our status as professionals would be undermined by the revelation and, although we discussed and sympathised with my notion that we open up the debate to the community to discuss possible next steps, the choice simply came down to the need to preserve our professionalism. My own thought processes (self-cognition) – to act sincerely, honestly and community-centred – were challenged by a desire to deliver an employment site for my authority (strategic action) while remaining loyal to my colleagues and retaining some professional credibility (normatively regulated behaviour). My personal and ethical pre-packaged views had been compromised.

Story 3: Public frustrations. What role should the professional planner take in wider public interests?

If I had uncertainties about planning at university, you can imagine that my experience of professional planning practice was not doing anything to enhance my enjoyment of the discipline. My principal frustrations with my career concerned interactions with the public, particularly duties undertaken when I was within the planning control section. The need for constant negotiations with applicants, appellants, inspectors, developers, architects, third party interests, through letters written in the third person, a never-ending stream of telephone calls, and weekly site meetings, was proving to be too much. It was not the principle of the interactions that I objected too; quite the opposite, since I firmly wanted to help the public. Rather, it was the manner in which the public treated professional officers. Constant demands, abusive conversations, threats and bad language, were all aspects of the planning controller's job that as local government servants we had to deal with and deal with in a polite, respectful manner even if beneath the surface all hell was breaking loose.[13]

The most common difficulty in development control was retention of professional credibility and esteem in the face of a torrent of abuse from people incensed at what their neighbours were proposing. Planners are in the firing line: we are an easy target as controllers in the 'winning' and 'losing' game of planning permissions. For the most part, it is not the failure of planners that warrants such abuse. There are delays, of course, and some of these might be caused by professional impediments. But, frequently, delay in delivering a planning permission is caused by professionals ensuring all the necessary facts are gathered, all the opinions are collected from the public, and adequate time spent on delivering a quality outcome.[14] The public's frustrations with planning are more related to planners' unique ability to frustrate some people's dreams and at the same time deliver dreams for people to the annoyance (envy, jealousy?) of other members of the community. There are many examples of this nature I can recall from my period in practice, but one stands out.

A colleague working alongside me in the planning control section was asked to visit a small community on the very edge of a coast and to meet a husband and wife ('Mr and Mrs M') who had asked for planning permission to erect a holiday cottage adjacent to their existing house. The site in question was an environmentally sensitive area, of great landscape value, a heritage coast, and an Area of Outstanding Natural Beauty. In our local authority, we possessed a policy presumption against any new dwelling in these protected areas. My colleague had to visit the couple and state fairly unambiguously that they would be unlikely to receive planning permission for their holiday cottage. Only Mrs M was home when my colleague called. She listened politely, expressed disappointment, but understood the problems over building anything in this part of the world. Shortly afterwards, Mr M returned.

His wife explained the planning predicament and asked my colleague to repeat the justification that had previously been explained to her. Mr M was not pleased and, in complete contrast to the placid character of his wife, turned extremely angry. Reasoned justifications went out of the window when, from the corner of their home, Mr M produced a shotgun and pointed it in the direction of my colleague, yelling to him, 'Get out of my house now! I do not want you planners here – we'll do what we want.' Despite the best efforts of Mrs M to calm matters down, my colleague fled rather rapidly with Mr M stalking him along the causeway until he reached his car and was able to drive away. Shaken and nerves on tenter-hooks, my colleague arrived back in the office to be summoned immediately by the chief director. Before he was able to explain the dangerous situation he had just been involved in, the director wanted him to explain everything that he had said during his visit to Mr and Mrs M. Apparently, Mr M had just telephoned the director to complain about the planner swearing and giving abuse to him and his wife during a visit to discuss their planning application.

From conversations I had with my colleague at the time, I knew that he was in a dilemma over the decision. His implicit reaction was to support Mr and Mrs M; they were – or at least had seemed – nice people with a genuine case, made even more heartfelt because of the number of letters and views expressed by their neighbours to the planning department *in support* of their application. My colleague had visited some of these neighbours prior to calling in to Mr and Mrs M's house. Explicitly, in the light of the authority's policies and political commitments, there was no possible way the holiday home would receive planning approval. He had to deliver the formal position and provide as a professional duty the authority's position. The apparent threat from Mr M and the later formal complaint to the director of planning were regrettable; my colleague was particularly upset at the inability he possessed to reject the authority's position and discuss the possibility of acting for Mr and Mrs M and in the wider local community's interest since the support and general views had been expressed. His view was that it was a political necessity to follow the line expressed by his employing department and it was a professional necessity to be seen to be accepting his superiors' judgements. My colleague's own thought processes (self-cognition) to support these people who possessed a genuine desire and had support from the neighbours were counteracted by the thoughts that (a) he needed to deliver the politically acceptable outcome (strategic); and (b) he had to be seen to be acting within departmental practice since it had been formulated out of professional discussions (normatively regulated behaviour). The personal dynamic – incorporating almost a communicative ideal in this case – was therefore incompatible with the strategic necessity to deliver a particular outcome and the professional necessity to be loyal to his colleagues.

Story 4: The loyalty card. In whose interests should professional planners work?

One of the most important skills I had to develop quickly in professional practice after graduation was keeping confidences, particularly in relation to potential projects, tentative early negotiations with developers interested in sites, and conversations with colleagues over making the 'right' or 'wrong' decision. Loyalty did play a significant part of the job. One believed that one had a sense of loyalty to one's employing organisation to ensure no bad press emerged about the activities we were involved with, some of which were – as the second story demonstrated – 'problematic'. Loyalty also existed to one's colleagues, in the form of support, advice and even a shoulder to cry on when things were getting tough, so there was a professional component to loyalty too. But there was another aspect of loyalty that existed: loyalty to the politicians the professional planners gave advice to.

I have discussed elsewhere (Tewdwr-Jones, 1995, 1996) how planners in a representative democracy need to allow for politicians' manoeuvrings during the course of debate on planning projects, particularly where that debate occurs in the public arena and/or in front of the press and media. Appreciation of the politician's role in the planning process is fundamental to understanding the difficulties that can arise and the nuances experienced as the routine successive overlapping wave of negotiation and bargaining occurs in relation to each project. The chairperson of the planning committee possesses a key role in ensuring that the planning process delivers to both applicants and the public, as numerous texts have demonstrated over the years (e.g. Friend and Jessop, 1969; Blowers, 1980; Underwood, 1980). A good chairperson understands how planning operates, appreciates the multi-audiences that planning is geared towards, and recognises the pressure that professionals are under on a day-to-day basis. The chairperson should also be able to work closely with the senior officer responsible for planning within local government, by expressing political views on what might be and might not be acceptable to a larger political audience in advance of public debate. Frequently, this has meant professionals adopting political skills (Catanese, 1984).

The chairperson of the planning committee in another local authority I used to work for was highly skilled in the sort of attributes I set out above. He was astute in professional requirements, politically aware, proficient in chairing meetings, and an excellent communicator. With long service in local government, he was adept at high local government practice, an activity he only became involved with after retiring quite early from the armed forces. A highly affable character, large in size and tall in height, and looking some twenty years younger than he actually was, he dominated planning meetings but was strongly supportive of community inter-action. He possessed an excellent relationship with professional planners at all levels, occasionally calling in to the department to discuss on-going planning issues on a one-to-one basis with case officers. He had been chairperson for six years and was intending to continue in that role for some time. Planners felt as though they could do business with him, and did possess some loyalty because of the harmonious working relationship that had developed.

The loyalty card is actually very problematic for the individual planner. He or she may possess some personal goals about enhancing public discourse on plan-ning matters, to debate issues in a much more open and inter-subject way, and to foster participatory democracy. But given that the public planner works with, and to a degree for, representative democrats in the form of local politicians, allegiances can be divided. Local politicians often view enhanced public participation as a threat to their own positions, as political representatives who have been elected to act on behalf of communities. Engendering enhanced debate between professional planners and the public directly in an open way actually places a question mark over the need for representative democrats. Experiences of more open democratic processes in planning have illustrated this dilemma at first hand, where politicians are vulnerable in the arena of public discourse and feel as though they need to be seen to be stating views (Tewdwr-Jones and Thomas, 1998).

As one of the planners in this authority, I sought to support the chairperson because of, I dare say, his affability, his strong sense of vision, his general demeanour, even his sense of humour. He was a very likeable person, and his per-sonal traits were qualities I appreciate in an individual. From a professional perspective, I also knew – just as my colleagues knew in their perceptions of him – that we had to retain a degree of distance between ourselves and the politicians in order not to feel compromised. This was because in the department there was an almost unwritten code that 'professional planners stick together' in some sort of normatively regulated way. This often gave rise to strategic behaviour on the same case, project, or policy, with individual planners in turn offering 'advice' or 'guid-ance' to a politician but having discussed an agreed position between ourselves first, so that it appeared that each professional was giving an opinion that they had formulated themselves individually and which was, coincidentally, exactly the same as that of their colleagues. My thought processes (self-cognition) were at variance with this strategic behaviour since it meant, at times, duping the chairperson. But these thoughts were determined by the normatively regulated behaviour I felt obliged to consider in order to remain loyal to my colleagues. The question of acting once the advice had been given was a successive step after pre-determined acting parameters had been set; sometimes – in the scope of difficult decisions – this permitted a degree of discretion to negotiate and communicate with the public to build in their desires but, on other occasions, the public's ability to express a divergent voice was intentionally limited. This, in itself, was ethically questionable in my own mind.

Representative democrats are indeed vulnerable to the pressures and expectations of high-profile political life. As a final aside, I should add that we have long had experience of the press and media reporting politicians falling from grace over delicate social and personal circumstances; those politicians at the local level are no different to those on the national or even international stage. It happened unfortunately to our chairperson.[15]

Following discussion of these stories, I wish to relate their more conceptual issues back within the discussion framed at the start of the chapter: the position of the personal dynamic or humanistic dimension in planning practice and its implications for theorising. In so doing, I utilise aspects of frame analysis and the matter of the theory–practice gap in planning before going on to suggest avenues we might explore in the future.

IMPLICIT AND EXPLICIT COGNITION AND THE PERSONAL DYNAMIC IN THEORY–PRACTICE

The stories discussed above indicate that (some) individual planners do possess autonomous thinking prior to considering whether and how to act. These personal preferences exist as the outcomes of beliefs, judgements and opinions formed in everyday contexts from family experiences, social learning, personal knowledge, and education experiences – they are in essence the outcome of pre-professional planning relational webs. Although they may be determined by past interactions, they remain in the individual's mind as thought processes and are the baggage that individuals take to decision settings, in interpreting events, and in deciding whether and how to act and for whom. Essentially, they occur prior to any attempt to interact with other planning actors. Once the interaction occurs, and there becomes a necessity to integrate other thoughts (such as group norms, strategic objectives, or social ideals), the individual finds it necessary to modify, abandon or ignore his or her pre-determined thought processes. The relationship between these different thought processes is illustrated in Table 4.1, that links together the dilemmas evident in the pre-action minds of the individual.

Table 4.1 illustrates the four value thought processes that exist in the minds of planners prior to making a judgement on whether to act or not. The personal

Table 4.1 Interaction of thought process values, behaviour and ideals in the planner's personal dynamic

	Value	Behaviour	Ideals
implicit	personal	cognitive	(variable)
	social	communicative	open/inclusive
explicit	professional	normatively regulated	loyal/ethical
	political	dramaturgical	strategic/purposeful

thought processes, implying implicit and explicit cognition, will vary from person to person and will either be vulnerable or principled in character as the three other thought process values impinge. The social thought processes imply a desire to act socially, for community interaction and inclusion in an open and fair manner. Planners working for the public sector will be more aware of this audience and what the individual planner believes to be the correct course of action. The professional thought processes revolve around the notion that the planner is a member of a professional group employing its own standards, codes of ethics and norms that have to be adhered to. This elitism could also yield loyalty between different members of the group. The political thought processes imply a deterministic dimension to work strategically for a given end for political purposes, and could warrant dramaturgical behaviour to attain an outcome. The explicit values of social, professional and political thought processes will impact or impinge upon, and possibly redefine or modify the individual's implicit personal thought processes. The ideals associated with each are those perceived to exist or to be worked towards; the extent of whether they do exist or are modified will rest on experience and individual circumstances. The individual will possess his or her own ideals and these are determined by characteristics and beliefs of the self.

It is the role of cognitive psychology to explain the unconscious procedures and processes that exist within individuals (Barsalou, 1992). It is not my intention here to dissect notions of cognitive psychology or to attempt to enter the mind of the individual. My sole purpose within this chapter is to show that the autonomous individual will possess personal thought processes stemming from pre-professional planning relational webs and that these will be vulnerable to social, professional and political thought processes prior both to determining whether and how action is to occur and to any interaction once new professional relational webs emerge. For the benefit of future planning theorising, it is first necessary for this distinction to be made and acknowledged. Once this understanding and appreciation have occurred, planning theory can then address notions of delivering more social and communicative forms of practice.

There already exists a body of work in planning theory that can assist us in our understanding of the world of differences and of the conflicts that exist within individual thought processes. Martin Rein and Donald Schön (1993, 1994) discuss the problem of 'framing' in policy or decision situations, a topic that is particularly appropriate in analysing the personal dynamic that gives rise to the planner's pre-packaged views and spinning or learning from social interactions. Framing is the phrase used for the integration of facts, values, theories and interests in decision settings.[16] It acknowledges that decisions are formulated on the basis of judgement and values, in addition to technical criteria, and that such decisions vary between institutions, individuals and situations. As Rein and Schön acknowledge:

> Framing is problematic because it leads to different views of the world and creates multiple social realities. Interest groups and policy constituencies, scholars working in different disciplines, and individuals in different contexts of everyday life have different frames that lead them to see different things, make different interpretations of the way things are, and support different courses of action concerning what is to be done, by whom, and how to do it.
>
> (1993: 147)

Here, then, we have an existing theory that neatly pinpoints the crux of the problem in identifying the influencing determinant on the planner that Healey (1996b) has distinguished. Frames arise from two sources: the implicit cognition of the autonomous individual possessing pre-packaged ideas, and the explicit cognition effect of the planner being influenced by spinning social relations. Both are relevant. On the one hand, there exists the possibility for individual planners to possess personal frames, or the implicit personal goals and objectives, they have developed outside the world of practice. These thoughts may emerge from relational webs stemming from upbringing, culture, learning, or personal knowledge acquisition; they may have developed in the family, in school, at university or in extra-curricula activities; they may not be tested, and remain hypothetical or theoretical. On the other, individual planners will possess professional frames, or the explicit goals and objectives, that have developed inside the world of practice: the professional relational webs. These may stem from organisation, politics, professionalism, experience and mutual learning. They may have developed at any stage but will be particularly prevalent and influential in the world of planning practice. These frames rest on experience and are therefore tested regularly. These give rise to the institutional and territorial dependencies and varying personal capacities that I mentioned earlier in the chapter. At times, the individual planner will possess a dilemma as the two sets of frames conflict with each other. All four stories discussed above are examples where the implicit and explicit frames collide. So how can we utilise frame analysis in planning theory to assist our development of planning theory generally and for communicative planning in particular?

The problem for the assessor is how to identify and act upon these different implicit and explicit frames when some of them are essentially dependent on personal motivation, on the subconscious take-it-for-granted world of individuals. Communicative planning theory calls on planners to act as they interact with wider social relations (Healey, 1996b; Forester, 1999c) but no one has yet adequately discussed the personal dynamic inherent within the individual that gives rise to the will, or the determination not, to act in the first place. There is nothing cynical or dramaturgical about individual planners possessing a dilemma over whether he or she should act. The planner is less concerned here with the presentation to an audience and more concerned with personal justification and reflection, although the perceived status attached by planners to professionalism can be the key determining influence in decisions on which way to act, since often it is viewed as a choice between the public and professional credibility.[17]

Explicitly, I would argue that it is not possible for analysts to uniform frames in decision settings since the personal dynamic is determined by social, professional and political thoughts that vary across situations and scales. Equally, it is impossible to standardise implicit frames developed within autonomous individuals; there must be a degree of acknowledgement that the two co-exist. In policy and decision settings, individual frames of actors form the principal issues for personal conflict, uneasiness and dilemmas. However, it is possible to focus on the personal methodology used by the individual in decision framing, on the problems associated with frames, and on the reasons why implicit and explicit frames are formed in particular ways. This is the subject that planning theory needs to focus on if more communicative forms of planning are going to be encouraged and professional planners persuaded in their own minds to adopt such practices.

CONCLUSION

The role of any discourse on planning theory–practice – particularly in planning education – is to assist students and practitioners to understand how the world exists and what theory might offer to our understanding of the world. Equally, we can learn from practice for the benefit of improving our theorising, and theory teaching to students. Educators need to identify the dilemmas and uncertainties, the problems and complexities within the translation from planning theory (implicit thinking) to planning practice (explicit thinking). In many ways, the translation process for individuals between preconceived knowledge and problem-solving (or action) necessarily involves planners recognising the impact of political thoughts, professional thoughts, and community thoughts, on the individual's thoughts in their problem-solving process. The translation process between implicit and explicit cognition in the individual is the power-player: it is both the strength of the translation from planning theory to planning practice and its hindrance. Making sense of the translation between theory and practice is an attempt to understand the dilemmas associated with the conflicts in implicit and explicit thought processes, not to remove it. By understanding the translation in these terms, the importance of any discourse on planning theory–practice switches attention to knowledge, language, discourse, communication, and – above all – cognitive determinants that influence, amend, delete, or sway the individual's thinking or translation process.

Theorising in planning in the UK at least has reached a happy medium where the individual will ultimately decide in his or her own mind whether a given situation warrants modifying personal thought processes and, if it does, to determine the choices available, the implications of those choices for personal ethics and values, and whether the individual's professional role will be compromised by taking particular courses of action. This approach bears some resemblance to the concepts discussed by social learning theorists (e.g. Argyris and Schön, 1978; Friedmann, 1987). Cognitive and experiential processes within individual planners are formed through individual frames (Rein and Schön, 1993; Schön and Rein, 1994) and are important in the formulation of strategies to enable particular tactics, which may take on some relevance within organisational settings.

Planners possess personal thoughts, knowledge and facts before entering into the translation process; they possess both implicit and explicit thinking and learning. Implicit thinking stems from beliefs and values derived from life and education. Explicit thinking stems from reaction to influences while one is making sense of the implicit. Divorcing the explicit thoughts from the implicit cognition during the translation of theory to practice is a theorising process in itself (Underwood, 1996). Different planners can react very differently within the process of translation from implicit thinking → explicit thinking → action, according to how 'passive', 'principled', 'vulnerable' or 'strategic' the planner is.

Communicative planning theory could benefit from this analysis: the theory is concerned with generating communities' desires and forming policy from a collective voice. Healey (1999a) has made a useful start by highlighting the importance of relational webs around actors but this style of thinking needs to be transferred from the institutional scale to the level of the individual. Little has been stated by communicative planning theory proponents about the translation process, how planners take communities' desires and translate them into practical policy responses. It seems to me that a focus on the translation, on the motives, values, and beliefs of the planner in this process is a natural step in discussing how planners can be per-suaded to both think and to act more deliberately. This may be difficult work for planning to embrace, and Alexander (1999b) might be correct in asserting that a more useful way to describe the relationship between the politically purposeful planner and the pro-community planner in the translation process is 'interdepen-dence'. But this does not devalue questions associated with knowledge and thought processes. If we view planning discourse and implementation as a transper-sonal activity constituted out of both socio-political reality and psychic reality (Samuels, 1993), we might better understand the translation or gap between plan-ning theory and practice that students of planning find difficult to reconcile.[18]

I am not advancing political cognition as a theory to enable us to understand planning practice; rather, I am striving to identify the factors that lead to dilemmas and uncertainties within the translation process between ways of thinking (which are often good intentioned) and the decision to act in a particular way. These are the factors that can cause the breakdown between theory and practice, between knowledge and action, and between intention and implementation. In other words, I believe that it is time to focus on and understand the individual's decision process. Such an analysis can also assist us in explaining to students why there is no grand theory of planning, and why there are so many different theories that have sought to provide planners with both the prescriptions and the ideal models for that text-book solution.

NOTES

1   I am less interested with the incidence of practice and the operation of the planning system and more concerned with thought processes within individual planners. This is how I define 'the personal dynamic'.

2   These other motivations might bear some similarity to the different types of action identified by Habermas (1984) in his development of a communicative theory of action. The four types of action identified were: teleological – the selection of means to bring about a specified end or desired state, being a decision among alternative courses of action; normatively regulated – the orientation of action by a group member toward the common values and agreed norms within a social group; dra-maturgical – the interaction and presentation of participants constituting a public for one another; and communicative – action orientated toward the reaching of an under-standing about an action situation. See Tewdwr-Jones and Allmendinger (1998) and Phelps and Tewdwr-Jones (2000) for discussion of the relationship between these types of action when they might be applied to planning practice. Note, however, that I make a distinction here between different types of *behaviour*.

3   Flyvbjerg (1998b) draws a similar comparison in his discussion of Goffman's (1959) backstage and frontstage analogy with 'rationality' and 'rationalization': 'On stage rationality dominates, if nothing else as rationalization presented as rationality. Backstage, hidden from public view, it is power and rationalization that dominate' (Flyvbjerg, 1998b: 98).

4   Indeed, when this perspective was first peddled, Philip Allmendinger and I were accused of acting like neo-classical economists, which we took to mean we were more interested, academically, in questions concerning how the self integrates in society rather than accepting at face value the need to continuously act in the wider interest.

5   Taking this opportunity to stand up for the planner that puts personal thoughts and preferences over societal needs is not necessarily a target for criticism; after all, I am merely acting – in the language of communicative theorists – on behalf of subjects that might otherwise appear to be a marginal voice.

6   This has yet to be acknowledged by planning theorists even if attention now seems to be starting to focus on how to put communicative ideas into practice (Forester, 1999c) and how to reconcile the various strategic and open inclusionary pressures over how to act (Alexander, 1999b).

7   The obvious next step towards implementing a more communicative approach to planning is for the protagonists of the theoretical pulses to call for the de-profession-alisation of planning, or at least the re-writing of Professional Codes of Conduct to ensure that achieving social aspects of inter-subjective action is the primary purpose of the professionally trained planner.

8   I can remember these events distinctly, in part, because of the humour contained within each story. I dare say that students may find them more interesting for the humour and controversy that are contained within them, although I wish to stress that these issues are of secondary importance to the theoretical principles that each case addresses.

9   This is a very British way of stating that it is in point of fact an issue of great indelicacy.

10 I quickly thought of reactions: from my bank manager – where did this £2000 come from, Mr Tewdwr-Jones?; from my colleagues – where did you buy a BMW?; or from my family – how come you've got a BMW when you don't even have a driving licence for a car?

11 In fact, I would probably go so far as to say that the team had already determined that the proposal would probably be retained regardless of the extent of public opposition, which says a great deal about professional planners thinking 'they know best' over public reaction. This *is* the sort of 'pre-packaging' that Healey (1996b) refers to.

12 I say 'overlooked'; in actuality, it was more a case of taking too many short cuts in site

selection four months previously, the most damaging of which was simply choosing a site on the basis of a map rather than unearthing the planning history of the site and even carrying out a physical survey of the land.

13   I have to admit that it is rather perverse perhaps to complain about the public's treatment of planners when I have just illustrated through a story how planners abuse the public through deception!

14   This aspect of the planning controller's work does not seem to be a feature in this and the last government's over-zealous approach to league tables of fast decision-making as performance indicators.

15   The chairperson of the planning committee was caught one late afternoon in the typing pool by two professional planning officers in, shall we say, 'a compromising position'. The compromising position was with a 21-year-old secretary who had been clearing away files after the planning committee meeting. It was very embarrassing, naturally, for everyone concerned but acutely so given that the chairperson's age was 82. The ruling political group described the chairpersons immediate resignation to the public and media as a consequence of failing health.

16   I have used frame analysis elsewhere to understand the breakdown in communication between different local planning actors in decision settings (Tewdwr-Jones, 1995).

17   One issue to emerge from this discussion is that some planners may align themselves professionally in the style of normatively regulated behaviour to an unwritten unspecified ambiguous set of parameters or codes of what being a professional is perceived to be concerned with.

18   My uncertainty over my translation from the world of academia to planning practice continued while I was employed in local government. I recall asking my main line manager for his thoughts on the subject of how to manage personal dilemmas in planning practice. His reply was short and to the point: 'Go back to university, Mark. You don't have time to think in planning practice.'

5

Values and Professional Identities in Planning Practice
Heather Campbell and Robert Marshall

INTRODUCTION

Our purpose in this chapter is to examine what it means to be a planning professional at the beginning of the twenty-first century. What is the nature of the activity
and what professional identities do practitioners bring to bear upon their everyday
concerns? Our analysis is based on a framework which focuses on the values and
obligations which shape practitioners' views of their roles and purpose. It explores
the interactions between the actors in the planning process and the constraints
and opportunities presented by the contexts in which they find themselves. The aim
is not to interrogate the appropriateness of any particular theoretical tradition but
to build out from the views and perspectives articulated by practitioners themselves. The primary source for these reflections are focus group discussions with
practitioners carried out in 1996 (Campbell and Marshall, 1998), but which has
been supplemented by more recent work (Campbell and Marshall, 1999, 2000b)
including a study of planning gain (Campbell et al., 2000), and work with which we
have been associated on planning education (Poxon, 2001).

The chapter begins with an overview of the current operational context of the
planning system in Britain highlighting, in particular, the way in which that context
has been materially altered by the reconfiguration of the relationships between the
state, society and the individual which occurred in the 1980s and 1990s. The
empirical work is then introduced. The main part of the chapter is devoted to a discussion of practitioners' perspectives which is developed through a framework
which explores: first, intrinsic values and outputs; second, process and appropriate
actions; and, finally, competing obligations. We end with a conclusion in which we
make a plea for members of the planning academy to engage more readily with
questions of value in their theorising.

THE END OF PROFESSIONALISM?

The establishment of the welfare state in the years after the Second World War
represented the apotheosis of professionalism in British society ushering in 'the
public sector ideal of an egalitarian, caring and compassionate state run by

well-paid professionals' (Perkin, 1987: 518). Indeed, the roots of the cross-party consensus on the need for collectivist solutions to a wide range of social and economic problems were to be found, at least in part, in an alliance between politicians and experts (Thornley, 1993). The creation of the post-war planning machine was an important part of the 'professional ideal' and of the Keynsian social democracy upon which consensus was built (Marquand, 1996). This adherence to a social democratic creed came to an end in the 1970s. The electoral triumph of the New Right in 1979 heralded in a new era in British politics. Important aspects of the post-war consensus had already started to crumble before this but it was the Thatcher years which saw the dismantling of a large part of the social contract and a backlash against the professions especially those embedded in the public sector (Perkin, 1987).

The impact of the restructuring of British society on the planning system has been profound. First, the resurgence of the free market has seen a realignment of the planning system with property and development markets and a reappraisal of client/service relationships. Second, there have been far-reaching changes to local governance with the consequences that managerialism has displaced professionalism as the organisational norm; departmentalism has given way to a corporatist approach to both structures and organisational goals; managerialism and corporatism have resulted in an audit culture of performance indicators and league tables with an emphasis on process rather than outcomes. Third, the places in which planners are employed have become more diverse. No longer is it the norm to find those employed in the public sector working in a single department headed by a chief officer who is also a planner. Instead, planners and the planning service itself are often divided between different parts of the local authority. Moreover, although the majority of planners are still employed by local government, there has been a steady growth in private sector consultants with the consequence that in 1996 almost one in five corporate members of the Royal Town Planning Institute (RTPI) resident in the UK were employed as planning consultants (Hague, 1996). The diversity of work places and the work that planners do, together with the other changes referred to above, have weakened the claims upon which a unitary professional identity have formerly been based.

Not only have the past twenty years seen major changes to the practice of planning but the theories underpinning the activity have also been in a state of flux (Fainstein, 1999). Significant in this has been the critique of planning emanating from postmodernism which seemed to undermine central tenets of the practice of planning as traditionally conceived including professionalism, technical rationality, political neutrality and a unitary public interest. As a consequence of the apparent collapse of the modernist planning project, planning theorists have been searching for a new foundation for planning (Beauregard, 1989, 1991; Milroy, 1989, 1991; Healey, 1997a; Fainstein, 1999) as the chapters in this volume demonstrate.

This turbulence has created significant tensions for practitioners as they grapple with multiple and, often competing, obligations (Campbell and Marshall, 2000b). The ethical terrain which they must now negotiate is more complex and problematic than it once was. Moreover, there would appear to be, at least in Britain, growing dissatisfaction with the planning system (Committee on Standards in Public Life, 1997) which is portrayed as negative, bureaucratic and incompetent (Grant, 1999). This view, in many ways, has been fostered by successive governments which have sought to speed up the planning process in the interests of entrepreneurial inventiveness or economic competitiveness. It has also been reinforced by the negative view of the planning service portrayed in the Final Report of the government-appointed Urban Task Force (1999). The current context of planning raises fundamental questions concerning its role and purpose.

Despite the changing nature of the intellectual and contextual environment for planning, there has been comparatively little published work which has attempted to examine values and ethics in planning practice and changing professional identities. Of the studies which have been carried out in Britain, the in-depth investigation by Healey and Underwood (1978) of the inter-relationships between professional ideals and planning practice is still of interest despite the fact that it was carried out in the mid-1970s. Based upon case studies of London Borough planning departments, the findings revealed major discrepancies between the claims made by planners concerning their roles and the reality of the tasks in which they were engaged. Also significant are the collections of essays edited by Thomas and Healey (1991) and by Thomas (1994) and the critical evaluations of professionalism in planning by Reade (1987), Evans (1993, 1995) and the more recent exploration of *planning as a learned profession* by Grant (1999).

PRACTITIONER PERSPECTIVES

Given the relative paucity of published material, we decided to begin our exploration of the ethical dilemmas facing practitioners through focus groups which offered the best method of gaining an initial insight into the current concerns and preoccupations of the practice community. We did not want to bring our own preconceptions to bear upon the research but to allow the participants to bring forward their own opinions, experiences and attitudes. Two focus groups were held. The first consisted of new entrants to the profession. The six members were aged between 23 and 30 and had worked in planning for periods of between two and seven years. Three were women and two were working in the private sector.

The second group represented senior members of the profession. This was a more homogeneous group. All of the five participants were men and all but one were currently employed in metropolitan districts. The exception worked for a shire district. They were aged between 45 and 55 and all had spent their professional lives in the public sector for periods ranging from 24 to 30 years.

Clearly, we do not suggest that the findings from the focus groups are in any way representative of the wider practice community but they do serve to highlight *some* of the dilemmas and concerns of contemporary practice and this view has been buttressed by more recent work with which we have had an association (Campbell *et al.,* 2000; Poxon, 2001). The remainder of the chapter presents an analysis of the dilemmas and concerns.

One of the key strands of debate within moral theory concerns the emphasis placed on whether good consequences can justify wrong actions. This distinction between the appropriateness of actions and the often associated stress on fair and just process in contrast to a focus on the intrinsic value of the underlying goals and therefore the resultant outcomes provides a useful way of structuring the reflections of practitioners. Perceptions of the nature of planning are not, however, entirely separable from context and experiences. The course of action and the emphasis chosen are influenced and shaped by an intricate web of obligations. It can be difficult in practice to distinguish precisely between appropriate action, intrinsic values and underlying obligations. However, this very difficulty helps to highlight the dilemmas confronting practitioners and the tensions and even contradictions which are often inherent to planning. The subsequent discussion of practitioners' perspectives of the current nature of planning practice and how this fits with their aspirations is structured around a framework focusing, first, on intrinsic values and appropriate outcomes, second, process and more particularly appropriate action and, finally, competing obligations.

INTRINSIC VALUES AND APPROPRIATE OBJECTIVES

The difficulty and unease practitioners exuded in discussing issues of value in relation to the practice of planning regardless of age or level of experience were hugely striking. All were convinced of the enduring relevance and value of an activity which went under the name 'planning' but what this activity was about, and even should be about, was far less certain and often somewhat confused. The underlying assumption that planning is about market intervention provided something of a starting point. However, the discussions revealed very different perceptions as to the role of planning in relation to market processes. Perceptions often seemed to be influenced by the prosperity of the local economy in which the individual had most recent experience. At one end of the spectrum were those working in demor-alised economic circumstances such as large conurbations which had suffered from industrial restructuring. Here overwhelming emphasis was placed on the need to secure development and jobs, an imperative which it was acknowledged would frequently override all other planning considerations. At the other end of the scale were those based in outer suburban authorities. They saw planning's role as strongly regulatory in nature, that is seeking to steer development to preferred loca-tions, a process moreover which often implied protecting existing property rights and values. Locational differences in experience did not entirely explain contrasting attitudes. One of the planners from a northern metropolitan district asserted force-fully that planning was 'quintessentially interventionist ... if we can't improve on how the market performs then we have no role'. This highly interventionist stance with regards to the market contrasted strongly with the analysis of a colleague also working in a northern metropolitan authority. He suggested that the restructuring of the 1980s had left planning in a position where all it could do was *manage* the market, that is to say 'doing work for it by consultation and bringing elements together to make development happen'. Whatever the experience and perspective, the way in which the planning system engaged with the development process was seen as fundamental to the values such a system articulated. Moreover, the contex-tual pressures and general uncertainty felt by individual professionals gave rise to a variety of ethical concerns which are discussed further below.

Newer entrants to the profession seemed more comfortable talking about the goals of planning in relation to a concept referred to as the 'environment' than market processes. Forceful comments were made about the crucial role performed by planners in defending the 'environment'. This was accompanied by an under-lying sense of frustration, often passionately expressed and summarised in the following, 'we're all undervalued for the job we do in society ... we're the only people defending the environment and trying to get the best for everybody'. The frustrations were several but included a feeling of being somewhat isolated, with politicians and the public not understanding the value of planning and what it is trying to achieve, the slowness with which decisions were taken and the incremen-tal nature of the gains made. Despite this palpable sense of irritation as to the lack of status accorded planning, combined with their enduring sense of the signific-ance of the activity, they found it extremely difficult to define what was meant by 'protecting the environment'. The term was used in a highly generalised sense, referring to the 'world out there' without ever specifying exactly which aspects of the world out there were important. This preference for ambiguity fostered consen-sus while also enabling difficult and even controversial questions to be avoided.

The claims of the natural environment and the need to achieve sustainable development were given prominence in all the discussions with practitioners. There were, however, major contradictions in the views expressed both in relation to the meaning of 'sustainability' and its implications for planning policy. On the one hand, there was the feeling that this was the one area where the planning system had, in the recent past, gained a more powerful and enhanced role and where intervention in the market would be more easily justified because there was a coming together of political and professional aspirations. On the other hand, some expressed the view that sustainability had been written into central government guidance as expressed in the UK Government's Planning Policy Guidance Notes (PPGs) but had not really filtered down to where it mattered at the local level because there was not the political thrust to see it through. This was particularly the case where the short-term needs of job creation would gainsay the longer-term needs of future generations for a clean and healthy environment. Encapsulated here are two ethical dilemmas for society and for the planning community. The first is the problem of balancing the needs of present and future generations. The second is the problem of balancing the claims of the natural world against those of human welfare. In operationalising the concept of sustainable development, concern was expressed as to the real opportunities for win-win solutions to be implemented, particularly in the context of major developments. There were felt to be profound tensions between the social, economic and environmental dimensions of sustainability with most associating sustainability with the needs of the natural environment. The competing claims of natural and social environments were expressed in the following way by one of the senior planners in respect of the major themes of his authority's Unitary Development Plan (UDP).

> The issue arises how far the social issue is brought in. To what extent we lose some of the edge of our social concern because of our concern for the future of the planet. There is a difficult issue of trading off the interests of poorer groups in our own generation against poorer and better-off groups in future generations. How far in rationalising the aims of our UDP was sustainability to be the big aim and how far it's a question of social disadvantage? My view is that people remain the centre of the picture but the environment is still an enormous issue.

The above quotation directly focuses attention on the planning community's responsibilities with respect to social, and perhaps even economic, disadvantage. However, in placing 'social disadvantage' centre stage, this participant in no way reflected the general sentiment. The newer entrants to planning were unanimous in their view that questions of social justice were not matters which planning could, or indeed should, address. The term social justice was reinterpreted into the more derogatory concept of 'social engineering', a process with which it was not regarded as legitimate for planners to become involved. The more senior planners on the whole were ambivalent to the role of planning in relation to matters of social justice. It was felt that planning should have a role but it was emphasised that the mechanisms and resources for effecting anything other than marginal change were not available. The way in which participants drew boundaries around what they considered to be planning tended to preclude an association with social or redistributive concerns. Consequently, while it was argued that social objectives were central to local economic development initiatives, they were seen as generally beyond the remit of planners. Moreover, the imperative of development which was associated with such initiatives was seen as directly at variance with planning considerations. Organisational practices therefore appeared to influence practitioner perceptions of the scope and goals of the planning activity. Central government was certainly seen as restricting the focus of the planning activity through a failure, on the one hand, to match resources to identified needs and, on the other, the allocation of an increasing element of public funding through various competitive bidding processes. One of the senior practitioners felt that the underlying impetus for concern about social and economic concerns had come from Europe through the 'social exclusion' agenda rather than from UK planning practice. Recognition of the fragmented nature of communities and of issues of diversity were not mentioned.

Overall there was a strong sense of unease amongst the planners involved in the discussions in dealing with issues concerning values and objectives in relation to planning. It is difficult to identify the source of this unease. Perhaps intellectual debates which have critiqued the modernist project combined with an emphasis within society on prioritising individual rights have left planners reluctant to articulate alternative futures and the underlying values on which they are based. The preceding discussion highlights the huge ambiguity surrounding the core purpose of the activity of planning. The one life-line seems to have been provided by the concept of sustainability. That said, it was evident that practitioners felt there to be considerable tensions in attempting to operationalise such a notion, particularly within market-based economies.

PROCESS AND APPROPRIATE ACTION

The strong popular association between the planning activity and bureaucratic forms of working might be expected to lead to a focus on due process. Certainly there was an emphasis on process and the linked issue of upholding fair procedure, however, there were many, not always compatible, dimensions to this discussion. Central to practitioner perceptions was the notion of planning as a process of argumentation between professionals on the one hand and on the other some concern about 'giving people a say'. A strong and perhaps even distorting influence on these observations was the increasing array of performance criteria being laid down and forcefully implemented by central government. Consequently a major tension which ran through all the discussions was between achieving 'efficiency' and 'quality'. These terms arose frequently, although as the discussion below highlights there were considerable differences in the way in which these attributes were interpreted.

Planning as a process of argumentation between professionals was implicit to much of the discussion. Regardless of whether individual planners were working for the public on private sectors the process was conceived in adversarial terms. Several of the public sector planners conceded that they felt the quality of the debate had been enhanced by the routine engagement of consultants by developers and even certain sectors of the public. Quality in this sense was envisaged as the requirement consultants were placing on local authority planners to justify their decisions and policies in arenas such as appeals into the refusal of planning permission and inquiries into the objections to plans. In the past it was argued that local authorities had generally had an advantage in such arenas, however, with declining resources and the often technically complex nature of planning matters it was felt that the balance had shifted towards the development sector. One senior practitioner whose local authority had just come to the end of a development plan inquiry observed that:

> the more widespread use of planning consultants had raised the quality of argument. But to make that work the authority needs to be resourced adequately. Trying to operate an inquiry on the resources we've had has put us in an invidious position. All the work we have put in could go down the swanny because we haven't had the resource to counter the arguments of private consultants.

There was widespread sympathy for this view and concern as to its implications. One effect of this process of argumentation was for the technical and legalistic bases of the discussion to become more prominent. Effective argument in such circumstances required specialist knowledge, something local planning authorities often did not have direct access to nor the resources to hire. More broadly this implies, at least in some of the key arenas of disputation, an increasing emphasis on instrumental and legalistic forms of reasoning. This is an issue we will return to later.

The underlying assumption that planning is a process of reasoned argument was extended and supplemented by an additional dimension which is best summarised by the phrase 'giving people a say'. The more senior planners, in particular, emphasised the importance of consultation as a means of improving the quality of decision-making in planning and therefore the outcomes of that process. In contrast, and somewhat surprisingly, those newer to the profession were less inclined to see public participation as a virtue. Given such divergent views the discussion surrounding public involvement exhibited huge complexity and inevitable contradictions.

Since the publication of the Skeffington report in 1969 (Committee on Public Participation in Planning) planning and planners in Britain have developed an enduring attachment to public involvement. It was evident from the discussions that for some this attachment was of such significance that it lay at the centre of what for them it meant to be a planner, while for others it represented a distraction from the proper tasks of being a planner. This difference in perspective seemed to pivot around the extent to which individual planners displayed a fundamental belief in the importance, perhaps even right, of all members of society to be able to articulate their views on planning matters or whether in contrast the difficulties of operationalising such a belief were felt to outweigh the possible virtues. For one individual his involvement in designing a programme of public participation linked to the process of plan preparation was one of the most important and satisfying aspects of his professional life. An initiative, furthermore, which explicitly envisaged public involvement as a compensatory mechanism. He stated that, 'Some interests are being bulldozed by the groups with money,' and then went on to reflect about the complexities involved:

> We made a special effort to make contact with the people who wouldn't normally comment and to help them understand the plan. I think we really only skimmed the surface of that ... Having said that, it has involved a major input of time, a major input of staff resources and with the resources we have now I question whether we could put in that effort. It grieves me to say that. It's one of the bits we have done so far I am really pleased about.

This perspective and the underlying rationale aside, most other planners characterised public involvement in far more instrumental or negative terms. One chief officer spoke of 'encouraging more participation' in terms of enhancing the 'respectability' of planning. The emphasis on the 'more' in terms of participation seemed merely to reflect some basic quantifiable measure rather than a detailed elaboration of the role and significance of participation. Moreover, in common with several others, there was considerable concern as to the time-consuming nature of such activities. This individual observed ruefully that the plan preparation process had taken seven years from central government's commencement order to the completion of the public inquiry. As a consequence of the time taken he felt the plan lacked credibility as it was becoming of less relevance to the issues of the day. Public participation was cited as one of the key contributors to the lengthy nature of the process and while respectability (and possibly legitimacy) would be sacrificed by reducing such involvement, the impact on the policies in the plan were felt to be minimal. Nor was it accepted that devoting time to securing consensus over policies in the short term would reap benefits later in terms of a reduction in the numbers of objections to the plan or when planning applications were submitted.

At the heart of the more negative attitudes towards participation lay a perspective of planning as an embattled activity. An activity which often placed its practitioners in situations of conflict and confrontation and that as far as was possible it was preferable, both professionally and personally, to avoid arenas where antagonistic debate was perceived to be inevitable. The newer planners all spoke of the disrespect shown to them by members of the public. Moreover, they were not convinced by the pertinence of the observations made to the decisions with which they were concerned. Doubt was not only cast about the contributions of the public. Politicians were also seen as presenting obstacles to achieving good decisions. It is perhaps not surprising that given this notion of an embattled activity stress was placed on an inward-looking conception of appropriate action; one which placed the ultimate emphasis on technical competence and professional judgement.

It is all too easy for an academic observer to castigate such views and to portray these individuals collectively as exemplifying the worse traits of the 'I know best' planning stereotype. This would be, however, to perform an injustice. In their reflections on the process of dealing with members of public and other interest groups, what many of these individuals were emphasising was the importance of not romanticising public participation. It is a natural human emotion to wish to avoid arenas where the planner becomes the focus of bitter and angry argument amongst entrenched self-interests. This is not to endorse or otherwise these attitudes merely to provide some explanation. The poorly developed reasoning as to why 'giving people a say' was important other than because it was self-evidently 'a good thing' perhaps further helps to account for the negativity. It is difficult to handle challenging situations if you are uncertain as to the underlying objectives which justify such a process. It is striking that only one of the planners seemed to have a clear sense of the underlying rationale for involving the public in decision-making.

The discussions concerning argumentation and the role of public participation highlight contemporary planners' perceptions of the nature of the planning
activity and how it should be conducted. However, there was lengthy reflection
on how pressures external to the planning community were having a significant
influence on shaping the choices available to practitioners. Of particular concern
was the initiation by central government of management through performance
criteria. Concern about this process frequently found expression in the notion
that 'quality' in planning was being sacrificed in favour of 'efficiency', most especially a pressure to speed up decision-making. This was exemplified in the
requirement central government has placed on local planning authorities to
decide 80 per cent of planning applications within eight weeks and the associated league tables showing the success rate of individual authorities. It was
evident that despite the general application of this principle the detailed
response of local authorities varied hugely. Some were keen to utilise all
mechanisms possible to ensure they topped the league tables such as immediately refusing poor applications they might otherwise have discussed with the
applicant to see if they could find ways to modify the proposal to render it
acceptable. Others were content to achieve a 'satisfactory' level of performance
using neighbouring authorities as a benchmark.

This detailed example highlights the extent to which a performance criteria
based approach can develop a life of its own; satisfying the performance criteria
becomes everything and the underlying purpose of the activity can become lost.
This sense of loss was strongly felt by all the planners who participated. However,
they found it much more difficult to articulate what had been lost and as the earlier
discussion has highlighted what 'quality' might mean with respect to planning. It
was clear that most felt the planning process was being distorted. Perhaps more
particularly that pressures external to planning were shaping, even determining, not
only the goals of the activity but the very nature of the process itself. The specification of the appropriate rules by which the planning activity should be conducted
were being established by others. Consequently, the responsibility and associated
autonomy of the professional planner to ensure fair and just process was not only
being questioned but were more actively taken out of the hands of the planning
community.

COMPETING OBLIGATIONS

Intrinsic to planning, as a profession which saw its status advance significantly as
part of the evolving welfare state of the 1960s, are a myriad of competing and at
times contradictory obligations. While the more traditional and long-standing

professions of law and medicine are not without their dilemmas this renders the nature of professional activity and the obligations placed on its practitioners as different. It was evident from the discussions with practitioners that tensions between the expectations of their employing organisation and a broader range of personal principles and professional obligations were strongly felt and with the restructuring of the state perceived to be becoming more acute and troubling. Closely linked to this was concern as to whose interests were being served by planning and, more interestingly in many ways, confusion as to whose interest *should* be paramount.

The majority of planners expressed a strong underlying assumption that their primary obligation was to some concept of professional competence, autonomy and independent judgement. It was unclear whether this was their desired end state or that given the pressures and changes confronting practitioners the classical concept of a profession providing some form of solace and sanctuary. Whatever the motivations, theirs was an essentially technocratic view of the planning process in which planners were the experts and best able to evaluate alternatives and make judgements based upon careful consideration of all aspects of the problem including the longer-run as well as the short-term implications of choices. As the earlier discussion highlighted it is not surprising therefore that public consultation and participation did not figure prominently in the discourse. When the question of public involvement did emerge it often did so in a critical frame of reference, in the sense that the dominant view was that those who were able to influence outcomes were from narrow and privileged segments of the community who could 'hijack the system' and whose aims were often assisted by press 'misinformation'.

The general primacy of the obligation to professionalism is entirely consistent with the perceptions discussed earlier concerning appropriate goals and processes with respect to planning. There was a widely accepted presumption that professional expertise in planning was essentially a matter of technical competence and that such expertise was underpinned by a distinctive body of knowledge and skills. However, defining the nature of that distinctive knowledge and skills proved a virtual impossibility. Notwithstanding this crucial area of ambiguity the discussion did provoke a particularly intriguing dynamic between those working in the public and private sectors. The contention by those working as consultants that the nature of their work accorded precisely with the notion of professional expertise and competence first articulated by those employed within local government proved both controversial and highly provocative. The latter questioned the integrity of private consultants as they felt their judgements were influenced by their financial dependence on their clients. This perception in turn encouraged the local authority planners to distinguish the activities with which they were concerned from those of the private consultants. At the heart of their concern lay a responsibility, as they saw it, to the wider community which it was not felt impacted similarly on the private sector. As a consequence it was in this context that the local authority planners came closest to associating professional responsibility in planning to an obligation to serve the public interest. This is exemplified in the following comment:

> Private consultants are like lawyers – they'll defend anything if paid enough – whereas we're meant to have values and defend concepts like fair play ... I feel as though I'm on the side of the angels ... [that] I'm on the right side which I couldn't in private practice.

The forceful, even impassioned, nature of the comments was the most striking part of the discussion, for as with earlier concerns the elaboration of who the 'angels' might be, in what was clearly envisaged as a confrontational process, was far more difficult to tease out. There also seemed to be a contradiction between the notion of planning as essentially about technical competence and the articulation of being on the 'right side'. For most of these planners it appeared that working in local government and the associated assumption of a public service ethic represented the 'right side'. More particularly this organisational arena was inextricably tied to the whole notion of what, for them, it meant to be a planner. Within this context, however, they saw the role of the planner as providing technically competent advice. It was assumed that this role would serve the general interests of society, as this was the presumed purpose of local government.

Those working in the private sector defended their role, seeing themselves not only as problem-solvers for clients but also fulfilling an obligation to serve the public interest by acting as a check on local authorities by ensuring they justify their decisions. Senior local government practitioners acknowledged that in certain circumstances the apparent independence of consultants could be useful in convincing politicians of the validity of a particular case. That said, while all the consultants relished the sense of responsibility they had some were not entirely comfortable with the implied obligation to meet the needs of clients. One individual in particular confessed that she found herself on occasions being required to do things with which she disagreed. The public sector planners were challenged that they too might find themselves in a similar situation. This was acknowledged but that the public accountability inherent to a local authority environment was felt to provide a more acceptable, if not entirely satisfactory, justification for the potential manipulation of professional judgement.

An important strand cross-cutting these discussions was the extent to which an obligation to the profession as outlined above was being comprised and distorted by the corporate goals of the organisations in which the planners worked. The public sector planners in particular spoke with regret of the often low priority given to planning considerations where they were not consonant with organisational objectives. Interestingly, and somewhat to contradict earlier observations, corporate interests were regarded as directly at variance with the public interest ethic local government planners intuitively associated with the activity of planning. There were various dimensions to this distinction but the key underlying tensions consisted of a tendency towards pragmatism over strategic thinking and between short-term political expediency as against longer-term notions of community benefit.

The tension between an obligation to professional competence and the employing organisation was particularly acute for planners working in the less prosperous localities facing economic restructuring combined with physical regeneration. In these circumstances the political imperative to 'go for jobs' cut across all other considerations, most notably the interests of the natural environment. While many of the planners felt uneasy about the resulting decisions, such a course of action was regarded as a defensible political choice. However, much more problematic was felt to be the conflict of interests which increasingly arise over financial considerations in the context of severe spending constraints on local authorities. A frequently cited example concerned the sale of council-owned land, more specifically where the imperative to maximise revenue through the sale of such assets came up against the professional judgement of the planners. The key question is whether the local community interest is best served through maximising revenue which often implies the sale of greenfield sites for large executive homes or whether it is better served by the maintenance of amenity and the natural environment and using the council's leverage over sites, for example to encourage the provision of affordable dwellings.

The senior planners tended to resolve the tensions between corporate and planning concerns by placing accountability firmly in the hands of elected members – 'the ethical thing is to continue to make our voice heard on planning principles and let members take responsibility for the ethics of their choice'. However, one individual in particular found such legitimisation impossible. He found himself compelled to move jobs as he could not reconcile his own personal values with the obligations he was expected to fulfil by his local authority. He expressed the tensions he encountered as follows:

> If you just see planning as a job – there's enough institutional need to keep you going and that has some value, but if you have some vision that's very different ... I lasted as long as I could in a hostile environment and then went somewhere else where I felt happier. That for me was the only practical way forward ... when I'm older perhaps I'll care less ... at the time I felt deeply and had to do something about it.

This individual felt that his professional autonomy had been reduced by the imposition of corporate objectives handed down not, in this case, by elected members, but by the chief executive. In moving jobs he was seeking an organisational culture which was still public service-centred and where principles of professional judgement and public accountability had not been prejudiced by organisational goals mediated through financial and performance targets. The concern as to the erosion of a public service ethic and the associated obligations this placed on planners was further specified in terms of the substitution of an overriding concern for the public interest by the customer interest. The following quotation from one of the senior planners effectively summarises the dimensions and implications of such a trend:

> If you treat planning as a service delivered to customers who make a demand on this service the trend is towards regarding the applicant as the customer ... Hence the emphasis on speed – you treat the transaction as a quasi-business relationship. Whereas the public interest ethic has been very different. It was the planning system interposing itself between so-called customers (or private interests) and the general public interests that is a completely different relationship.

The perceptions of these practitioners highlight the enduring primacy of an obligation to professional competence and autonomy. It was unclear from the discussions whether this represents a defensive response to the difficult circumstances in which planners find themselves or a desired end state. Certainly any further specification of what this implied proved problematic with the exception of the intuitive response by the planners employed within local government that they had a responsibility to the wider community. However, a professional, and for some a personal, obligation, was being severely tested if not comprised by the increasingly vigorous pursuit of corporate and customer interests as a consequence of the restructuring of local government.

CONCLUSION

Uncertainty and disquietude concerning the current operational context of planning in Britain was a constant undercurrent in our discussions with practitioners. A picture emerged of a beleaguered and embattled profession which is misunderstood and maligned both by politicians, especially at central government level, and by the public. All members of the focus groups were struggling with their professional identities in an increasingly broken and shifting terrain of practice. Paradoxically, given intellectual developments, the one thing which seemed to provide a stable and legitimising frame of reference as they faced the frustrations and challenges of their everyday practical concerns was a professional idealism premised on the traditional claims of a unique body of knowledge and skills which equipped them to make expert judgements on technical matters. It ought to be added that this idea of professionalism was for many, and especially the young planners, quite independent of any attachment or loyalty to the professional association, the Royal Town Planning Institute, which, indeed, some saw as largely irrelevant. Although there was this deeply held commitment to professionalism, they were largely at a loss to articulate exactly what constituted the distinctive knowledge and skills base upon which their notions of professional competency and independence of judgement rested. Alongside this enduring sense of professionalism was an affirmation of an ethic of public service at least in the sense that they saw themselves engaged in a task which had the general interests of society at its heart. Despite this, however, most were reluctant to engage in any discussion of values particularly normatively in relation to what values *should* underpin the planning system as opposed to what were perceived as some of the current obstacles and frustrations to achieving 'good' planning.

Reluctance to engage in debates about values, except in very general terms, is something which also afflicts, we would argue, the planning academy. By and large, academics stand aloof from questions about purpose and ends, preferring the safer and less embarrassing territory of procedure and means. We agree with Forester (1999a: 8) that academic 'theorists' should 'take practice more seriously' in order to produce stronger and deeper theories. The practice community has not been helped, by and large, by the intellectual debate which has accompanied the turmoil which has afflicted planning practice over recent years (Campbell and Fainstein, 1996). The acuity of Forester (1999b: 177) again serves to explain the poverty of much of our theorising:

Planning theory today gives us too little analysis of better and worse planning, as if notions of good and bad, right and wrong, were the province of simple relativists, as if better were only matters of perspective. Planning theory today gives us too little analysis of real, if tragic, choices, acting when all our options involve doing harm; too little analysis of public suffering and abiding humiliation, anger and resentment. A planning literature that remains intellectually inarticulate about questions of value, questions of better and worse processes and outcomes can hardly be worth much ...

6

Direct Action and Agonism in Democratic Planning Practice
Jean Hillier

> We have got on the slippery ice where there is no friction and so in a certain
> sense the conditions are ideal, but also, just because of that, we are unable to
> walk; so we need friction. Back to the rough ground.
>
> (Wittgenstein, 1958: 46)

INTRODUCTION

Since the late 1960s in the Western world, waves of interest-focused citizen
activism have been represented through formal processes of public participation in
planning, such as making written submissions or attending public meetings,
through advocative processes such as lobbying (Hillier, 2000), or through intimida-
tory processes (Smith *et al.*, 1997) such as civil disobedience. As Smith *et al.*
(1997: Fig. 1; 141) illustrate, convergence towards a form of interest representation which facilitates participation, in the interests of accountability and empowerment, and generally what are regarded as more efficient processes (such as
environmental dispute resolution), has gradually overcome bureaucratic constraints
such as reluctance to share power and technocratic inertia.

The recent 'communicative turn' in planning theory has recognised the
importance of communication in planning decision-making and the role of collaboration between as many actors as possible in working towards 'a political democratisation of daily communication' (Forester, 1989: 21). Most authors interested in
communication and collaborative planning concentrate on formal participatory planning processes (with notable exceptions of John Forester and Bent Flyvbjerg),
including committee and other meetings, public participation strategies, such as
search conferences, and the texts produced for and by these processes. Judith
Innes' work on consensus-building (1999a; Innes and Booher, 1998, 1999a, b)
offers a collaborative process in which all actors and interests may be able to
agree on an outcome which they can accept.

I am concerned here with giving more than simply voice to the voiceless with
regard to interest representation in land use planning decision-making processes.
Building on results of empirical research into the power and influence of informal
direct action on planning decisions and recent Habermasian (1996a, 1998) ideas

which place the weight of political legitimation on informal and legally institution-alised procedures of opinion- and will-formation, I am concerned in this chapter with attempting to build inductive theory addressing issues of both:

- legitimation of informal direct action by opening up planning processes and public protest to all; and also
- to consider briefly potential 'institutionalisation' of community mobilisation through forms of associative democracy sensitive to those involved.

I attempt a reconciliation of the two in a theoretical conception of associative/agonistic planning which incorporates both informal direct action and institu-tionalised practices. In this chapter, I explore processes which offer the flexibility to be issue-dependent, to include those groups and individuals affected by the context and which welcome, rather than attempt to suppress, conflict. In so doing, I examine the implications of Benhabib's (1996a) distinction between asso-ciational space as a space in which people work together in concert, and agonistic space, which she regards as competitive space. If, as Mouffe (1996) suggests, all space is inherently conflictual and agonistic once we go beyond the moral to con-sider the political dimension, does this imply that consensual democratic decision-making is impossible? Does it mean that there is always 'more than reason', something beyond the 'slippery ice', and that insider (associative democratic) and outsider (informal direct action) strategies should be legitimated to take place in parallel?

ROUGH GROUND AND SLIPPERY ICE

My previous work has deconstructed processes of public participation in local land use planning decisions to identify a variety of events chained together by the expectations, interests, fears and desires of the actors involved (Hillier, 1995, 1998a, b, 2000). These chains are communicated along networks as energy flows of varying intensities and power. The political opportunity structure[1] in place at a particular point in time may act to determine the relative intensity of the various approaches to interest representation which are used.

I have identified that networks of actors are contingent and dynamic as associations and coalitions form and disband according to the issue under consideration. Traditionally antagonistic actors may work together, for instance, in the face of some other, mutual threat. As different forms of interest representation take place contemporaneously, planning processes may become replete with con-flict and antagonism. I build here on three particular aspects of communication in planning processes identified from practice and theory: direct action, networks and consensus-building.

Direct action and lobbying

My previous work (Hillier, 2000) has demonstrated a case in Western Australia in which, through astute channelling of energies, a small group of actors successfully lobbied elected representatives and used the media to manipulate a new situation definition away from what would have been a better technical planning response to a 'problem' of housing over 100,000 people to a 'solution' which suited themselves (developing the housing elsewhere; not in their backyards). I demonstrate how the formal channels of communication in the planning process were essentially hierarchical, representative and state-directed. In contrast, informal networking activity involved a far wider range of actors, and was far more effective in influencing the planning outcome. Forms of informal direct action included targeted activities, such as telephone calls and conversations with relevant government ministers and the enrolment of the editor of the state daily newspaper to the cause. The newspaper ran front page articles for a week, using romanticised photographs, aimed at maintaining the status quo in the area. In this way, the capacity of the eight or nine people involved in the 'Friends of the Valley' lobby group was increased exponentially to include the weight of public opinion throughout the urban area, if not the wider region.

This empirical study indicates how actors may communicate via traditional forms and institutions (such as the formal planning approach to public participation), but they also communicate and generate energy flows along new areas of activity and identity (use of media, direct action, etc.). The relational resources of the actors involved are also important. The successful 'Friends of the Valley' group had good contacts with influential people and used them to best advantage. A second lobby group had very little influence on the outcome. Its relational resources were weak in that there was a low number of people involved, they had few influential contacts and the group was formed far too late in the process to make much impact. The capacity of this second group to achieve its aims was thus extremely low.

My study illustrates how communicative rationality yielded to strategic action and power. It indicates how the 'political' aspects of direct action or lobbying can subvert the more 'moral' theoretical framework of communicative action. There is a fundamental difference between moral and political considerations, as noted by Tewdwr-Jones and Allmendinger (1998: 1981) who state that communicative action is inherently unable to 'guarantee that all participants will act in an open and honest manner all the time'.

Networks

Although individual actors may occasionally be able to lobby decision-makers successfully, most forms of direct action (e.g. rallies, telephone blockades, etc.)
require a co-ordinated network of participants. Networks are relational links
through which people can obtain access to material resources, knowledge and
power. Although some networks will be formally incorporated (such as the Round
Tables mentioned above), others will be informal and *ad hoc*, mobilising various
actors on a perceived 'as needs' basis. Actors may draw upon several of their individual multiple relational networks (such as a lawyer golfing partner, a planning
officer from the Parent Teacher Association, in addition to more formal ties with
others through business and/or political contact) in selecting interaction on a
particular issue.

The institutional capital and capacity (Amin and Thrift, 1995; Healey, 1999a)
generated by such networks thus embrace the collective abilities of the
actors' relationships, alliances and coalitions tempered by the contexts and
arenas in which they come together. A major factor leading to inequality
between actors and their ability to influence policy outcomes may therefore lie in
the socio-economic and political richness of the networks to which they have
access.

It is apparent that different types of actors, rationalities and networks often
coexist. As Hunter and Staggenborg (1988) and Amin and Hausner (1997) indicate, however, it becomes important not simply to recognise the existence of such
links, but also to consider the form, type and qualities (including strength of ties,
form of power relations, etc.) of the networks involved if we are to understand the
complexities of policy-making activity.

Rhodes and Marsh (1992) identify different types of networks by degree of
openness ranging from tightly knit policy communities to loosely integrated issue
networks (see Table 6.1).

As indicated in Table 6.1, policy communities have restricted memberships
and arrangements are characterised by a shared understanding of policy problems
with limited disagreement over the possible range of solutions (Dalton, 1996: 201).
In contrast, issue networks are open to the entry of any groups able to claim an
interest in an issue. They are often temporary and *ad hoc*, existing while the issue
remains important, and bringing together a wide range of actors often with little in
common other than the issue at hand. Conflict between actors is rife. These concepts would appear to embrace the activities of professional officers, perhaps in
conjunction with an elite of societal actors, often economic agents (a policy
community) and of the various groups and individuals involved in participating in a
local planning decision (an issue network).

Table 6.1 Types of policy networks: characteristics of policy communities and issue networks

Dimension	Policy community	Issue network
membership number of participants	very limited number, some groups consciously excluded	large
type of interest	economic and/or professional interests dominate	encompasses range of affected interests
integration frequency of interaction	frequent, high-quality, interaction of all groups on all matters related to policy issue	contacts fluctuate in frequency and intensity
continuity	membership, values and outcomes persistent over time	access fluctuates significantly
consensus	all participants share basic values and accept the legitimacy of the outcome	a measure of agreement exists, but conflict is ever present
resources distribution of resources (within network)	all participants have resources; basic relationship is an exchange relationship	some participants may have resources, but they are limited, and basic relationship is consultative
distribution of resources (within participating organisations)	hierarchical; leaders can deliver members	varied and variable distribution and capacity to regulate members
power	there is a balance of power among members, although one group may dominate	unequal powers, reflecting unequal resources and unequal access. It is a zero sum game

Source: Rhodes and Marsh (1992: 25)

The case study referred to above identified three distinct active networks in the planning process:

1   A 'development' network comprising the landowners/developers and relevant State government Ministers and planners: a classic policy network.

2   The 'Friends of the Valley' network which lobbied intensively, made strategic use of the media and significantly influenced the planning outcome. This issue network was not involved at all in the formal public participation process organised by the local authority and State planning departments.

3   The 'Swan Valley Residents and Ratepayers' Association' (SVRRA) network based on an existing ratepayers' association. The network's energies were primarily channelled through the formal representative process, supplemented by letter-writing to the press, planning officers and elected representatives. Although extant prior to the urbanisation proposals, the SVRRA is also predominantly an issue network.

Issue networks are contingent and dynamic as actors form and disband associations and coalitions according to the issue under consideration and the strategic alliances they believe will assist their cause. While policy networks are generally more stable, actors nevertheless selectively choose communication partners from among their multiple networks according to the perceived 'demands' of the circumstances.

Citizen interest representation through direct action has the potential to undermine dramatically the capacity of planners to plan. Is this necessarily a 'bad thing', however? If informal direct action is taken by the otherwise voiceless, is it not a legitimate means of obtaining voice? Although unlikely to take to the streets in demonstration, planners do have less *public* opportunities to 'gain the ear' of elected representatives.

What action should planners take in circumstances when their recommendations for a technically sound policy are opposed by an influential network of articulate actors with a less viable, self-interested alternative? Can and should planners use what powers they have (and their networks) to fight for an outcome in which they believe? Should they fight fire with fire and engage in informal leaks and direct action? This raises no small matter of ethical questions.

This research, and the work in Europe of Louis Albrechts (1997, 1999) and Bent Flyvbjerg (1998a, b) helps to expose the clientelistic tendency of governance systems and the informal activities of actors which both underpin and undermine such structures. Clearly, 'the whole apparatus of adverse bargaining, negotiation, compromise and deadlock which normally surround the planning process is undervalued' (Albrechts, 1997: 8) in both practice and theory. Such pragmatic considerations should be integrated into theory which aims at eventual implementation or praxis. The question is how? Direct action/lobbying has become part of decision-making behaviour. I certainly do not advocate its abolition. I firmly believe that preserving people's right to lobby is important. Yet at present (in Western Australia at least) it appears to be somewhat more of a 'fight with few holds barred than ... a contest under well-defined rules' (Gamson, 1995: 142), with the odds heavily weighted in favour of the already-advantaged groups in society.

Consensus-building

Grounded in Habermasian communicative theory, consensus-building is becoming an increasingly popular practice as a means to 'search for feasible strategies to deal with uncertain, complex, and controversial planning and policy tasks' (Innes and Booher, 1999a: 412). The aim of communicative theory is to achieve 'emancipatory' knowledge through dialogue between actors. Common principles allow dialogue and exchange of ideas to take place. Such principles include access to information, listening to and respecting other participants, having equal power to speak and challenge others, speaking sincerely, accurately and so on (Habermas, 1984; Innes and Booher, 1999a, b; Healey, 1999a).

As Innes and Booher (1998: 17) explain: 'The consensus process cannot change the deep structure nor take power away that stakeholders have in the outside world.' However, consensus-building groups often aim to equalise power at the discussion table by requiring a super-majority agreement before they make a decision and through the power of veto or withholding agreement, so that particip- ants have an incentive to find acceptable solutions.[2]

In this way, actors build shared meanings and interests and generate new ideas for framing problems and approaches to moving forwards. Consensus-build- ing is regarded as being transformative. Through participants' thinking and acting together, they may transform their ideas, values of what is important to them, their ways of working and organising.

Figure 6.1 represents a tentative attempt at illustrating diagrammatically the organisational landscape of participatory processes in planning. The vertical axis represents a political distinction between informal direct action and institutionalised

POLITICS:
INSTITUTIONALISED

Associative Democracy
(Cohen and Rogers)

Neocorporatism Policy Networks	**Radical Pluralism**
e.g. Concensus-building, development coalitions (Innes, Rhodes and March)	e.g. Small reciprocities/fixing (Mouffe)

CONSENSUS   **AGONISM**

Issue Networks	**Direct Action**
e.g. Coping networks (Burns and Taylor)	e.g. Resident action groups, environmental movements (Melucci)

INFORMAL

Note: Within individual groups/networks, etc., there may also be institutionalised-informal and consensus-agonistic activity.

6.1 Organisational landscape of participatory processes in planning.

community mobilisation. The horizontal axis represents two types of space: consensus and agonistic.[3] Within the diagram I offer some possibilities for types of action drawn from the above discussion and show how they might be represented in each area (recognising the non-exclusivity of each domain) and point out that *within* individual networks there may also be activities/behaviours taking place which are institutionalised-informal and consensus-agonistic in nature. Any patterns in practice would be extremely messy, containing various levels and intensities of networks nesting inside/overlapping with each other, changing over time.

I raise the questions: if we want to move towards more consensual planning decision-making, or at least decisions with which most stakeholders can live, do we want to impose some formal institutional structure on what is essentially a largely interpersonal framework? (see Mansbridge, 1992.) Can planners really not feel comfortable (less vulnerable?) unless there is 'an awesome and incontestable authority' (Bauman, 1991: 251) hanging over everything? Even if this means inventing and imposing an artificial order which may serve to reinforce, obstruct or fragment already existing organised coping mechanisms which planners cannot see.

Melucci (1989, 1996) is a strong advocate of conducting debate in public spheres independent of the institutions of governance, in order to provide guarantees of non-corporatism, non-tokenism and non-cosmeticism to local people, and to ensure that society's issues, demands and conflicts are subjected openly to negotiation. Non-institutionalised public spheres, he argues, make possible 'a democracy of everyday life'.

There are strong arguments for the encouragement and legitimation of informal direct action as a means of giving voice to the traditionally voiceless in planning decision-making processes. The implicit assumption, which runs through much of my analysis above, that if public protest takes place, the formal participation processes have failed ('campaigns are the currency of unsuccessful groups', Richardson and Jordan, 1979: 123) is open to question. An open process, in which all actors can protest publicly, could be an alternative.

Questions for consideration include: if we are aiming to overcome a situation in which the more affluent and connected are able to exercise greater power over planning decision-making, and to give voice and power to the voiceless, what are the relative merits of the following?

- opening up the decision processes to outsider strategies of direct action;
- attempting to restrict decision processes to consensus-oriented institutionalised insider strategies;
- enabling insider and outsider strategies to take place in parallel.

We may well need to consider introducing new affirmative principles which aim to avoid the mere institutionalisation of effectively mobilised networks of power, which is then legitimately exercised over weaker, less able networks. We would require new arenas which are perhaps less rule-directed than rule-altering/reflexive. To what rules should we switch? How may we create a 'form of articulation between individual freedom and civic participation' (Mouffe, 1992: 231) which respects the priority of the socially just over the socially and economically powerful? Who is likely to gain and who to lose? I am confident that we need local strategies, which are contextually appropriate rather than centralised solutions. We need to rethink the frames of reference about our thinking about place (see Hillier, 1998b) and about process. We need to open up new discursive spaces in the interstices of society. I now turn to explore the possibilities outlined above in more detail.

ONTO ROUGH GROUND: OPENING UP DIRECT ACTION

The concept of direct action embraces various forms of action including marches, demonstrations, sit-ins, refusal to pay taxes and other acts of civil disobedience which Routledge (1997) terms the postmodern politics of resistance. Yet, as Cohen and Arato (1992: 566) ask, is there any justification for activities which bypass existing procedures and institutions for expressing (planning) concerns? Do acts of civil disobedience violate the rights of elected members to make binding law, thus challenging both liberal and democratic principles? Or, as Walzer (1999) argues, do such non-deliberative (yet strongly communicative) political activities belong at the centre of democratic politics?

Direct action is located at the seam between Habermasian system and lifeworld, in the interstices between the boundaries of insurrection and institutionalised political activity. As such, it may offer the traditionally marginalised and planning-voiceless the opportunity to participate and to speak.

Empirical evidence of direct action in planning debates (see Petracca, 1992; Hillier, 1995, 2000) suggests that most activity is aimed at either providing information about ramifications of a certain policy and/or attempting to persuade decision-makers to a particular course of action. The logic of direct action is to discursively gain decision-makers' attention and to make them consider alternative arguments and options rather than to seize political power.

Although in certain circumstances, direct action may be a strategy of last resort as Cohen and Arato (1992: 601) suggest, research in the planning (Hillier, 2000) and community development (Tilly, 1975; Ostrom, 1992) fields indicates that it can also be regarded as an 'up front' activity, a valid and normal political resource to be used by actors in pursuit of their objectives: 'lobbying is as ancient as governing . . . it is also as legitimate and necessary' (Parton, 1869: 361).

Melucci (1988) advocates the encouragement and legitimation of direct action as a means of giving voice to the traditionally voiceless. By speaking out or acting directly in public spheres which decision-makers cannot ignore, one avoids the problems of corporatism, tokenism and cosmeticism which may arise with panel or committee membership. Open processes, in which all actors can protest publicly, could be an alternative.

The practical difficulties of operationalising such public spheres and ensuring they are just, are problematic, however. How do we overcome situations in which the more affluent, articulate and connected are able to generate greater 'noise' and to exercise greater power over decision-making? Not everyone is prepared to take direct action in a political culture which generally operates to produce quiescence and passivity (through family, school, workplace and law and order disciplinary traditions). Those who participate tend not to be the disenfranchised, the marginalised and excluded, but those able to devote resources (time, money, contacts, etc.) to the 'cause'.

There are important questions of inclusion and exclusion. If direct action favours some individuals and groups over others, who misses out? Does direct action simply 'buttress many relations of inequality' (Mouffe, 1993: 151)? How can the interests of the majority be protected in the face of vociferous minorities? Should populism be allowed to reign?

My argument so far has concentrated on citizen action. What about planning officers? My research (Hillier, 2000) indicated planners are irritated and frustrated by citizens taking direct action. Some regarded it as 'unfair' and 'going round the back' of formal participatory processes, even 'cheating'. Yet, these planners clearly overlooked the traditional practice of officers writing or summarising reports to suit preferred ends, or having a discreet 'word in the ear' of key elected members such as Committee Chairs and Ministers.

Albrechts' (1997, 1999) empirical work has brought such activities into the public arena for probably the first time. Albrechts demonstrates the *necessity* of planning officers engaging in 'delicate lobby work (talking to members of parliament, to several ministers, leading civil servants, leaders of the trade-union, . . . consultants, the press)' (1997: 17–18). Occasionally, as Albrechts indicates, stronger measures of leverage may be required. 'We refused to sign the contract. . . . Without us and our planning team the process would have come to an end, this would provoke major discontent with [some] important actors in society' (ibid.: 18).

Albrechts' focus on the 'highly political role' (ibid.: 24) of planners in Flanders in Flyvbjerg's (1998a) depiction of the 'stroking strategy' which officers in

Aalborg, Denmark employed, raises the question of how planners can justify their own lobbying activities as legitimate while condemning those of citizens' groups as illegitimate, and undermining their capacity to plan. It may be a matter of perception: that the planners interviewed (in Hillier, 2000) perceived the public displays of influential actors to have been successful and that such public displays are not a course of action open to themselves. Planners are unlikely to carry placards and march on parliament.

We also need to recognise that:

> the more conflicts of interests there are the more it is important to have procedural solutions of conflict adjudication through which parties whose interests are negatively affected can find recourse to other methods of the articulation and representation of their grievances.
>
> (Benhabib, 1996a: 73)

We therefore need to develop new debating and decision-making forums and arenas, outside, perhaps, of formal politics, in which marginalised groups have voice and power:

> [a] medium of loosely associated, multiple foci of opinion formation and dissemination which affect one another in free and spontaneous processes of communication ... a *plurality of modes of association* in which all affected can have the right to articulate their point of view.
>
> (ibid.: 74, 73, emphasis in original)

ON SLIPPERY ICE: BEYOND CONSENSUS

In this section I ask whether an objective of reaching deep or thick consensus rather than simply superficial or thin consensus is unattainably utopian. Does a proposal become so diluted in becoming consensual that it loses meaning? Are actors' interests not transformed *per se* through collaboration but rather submerged or induced into conformity with group norms? (Allmendinger, 1999).

I believe that planning theorists need to recognise that differently formulated identities, values, claims and arguments may find any common links extremely precarious and that there may well be substantive and even intractable disagreements over basic issues (see Hillier, 1998b). The key issue concerns the implications of a distinction between what Benhabib (1996b) terms associational space (consensual space in which people work together in concert) and agonistic space (competitive space). Associational or consensual space is essentially a moral space of interactive rationality based in Habermasian communicative action. As Benhabib emphasises:

> It is through the interlocking net of these multiple forms of associations, networks, and organisations that an anonymous 'public conversation' results. It is central to the model of deliberative democracy that it privileges such a public sphere of mutually interlocking and overlapping networks and associations of deliberation, contestation and argumentation.
>
> (1996a: 73–74)

Such deliberation, contestation and argumentation take place in situations, similar to those identified by Innes above as necessary for consensus-building, of universal moral respect and egalitarian reciprocity to speak, to initiate new topics, to question other actors and to challenge the rules as well as the agenda of public debate (ibid.: 78–79).

Reciprocity, or 'recognition of the other as one in whose place I can put myself' is essential as the 'core of democratic principles and practice' (Gutmann and Thompson, 2000). However, as is practically recognised by Throgmorton (2000), and persuasively argued by Young (1995, 1997), reciprocity is unlikely in situations where differences are well entrenched and where there is mistrust and suspicion. Benhabib's associational space is counterfactual. It is an utopian ideal which excludes the possibility of power-plays and of politics and which conceals the impossibility of its own realisation.[4] It lacks an awareness that 'for humans, resistance, transgression, and agonism are fundamentally vital' (Coles, 1995: 32) and that dissent is as important in dialogical relationships as the idea of agreement.

Agonistic space is 'a competitive space, in which one competes for recognition, precedence and acclaim' (Benhabib, 1992: 78). It is the view of space engaged by Nietzsche (1954) and Foucault (1983, 1984b) and by subsequent authors such as Connolly (1991), Mouffe (1992, 1993, 1996, 1999), Young (1995, 1997), Mansbridge (1995) and Wolin (1996). It is a political space embracing legitimate and public contestation over access to resources (Wolin, 1996). Its pluralism is axiological, recognising the impossibility of ever adjudicating without contest and without residue between competing visions (Mouffe, 1996). Conflict between different viewpoints, interests and values is inescapable.

Mouffe (1996) regards a belief in the final resolution of conflicts to be a dangerous and simplistic illusion. She argues that 'acting in concert' requires the construction of a 'we', a political unity, but that a fully inclusive political unity can never be realised since wherever there is a 'we', there must also be an excluded 'them', a constitutive outside. Any agreement reached will thus be partial, based on acts of social regulation and exclusion. The 'surplus of meaning' (Dyrberg, 1997: 196) which remains uncontrolled is liable to challenge from the excluded other.

For Connolly (1991) and Mouffe (1997, 1998, 1999), a pluralist democracy must allow the expression of dissent and conflicting interests and values. Since we cannot eliminate antagonism, we need to domesticate it to a condition of agonism in which passion is mobilised constructively (rather than destructively) towards the promotion of democratic decisions which are partly consensual, but which also respectfully accept unresolvable disagreements. While agonism is generally construed as a struggle against, it may also be construed as a struggle for. Hence, Foucault's (1984b: 379) remark that 'one must not be for consensuality, but one must be against nonconsensuality'.

Agonistic space, then, does not eliminate power by subordinating it to rationality in a search for consensual agreement. There is always 'more than reason' with regard to strategic policy-making, whether this be contestations of power, non-negotiable and axiomatic value differences, or the never-ending assertions of competition, conflict and alterity (Mouffe, 1996; Walzer, 1999). Once we consider the political dimension of deliberative policy-making we may find that rational (rather than rationalised) outcomes are impossible to achieve. 'Why use the force of the better argument when force alone will suffice?' (Flyvbjerg, 1998a: 80). What does this imply for democratic decision-making and planning?

Since attempts to establish a rational consensus may result either in a thin agreement at the lowest common denominator on the few issues about which parties can concur and/or be simply a 'front' (Allmendinger, 1999: 12) for powerful interests to maintain influence and capacity to get what they want while seeming to act more deliberatively, we need to understand and incorporate power into our framework. We need to provide channels of expression in which conflicts can be expressed while limiting the use of abusively confrontational antagonistic behaviour; channels which enable participants to move beyond potentially entrenched rights-based positions to constructively uncover each side's interests and expectations from outcomes and what aspects are critical to them; channels which offer more in various ways than participants might otherwise obtain by pursuing their interests in legal, political or other arenas. Competition and co-operation are often inextricably entwined in deliberative processes, as Innes' (1999b) empirical work confirms. The two often cannot be separated and 'neither denial nor discomfort will make it disappear' (Lax and Sebenius, 1986: 30).

In the philosophical sense we need 'a deliberative vision of democratic politics which can also do justice to the agonistic spirit of democracy' (Benhabib, 1996a: 9). Benhabib, however, fails to achieve such a vision, finding associational and agonistic space theoretically incompatible. Similarly, Gutmann and Thompson struggle to include antagonism and disagreement in what is essentially a moral deliberative paradigm. Despite acknowledging the existence of disagreement, they still seek consensus, however: 'deliberative democracy seeks not consensus for its own sake but rather a morally justified consensus' (1996: 42), proposing six universalist principles to be achieved: reciprocity, publicity, accountability, basic liberty, basic opportunity and fair opportunity. Of these, reciprocity, with all its problems, is regarded as key.

Given these moral conditions, mutually acceptable reasons for unresolvable disagreements are permissible. Gutmann and Thompson term such outcomes, when there is agreement to disagree, as 'moral or deliberative disagreement'. Their prescription for deliberative democracy is thus that citizens should 'deliberate with one another, seeking moral agreement when they can, and maintaining mutual respect when they cannot' (1996: 346), a concept similar to Connolly's (1998) notion of agonistic respect.

It is in this area of moral disagreement (which, together with that of disagreements governed by self-interest, I would regard as political disagreements) that Gutmann and Thompson (1996, 2000) call for prudence, whose 'distinctive method' is bargaining. They suggest that bargaining is justifiable when the universals governing moral deliberation fail; 'bargaining is a legitimate way of resolving political conflicts that would otherwise remain unresolved' (Gutmann and Thompson, 1996: 71). It should, however, be a strategy of last rather than first resort; not the principle of least effort. Bargaining is considered second-best behaviour, based as it is in self-interest and conflict rather than reciprocity and consensus, yet, Gutmann and Thompson (2000: 175) suggest that if the consequences of bargaining can be shown to be mutually justifiable to the people bound by them, 'then instituting self-seeking bargaining in place of deliberation can satisfy the principles of deliberative democracy'.

Gutmann and Thompson have attempted to deal with agonism by separating it out from their theory of moral deliberation and incorporating it through bargaining in special circumstances of moral disagreement or immutable self-interest.[5] I would argue, however, that such a conception is of relatively limited use to the highly politicised activities of planning practice. Elster's (1998) consideration of bargaining, however, is different from that of Gutmann and Thompson and may offer us a way forward. Elster (1998: 5) identifies three different modes of decision-making in conditions of unreachable consensus: arguing, bargaining and voting. Importantly to my argument here, he suggests that *political* decision-making usually involves all of the procedures in combination. Taking this issue further, Gambetta (1998) writes that it is sometimes difficult to separate bargaining from argument, although essentially he defines bargaining as involving negotiation through the exchange of promises and/or threats or warnings, while argument is an attempt to persuade others of the values of one's views.

By way of example, Aboriginal groups in Australia are increasingly negotiating directly with developers rather than the governmental planning system (Robert Bropho, 1996, pers. comm.). The thinking behind such a strategy is that both groups have vested interests in achieving an outcome and therefore have a stimulus to negotiate (unlike planning officers of governance to whom the issue may well not be so important). Although the participants may not like or respect each other and are unwilling to engage in reciprocity (imagining themselves in the other's position), communicative action or procedural justice, the necessary interaction between them for an outcome to be achieved is sufficient to stimulate negotiation: a transaction of enlightened self-interest (Rubin, 1991: 4) in which actors hold attitudes of 'I don't care what your values are, I don't have to like or trust you, but let's negotiate a compromise.'

Can we do this philosophically? My Aboriginal example appears similar to Elster's (1998) and Gambetta's (1998) notions of bargaining. As such, we should be able to work through transactions of enlightened self-interest or bargain to reach a compromise. Here I stress the difference between *compromise* and *consensus*. Compromise is reached through a *transaction* or through *bargaining*. Consensus is reached through *argument* or *deliberation*. Both have elements of agreement and differences of viewpoints and values. Transacted or bargained outcomes may not be strictly 'moral' (following Gutmann and Thompson's reasoning), but they may, nevertheless be socially just.

Even Habermas has begun to acknowledge that complex processes of bargaining and compromise have a legitimate role to play in democratic decision-making in deciding conflicts between interest groups about distributive problems. He suggests that a compromise is 'fair' if it provides advantages to each party; if it tolerates no 'free riders'; and no one is exploited in such a way as to force them to give up more than they gain by compromise (1996a: 165–167).

WHERE ARE WE? WHERE ARE WE GOING?

The question which remains is that if we conceive of planning policy-making as a political medium through which the antinomies of difference are expressed and contested and we reject an Habermasian consensual teleocommunitarian morality as utopian and counterfactual, can we achieve an agonopluralistic ethic in theory and practice, and what would agonistic democracy look like at an urban scale of decision-making?

If we can understand the circumstances and conditions which tend to lead to argument or bargaining in policy disputes, we may become more able to steer participants towards agonistic argument to the benefit of the traditionally marginalised. I suggest that there may be three key variables involved: actors' values, their perception of the other actors and their outcome preferences.

Forester (1999d) suggests that much hinges on actors' values; that value differences are sometimes irreconcilable, but that this should be the end-point of negotiation rather than a presumption. We should be asking questions of what makes disputes irreconcilable. How do different value claims matter practically to participants and to all those affected by the decision? We need to tease out differences in participants' values between those which they simply like, want, need, have a commitment to and so on, i.e. between their *core* and *secondary* values. In this vein, Sabatier (1987) proposes that actors' value-systems have a three-fold structure, comprising a deep core of fundamental normative and ontological axioms, a policy core of basic choices and secondary aspects which actors are more likely to compromise for various reasons.

I suggest, therefore, that participants are likely to reach consensus if large areas of their core and secondary values overlap/are commensurate, but that incommensurability of both will lead to situations of bargaining within the formal process and tactics of informal direct action outside. In circumstances where core values are incommensurable but there is agreement between secondary values, agonistic deliberation or argument may take place.

Forester (1999d) also argues the importance of participants' perceptions of the other actors involved. He offers a four-box matrix in which one side either believes the other's value statements or suspects them of posturing, against whether the other side is actually expressing itself honestly or is bluffing. While I argue that Forester's matrix should be multi-way rather than one-way, it does nevertheless, help us to understand more about conditions and circumstances in which positional bargaining is likely (suspicion on one side and bluff on the other), collaborative dialogue is possible (conditions of trust and sincerity), or anger, resentment and escalation of conflict is probable (suspicion on one side and honesty on the other).

Thompson and Tuden's (1959) typology of decision processes has been resurrected by Lee (1993) as it forwards comprehension of the important dimensions about participants' beliefs and outcome preferences. Thompson and Tuden (see Figure 6.2) suggest that irreconcilable conflict and direct action are likely when actors disagree over both their understanding of the causation of the dispute and their preferred outcomes. However, when there are levels of agreement on outcomes, bargaining may occur, while agreement as to causation makes

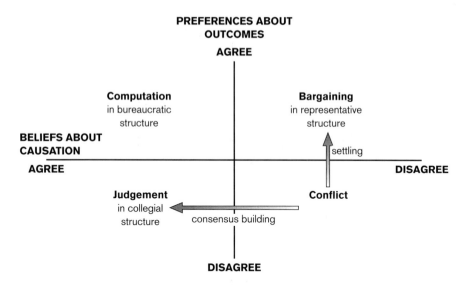

6.2 Social decision processes.

Source: Thompson and Tuden (1959) cited in Lee, 1993:106.

negotiation more probable. Translating these ideas into my base diagram (Figure 6.1) gives Figure 6.3.

However, as Joe Springer (1998, personal communication) has astutely commented, and Pruitt's (1991) work supports, my horizontal axis remains an inadequate explanation of reality. Not all actors choose to participate. Some may remain ignorant of the issue completely, some may be apathetic, unconcerned about the outcome and others may be alienated by the process, the players or other considerations. Some participants may withdraw from the process before its completion, to retire into inactivity or, at the other extreme, to ferment revolution outside of the formal process. My horizontal axis should therefore be extended to that depicted in Figure 6.4.

CONSENSUS V. AGONISM: CAN WE REACH A RECONCILIATION?

Consensus-building procedures described by Innes (1999a) and Susskind *et al.* (1999) resemble the practical realisation of aspects of Cohen and Rogers' (1995) conception of associative democracy. Embracing, as it does, the four core elements of decision-making pluralism; a combination of authority with consensus; processual, dialogic rationality and interactive governance; and concertation or decision-making through negotiation (Amin, 1996), associative democracy is similar to Habermas's suggestion for a model of deliberative democracy, consisting

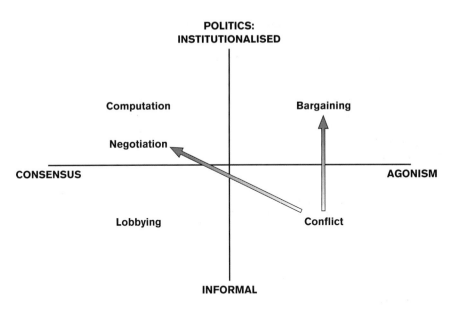

6.3 Social decision processes and participatory processes in planning.

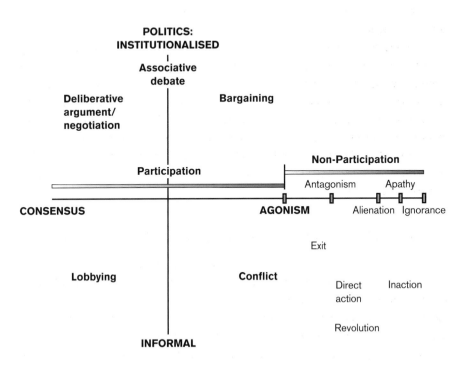

6.4 Participation in planning activity.

of a public sphere of political communication whose institutional basis is provided by voluntary associations of civil society together with inputs of expert information.

It is not my task here to suggest normative institutional details for actualisation of associative democracy (see Amin and Thrift, 1995; Amin, 1996; Amin and Hausner, 1997). I do, however, highlight some of the problems which may emerge to affect the potential of associative democratic, and by implication, consensus-building processes.

Young (1995) regards the necessary artifactuality of associative democracy as problematic and suggests a need for social solidarities to be formed and develop naturally rather than be conveniently fabricated or rationalised. Other important problematic issues should also be noted, including problems of representation. Is it inevitable, as Mulgan (1997: 204) suggests, that 'representation separates citizens from decisions' or is it physically possible for *all* stakeholders to have a voice? What about the not-yet-present, the deceased and those (e.g. gypsies) who gain specific advantages from 'living on the edge' (Sibley, 1998: 99) and who may suffer from incorporation into a regulatory system? These problems, and those of size, will necessitate some absences from the negotiating arena and some form of representation. As is now generally recognised (Young, 1995, 1997; Laclau, 1996; Dyrberg, 1997; Hillier and van Looij, 1997), it is impossible to represent accurately anyone or anything else. Representation is indeed re-presentation. The act of re-presenting confers power on the representer to act in the name of an absent totality, to stand firm or to concede points of debate. In other words, the conditions of possibility of the system (i.e. representation) are also the conditions of its impossibility (see Laclau, 1997).

There are also important problems of achieving representation of traditionally less articulate, less organised groups as compared to those who tend to lobby and take direct action in any case. 'For many people in excluded communities, joining a formal organisation is not a natural thing to do' (Burns and Taylor, 1997: 10). Outreach mechanisms, including, where appropriate, facilitation of group formation through a process of active listening for latent agency and nurturing its evolution (Gamson, 1995) may be crucial to achievement of fair representation.

Furthermore, representatives should not be able unilaterally to decide to abandon the commitments they brought with them to the negotiating table in the light of persuasive argument. There should be some mechanism by which representatives can either take ideas and proposals back to their groups[6] or be fully accountable for their actions.[7]

Acceptance is another problematic issue. In order for associative democratic institutions to fulfil their potential as a springboard or participatory resource for marginalised groups, they must be accepted in good faith by the 'mainstream' (officers of governance, elected members, organised interest groups, etc.) without attempts at neutralisation by co-optation and incorporation into a highly bureau-cratic, jargonistic, technocratic system.

How might associative democratic forums be established? Cohen and Rogers propose a deliberate use of public powers to promote the necessary organisational bases, involving the construction of temporary, context-related 'new arenas for public deliberation that lie outside conventional political arenas' (1995: 250). Burns and Taylor (1997), in this vein, identify the need for creation of 'social relays' to link actors' networks to one another and activate dormant links.

Real 'democratic associationalism' entails far more than the 'currently fash-ionable but nebulous idea of stakeholder democracy' (Amin and Graham, 1997: 425), exemplified by most 'partnership' and consensus-building arrangements. I support Amin's (1996) interpretation of associative democracy and emphasis on the importance of commencing with the socially excluded, as the greatest potential for innovating change lies in the interstitial spaces of society, those spaces which often resist mainstream interference and establish their own networks of mutuality, interaction, dialogue and negotiation.

However, organising political life using associationality as a regulatory prin-ciple of freedom and empowerment can itself involve a sort of imposition. Power is necessary to limit power (Flyvbjerg, 1998b: 209). We here encounter Connolly's (1991) paradox of difference, that some form of social order is necessary, but any social order is repressive to some. Would associative democratic institutions be simply another form of Foucauldian normalisation? Their so-called 'empower-ment' merely another instance of governmentality, with marginalised people partici-pating in their own further subjectification by exercising power over themselves, tying themselves to some form of definitional logic of who they are? Would asso-ciative democracy be little more than neocorporatism, a way of managing 'the pres-sures of interests on the state' (Wilson, 1990: 150) in an institutionalised framework of bargaining which renders conflict 'tolerable' by domesticating and neutralising any potentially serious challenge to the requirements of capitalist rationalisation? As Mouffe (1999: 753) writes, the main question 'is not how to eliminate power but how to constitute forms of power that are compatible with democratic values'.

Should attempts at associative democracy prove to be a means of institu-tional manipulation, as above, I would envisage them to also produce their own countertendency – pushing social conflict outside of the associative arena, back into direct action, resignation or apathy.

Rather than associative democracy, therefore, my belief is that agonistic democracy can incorporate elements of both associative debate and direct action; that insider (associative) and outsider (direct action) strategies are legitimate. But does this leave us in a political free-for-all in which the strongest, the most articulate, those with the most influential contacts, or the most violent win?

Is it impossibly utopian to realise an agonistic forum in an urban policy-making setting? Would it necessitate 'some fictive model of political agency that has never been instantiated anywhere' as Connolly (1998: 124) concludes? A political imaginary?

There cannot, and should not, be any 'model' of agonistic democracy as ways of working need to be contingent on circumstances, time, place and stakeholders. As Flyvbjerg (1998a: 234) writes, 'When we understand power we see that we cannot rely solely on democracy based on rationality to solve our problems.' For this reason I prefer a theory of democracy which incorporates both associative and agonistic aspects.

I recognise that if any actors believe that they can improve their outcome through any potentially viable alternative to a negotiated agreement, they may be expected to try to do so. This means that agonistic democratic procedures will not alter fundamental power relationships in a society, no matter what our desires. Powerful actors may simply resort to using other powers (of connections, financial wealth and other forms of leverage) available to them instead of, or at the same time as, engaging in a collaborative, associative strategy of consensus-building decision-making.

In terms of institutional organisation, given the theoretical debate above, it follows that the practical nature of associative participation and the nature of procedural rules (Bohman and Rehg, 1997: xviii; Weber, 1998) should be articulated in such a way that the inherent agonism and undecidability (Dyrberg, 1997) of political/planning decisions are embodied in an institutional setting which offers all actors a real possibility of participating in planning policy decision-making and which recognises the ultimate non-consensual undecidability of decisions and hence makes it possible to disagree.

We need to recognise the messiness of politics and to 'reconfigure the political' (Walker, 1994: 669) in societies currently 'strangled by insidious webs of alliance between the dominant political, economic and social institutions' (Amin, 1996: 329). Is this possible? In societies where the performance of bureaucratic administrations is increasingly measured in efficiency terms, administrators are seeking to discover and undertake activities instrumental to the achievement of such ends. As such, the nature of administrative power would appear paradoxical to, and perhaps incommensurable with, the logic of communicative power, based on relations of mutual recognition, respect and reciprocity.

We also need to remember that while new institutional forms may offer previously ignored interests an opportunity to enter planning debates, the pattern of the institutional form constrains the changes it enables (see Morone, 1990). Furthermore, we need to remember the essentially political rather than moral nature of much of what will take place. An emphasis on reciprocal deliberation alone attends too little to the degree to which disagreements are shaped by political differences of interest and power (Shapiro, 1999). It is all too common to see collaborative round tables disintegrate from being forums of co-operation, deep democracy, individual dignity and personal fulfilment to virtual battlefields of competition, domination, control and greed (McArdle, 1999: 38–39).

CONCLUSION

Is there some terrain between Wittgenstein's slippery ice of collaborative consensus-building and the rough ground of conflict? Planning practice is 'a field where interests and social groups meet and clash under conditions created by the interaction of multiple forces' (Melucci, 1996: 92). Planning practice will always be agonistic; a system of 'interweaving opposites, of ambivalences, of multiple meanings which actors seek to bend to their goals so as to lend meaning to their action' (ibid.: 95). While recognition of agonistic reality is important, as Benhabib (1996c: 8) points out, without some form of agreement or consent to an outcome of the debate, it is impossible to be sure that the (planning) decision will be 'good and just' rather than 'unjust, racist, fickle, and capricious'; a victory for the most organised, vociferous or having the 'best' contacts as in my Western Australian example.

Grounded in traditions of networking, through associative/agonistic practice, we may nevertheless make relational links, across cultural barriers, organisational divisions and fractures in the distribution of power (Healey, 1997a: 311). While actors may never reconcile fundamental differences, they may, nevertheless, be able to balance interests and compromise (Habermas, 1998: 245), to convert relations of antagonism to those which Mouffe (1999: 756) terms 'conflictual consensus' and which Connolly (1998: 122) calls 'agonistic respect': 'a social relation of respect for the opponent against whom you define yourself even while you resist its imperatives and strive to delimit its spaces of hegemony'.

All the above involves opening up the opportunity structure for involvement in planning policy-making. To achieve this, stakeholders with vested interests and established mindsets (elected members, private sector entrepreneurs, planners and other officers of governance and even public sentiment) need to be persuaded of the benefits of collaboration and that it is concerned with 'engagement and negotiation, not a political doctrine of ... consensus and resolution' (Connolly, 1998: 123). We also need to recognise that networking means far more than having contacts; that co-operation and collaboration mean far more than knowing people or sitting on the same committee (Marilyn Taylor, 1997, pers. comm.).

Any associative/agonistic practice must be context contingent (in terms of place, time, representation, resources, etc.). There would inevitably be problems with attempts at associative/agonistic democratic policy-making. It is likely that local citizens would either expect to achieve too much, ignoring the inertia of actors' vested interests, or mistrust governance intentions and refuse to particip-ate. Formalisation of networking could actually serve to destroy the informal coping systems of marginalised communities. There may well be attempts by some actors at exclusivity, at co-optation and corporatism, particularly if the public sector is pro-viding financial support and infrastructure for the practice. We would need to be careful not to create yet another system which serves to colonise people's life-worlds. There will almost certainly be direct action or bargaining activity taking place contemporaneously with associative debate.

Is this last necessarily a bad thing? I think not. Planning officers should relax their need for control and certainty. They need to learn to live with inconsistencies, contradictions and the fact that some actors will refuse to be 'mainstreamed' as they regard it, remaining 'outsiders by choice' (Maloney et al., 1994), while others will place their bets both ways, participating in associative forums and in direct action:

> in a world where negotiation, instrumental trade-offs, and strategic bargaining are the most common routes to reaching collective 'agreement', and resolving disputes, it is plausible that the most serious barrier (to associative debate) can be found in the con-versational habits that citizens have become used to.
>
> (Chambers, 1995: 247)

After all, if planning officers themselves engage in lobbying elected members and negotiating trade-offs with developers, why should they begrudge others the practice?[8]

Associative/agonistic practice, as conceptualised and represented in Figure 6.4, should recognise the inherent undecidability of decisions and accept unresolv-able differences of values and opinion without passing moral judgement on them. There should be freedom of dissent as well as of agreement. Where consensus cannot be achieved through negotiation, bargaining or transactions may take place to reach compromise agreements. As Mouffe (1999: 755) comments, 'Compro-mises are possible; they are part of the process of politics.'

Practice should be open to agonistic struggle and resistance to totalising hegemonic 'solutions'. Obviously, there is no guarantee that any outcome(s), produced by resistance and direct action, will be 'better' for traditionally margin-alised peoples than other outcomes. There will always be losers from planning decisions. As such, this is a tragic view of political life and its possibilities with regard to planning in that it recognises the inevitability of conflict and the experience of imposition on those whose wishes are denied. My ambition is to realise situations in which it is not usually the powerless and marginalised who lose.

It may well be that the creation and survival of associative institutional forums would be less important than their role in the development of networks which can hold 'organisational intelligence' (Milofsky, 1987) and the 'stirring up' of actors to respond to particular opportunities and challenges. If attempts at associative/ago-nistic democratic policy-making establish a tradition of forms of action that mobilise those actors in the interstices of society who are directly affected by a planning issue, then I would regard the experiments as having been successful.

Planning decision-making in practice is replete with overt and covert network activity, as people activate political networks, intra- and inter-organisational net-works and 'local residents' ' networks to further their own purposes. What I have attempted to do in this chapter is to engage in the theoretical struggle for a new discursive terrain of planning activity, with new principles of legitimacy of agonism (incorporating direct action) contesting the old principles of formal participation processes.

I have attempted to mark momentary convergences but also fundamental divergences between teleocommunitarian approaches to associative consensus-building and an agonopluralistic ethic. I have suggested that the two approaches can live together. Some form of radical pluralism and forums for expressing simil-arities, negotiating agreements or bargaining compromises is necessary. Yet plan-ners should be aware of the existence of intractable opposition and resistance as well as searching for agreement. By 'stirring up' stakeholders to action, we may encourage airing of a fuller range of views and knowledges than would otherwise take place.

We should refuse to close off the options that direct action and other forms of 'resistance' might make available. For some agonal subjects, direct action may be the only form of representation and empowerment open to them. As in Niet-zsche's (1954) agonistic contest, the point is to prevent the solidification of stra-tegic relations into states of domination.

My diagram of potential planning activity represents the terrain hosting the contest between two urges: the one, of direct action, seeking a site of untram-melled freedom beyond all limits, and the other, of formal associative democratic structures, representing the safety of life rendered meaningful by its inescapable limits. It is a terrain of experimentation and diversity in which a contestation of views can occur and in which new coalitions and alliances, of friends and some-time adversaries, can form for limited and localised initiatives in order to be able to walk forwards across both ice and rough ground.

ACKNOWLEDGEMENTS

My thanks to all those off whom I have 'bounced ideas' for this chapter and who have enriched my thinking, particularly: Chantal Mouffe, Marilyn Taylor, Patsy Healey, Margo Huxley, Nola Kunnen and Joe Springer. Thanks also to Theo van Looij for computerising my scribbled diagrams.

NOTES

1   See the volume by McAdam *et al.* (1996) which contains several chapters exploring aspects of political opportunity structures. Most authors seem to list the following as dimensions of political opportunity:
  • the relative openness or closure of the institutionalised political system;
  • the stability or instability of that broad set of alignments which typically underpin a polity (e.g. tradition, mass media access, etc.);
  • the presence or absence of elite allies;
  • the state's capacity and propensity for repression.

(McAdam, 1996: 27)

One major and obvious difference in political opportunity structure, for example, would be between the more fragmented political structure of the USA which would offer opportunities for communicative consensus-building, and the strong state struc-tures in the UK and Australia which tend to encourage more strategic, adversarial rationality.

2   I question the effectiveness of veto power across all participants. I believe that actors who have little which other actors may want or need, would have minimal power to effectively veto an outcome.

3   I prefer poles of informal and institutionalised action to Ravetz's (1999, Fig. 6) nomen-clature of illegitimacy and legitimacy.

4   Young (1997) suggests a way forward in terms of *moral* rather than political respect, with the idea of asymmetrical reciprocity. Communicating parties mutually recognise one another, even if only to recognise irreducible or asymmetrical points of view.

5   Their work has generated much debate, e.g. Macedo (1999) and the special issue of *Social Philosophy and Policy* (2000) devoted to the subject.

6   However, the groups will not have had the benefit of exposure to the discussion and

may not agree with the arguments of their representative. Deliberation may thus be lengthily protracted.

7   An alternative strategy, of mandating representatives to vote in accordance with agreed group desires, severely limits any ability for representatives to negotiate effectively.

8   I recognise that planning officers would probably argue that they are politically neutral and lobby in the nebulous 'public interest' as a whole, in contrast to the self-interested lobbying and activities of others. While it may be that planners do take a wider range of issues into consideration than do other actors, I would contest any suggestion that planning is a politically neutral activity and that planners can make politically neutral recommendations. I would also argue that planners may overlook the interests of some actors or underestimate the impact of a policy on them. It would appear that judgements of fairness of practice may well come down to the issue of the outcome achieved. But what would be a 'best' outcome? In whose opinion? How would it be 'measured' as being best?

7

Governmentality, Gender, Planning

A Foucauldian Perspective
Margo Huxley

INTRODUCTION

> [H]istory serves to show how that-which-is has not always been; i.e. that the things which seem most evident to us are always formed at the confluence of encounters and chances, during the course of a precarious and fragile history. What reason perceives as *its* necessity, or rather, what different forms of rationality offer as their necessary being, can perfectly well be shown to have a history; and the network of contingencies from which it emerges can be traced. ... [T]hese forms of rationality ... reside on a base of human practice and human history; ... since these things have been made, they can be unmade, as long as we know how it was that they were made
>
> (Foucault, 1988a: 37)

Feminist critiques of planning theory and practice have been at the forefront of the debates on planning and the city since at least the 1970s. In 1978, the *International Journal of Urban and Regional Research* (Garmanikow, 1978) marked the growing field of feminist research into the city with a special issue, and by the early 1980s, books, special issues of journals and articles abounded in the English-speaking academic world. In these, planning was criticised for its gender-blindness, its unresponsiveness to local needs and its technical-rational orientation.

These fundamental critiques of planning joined those from Marxist and Weberian theoretical positions and with those of activists against high-rise housing, road building, inner city neglect or redevelopment across the Western world. Critique was as much practical as theoretical, and for reformist positions, revolved around attempts to extract from planning the promise of progress and improvement that underpinned its public pronouncements and rationale.

For feminist activists, the task was to demand that planning take into consideration the needs of women in the capitalist city, in suburban environments that rendered invisible the work of domestic management and labour and to ensure these needs were understood in the education and practice of professionals.

There were calls for more women to be employed in planning, for more and better child care facilities, for more flexible and responsive transport services, for more accessible and responsive building designs. Many of these proposals had positive effects in local government programmes in the UK, the USA, Australia and Canada, and in mobilising women in community-based initiatives (which often led to women gaining positions in state bureaucracies or politics) (Franzway *et al.*, 1989; Watson, 1990; Savage and Witz, 1992).

Notions of local empowerment, collaboration and giving voice to marginalised groups, now seen as fundamental to communicative, collaborative or 'multicultural'[1] planning (e.g. Forester, 1989, 1999d; Healey, 1998; Sandercock, 1998a, b), owe much to strands of feminist thinking and to action based on forms of identity politics, on beliefs in progressive change, and have much in common with forms of critical theoretic conceptions of 'praxis' – the necessary connections between theory and practice.

Calls for equality within the existing system or changes in the valuation of difference are necessarily enmeshed in debates about the existence and/or nature of 'the system' itself, about the nature of gendered identities and the relation of feminist theory and practice to the marginalisation of other groups based on sexuality, disability, race, etc. (I shall return to this 'etc.' later). Gains made by white professional women in organisations and bureaucracies were seen to be at the expense of poor women of colour: or they were seen as male-identified sell-outs to patriarchy and/or capitalism. Reforms to cities, suburbs and buildings seemed slow and inadequate, and unrelated to the demands of the various groups struggling for change. The ability of the state to bring about positive changes for women, or any other groups, was increasingly called into question by both the Left and the Right. The multiplicity of 'differences' based on identity politics challenged planning – in practice and in theory – to reassess the idea of a homogeneous 'public interest'. But these debates and demands also challenged feminist strategies for the empowerment of 'women' by calling into question essentialised understandings of the homology between sex/gender and identity.

In this chapter I want to examine, from a Foucauldian perspective, two aspects of these challenges to the practices and effects of urban planning; and offer this perspective as an alternative to the debates about modern/postmodern planning theory and about the problems of acknowledging difference, diversity and gender in planning practice. First, I want to suggest that planning can be seen as a form of what Foucault (1991a) calls 'governmentality' – practices shaping the actions of others and strategies for the management of a population. Such a view of planning provides a genealogy of its rationalities and their effects, which are radically different from attempts to provide the kinds of normative justifications or practical prescriptions which seem to underpin most current debates in planning theory, postmodern or otherwise (see Huxley and Yiftachel, 2000; Yiftachel and Huxley, 2000).

Second, if planning can be seen as a strategy for governing the 'conduct of conduct', what does this means for (small-l liberal) feminist calls for more women in the profession, for greater attention to women's needs and, theoretically, for dismantling the masculinist rationalities underpinning the planning project? Foucauldian post-structuralist feminists such as Judith Butler (1990, 1992, 1993) have argued that the taken-for-granted norms of sex and gender are regulatory discourses that maintain dominant practices of 'compulsory heterosexuality', and produce 'docile bodies'. Butler's radical take on the contingency of identity suggests the possibility of unsettling normalising practices through 'subversive bodily acts'. The idea of the instability and constantly re-enacted nature of identity has implications for feminist and other forms of identity politics making claims on a 'planning-as-governmentality' which is itself a mode of social regulation of these identities and the spaces of their performance.

But, first, I want to situate these ideas in the context of debates about modernism/postmodernism in order to problematise the links between modernism, government, feminism and identity, and to indicate the possible effects of these approaches for contemporary planning theory and practice.

THE QUESTION OF 'POSTMODERNISM'

> I've never clearly understood what was meant ... by the word 'modernity'.... I feel troubled here because I do not grasp clearly what it might mean ... neither do I grasp the kinds of problems intended by this term – or how they would be common to people thought of as 'postmodern'. While I see clearly that behind what was known as structuralism, there was a certain problem – ... that of the subject and the recasting of the subject – I do not understand what kind of problem is common to the people we call postmodern or post-structuralist.
>
> (Foucault, 1988a: 34)

> The question of post-modernism is surely a question, for is there, after all, something called postmodernism? Is it an historical characterisation, a certain kind of theoretical position ...? Who are these postmodernists?
>
> (Butler, 1992: 3).

Foucault (1988a), and following him, Butler (1992) are arguing here against the characterisation of either periods or theoretical positions as 'modern' or 'postmodern'. They argue that the term 'postmodern' applied to theory subsumes a disparate variety of positions, covering post-structuralism, French feminism, deconstruction, Lacanian psychoanalysis or Foucauldian analytics, many of which accept ideas of modernism and the avante-garde and some of which (e.g. Kristeva) reject the idea of postmodernism altogether (Butler, 1992: 4–5). Butler suggests that the term 'postmodern' is often used in opposition to the 'modern' in order to undermine modernist claims to the primacy of rationality and to privilege the claims of alternative forms of knowledge. But this strategy often results in unproductive attempts to patrol the boundaries of what is sayable, setting up normative dualisms: e.g. modern = bad; postmodern = good.

But debates about modernism or postmodernism, whether as epoch or attitude, are not questions of 'subjects who claim to know and theorise under the sign of the postmodern pitted against other subjects who claim to know and theorise under the sign of the modern' (Butler, 1992: 8). Rather, Butler endorses Foucault's (1984a, 1988a) position that the question of (post)modernity is better left to one side, for modernity is not only (or even mainly) the triumph of a universalised scientific rationality and the rationalisation of doubt, but also the celebration of the 'new', of change, of 'the ephemeral, the fleeting, the contingent' (Baudelaire, quoted in Foucault, 1984a: 39; see also Rabinow, 1994). It is this aspect of modernity that Marx equates with the restless expansion of capitalism (see Harvey, 1989a) and Marshall Berman (1982) delineates in *All That is Solid Melts into Air*: postmodernism, then, in emphasising change, instability, novelty, is an expression of modernism (in the sense of the 'modern' being an apprehension of the present), rather than a radical break with it. In political practice, demands for the recognition of 'difference' and projects for conducting politics based on stable identities of liberal subjects as the authors of these demands, are co-extensive/coterminous with modernity and can be read, as Habermas (1987a) does, as moves towards the fulfilment of its promise of progress.

Foucault has little sympathy with a Habermasian construction of progress and modernity (1984a, 1988a; Rabinow, 1994). Nor does he accept the characterisation of (post)modernism as an era. He says:

> I know that modernity is often spoken of as an epoch ... Situated on a calendar, it would be preceded by a more or less naïve or archaic 'premodernity', and followed by an enigmatic and troubling 'postmodernity'.
>
> (Foucault, 1984a: 39)

Rather, modernity is an attitude, a way of thinking and feeling, acting and behaving which raises the question of what our relation is to the present. This present we inhabit is not 'a rupture, or ... a high point, or ... a completion, or ... a returning dawn, ... [On the contrary], it is a time like any other, or rather, a time which is never quite like any other' (Foucault, 1988a: 35, 36).

But, above all, the present is a time about which we can ask questions. For Foucault, philosophical questions about the present begin with the ability to self-reflexively trace the genealogy of these questions themselves. In asking what is our relationship to the present, Foucault (1986) distinguishes between modernity, humanism and the Enlightenment. If being modern is a relation to the present and a task of self-actualisation in that present, humanism takes different forms at different times, being at some times a critique of Christianity, at others, a critique of science, and at others, seeing the future of humanity in science itself. According to Foucault (1984a: 44), humanism has sought the good of human beings under many guises: Marxism, existentialism, National Socialism, Stalinists have all claimed to be motivated by humanist values (to which one could add, forms of feminism, and indeed, the welfare state). This is not to say that humanism should be rejected *tout court*, but that its history shows how it is used to justify particular value judgements that then tend to be imposed in the name of humanity.

Foucault sees the critical Enlightenment attitude to authority, custom or religion as being in tension with humanism, and through that tension the seeds of a 'counter-modern' critique of 'what we are saying, thinking and doing' (ibid.: 45) can be sown. Foucault reframes Kant's questions posed in relation to the Enlightenment – what are the relations between authority and reason, between the unconstrained use of reason and the continuity of social institutions, and how can universal reason be freely exercised in a polity that requires obedience? Foucault develops this insight into the genealogy of the Enlightenment to examine how the limits to reason and knowledge are constructed.

That is, questions about the specificity of particular rationalities and the contingency of identity are no longer 'off limits': the logic and rationality deployed in Enlightenment thinking can be turned on itself, without succumbing to the 'blackmail' of the Enlightenment.

> One does not have to be 'for' or 'against' the Enlightenment ... [it is not] an authoritarian alternative [in which] you either accept the Enlightenment and remain within the tradition of its rationalism ...; or else you criticise the Enlightenment and then try to escape from its principles of rationality.
>
> (Foucault, 1984a: 43)

So, to ask questions about the histories and rationalities that produce what we now call 'science', or 'social science' or to investigate the genealogies of particular identities is not to dispense with all forms of rationality or to deny the political significance of identity. Rather, it is to point to the contingency of the present and to critically speculate on how things might be otherwise. A Foucauldian, Nietzschean 'history of the present' can be applied to planning practices (of which theorising is one), to ask what are the rationalities at work in the regulatory discourses of planning and with what effects on subjects and spaces. Seeing planning as a mode of governmentality opens up its rationalities and effects to critical scrutiny.

GOVERNMENTALITY AND PLANNING

The 'dark side' of planning, as Yiftachel (1995b, 1998) and Flyvbjerg (1996, 1998b) have called it, is its entanglements in practices of social control and mobilisation of political rationality or *Realrationalität* (Flyvbjerg, 1998a). However, both Yiftachel and Flyvbjerg imply that this 'dark side' can be minimised to the point where planning can act in accordance with its reforming rationales. If control and *Realrationalität* are reflexively acknowledged by appropriately motivated individuals, the negative effects of planning can be minimised, and planners will be able to respond to demands for inclusion from oppressed minorities and able to wrest progressive outcomes from the murky world of politics.

Similarly, Raphael Fischler (e.g. 1995, 1998, 2000) carries out meticulously detailed examinations of the regularisation of zoning and of the representations contained in planning documents in a thoroughly Foucauldian spirit, uncovering discourses of power in the everyday histories of planning, with a rare critical eye. But nevertheless, these histories of planning practices, like Yiftachel's and Flyvbjerg's studies (see also, Huxley, 1994a), tend to leave unexamined the suppositions of progressive practice and autonomous (liberal) identity that lie behind them.

But what if 'improving planning practice' produces more of the same? What if the 'empowerment' of disadvantaged groups leads to further extensions of regulation? What if planning practice involves the 'making up' of subjects whose identities are shaped in the course of these 'empowerments', 'so that they come to recognise their common being within a common ... category'? (Brown, 1995; Cruikshank, 1999; Dean, 1999: 70). Seeing planning as a form of governmentality brings into the foreground the need to confront head-on the logical and conceptual possibility that planning itself is what needs to be resisted (Lewi and Wickham, 1966; Yiftachel and Huxley, 2000).

Seeing planning as governmentality is an illuminating, if difficult and dangerous, way of speculating upon some of these questions since they are similar to the critiques of planning coming from the economic and political 'Right'. So it is important to examine the notion of 'governmentality' to understand where Foucault's criticism differs from these.

Governmentality can be understood both as a 'mentality of government' and as the 'will to know' through 'governmental rationality'. Governmentality is a coalescence of various tactics and strategies for the 'conduct of conduct' – practices that define, shape or have effects in creating particular behaviours and identities within a given space or territory, and which only contingently and unevenly come to be exercised by the state.

GOVERNMENTALITY LINKS

> First, ... the continuities of the microphysics of power (and the political technology of the body) and the concerns of the government of nations, populations and societies. Secondly, there is a continuum established between both of these and the practice of ethics as a form of government of the self.
>
> (Dean, 1999: 176)

Governmentality moves beyond the disciplinary microphysics of power to a deployment of power that seeks the direction of the conduct of the governed, while assuming a particular kind of active subject (Dean, 1994, 1999; Rose, 1999).

Foucault traces these techniques of governmentality to the emergence of the human sciences in the seventeenth century, when humanism replaced religion with the science of Man: the 'discourses of life, labour and language became structured into disciplines' (Foucault, 1970; Rabinow, 1989: 9). Disciplines of the 'human sciences' converged in the ability to produce 'scientific classifications' of bodies and subjects that reinforced the 'dividing practices' of the disciplinary regimes of the asylum, the prison, the workhouse, the factory, the school, the barracks.

In parallel developments, the conception of the role of government changed from that of the rule of the sovereign over subjects to that of management of a population. The sovereign's connections were to his (sometimes, her) territory – inheriting it, defending it, deploying it in alliances, disposing of it. As long as subjects paid taxes and did not rebel, their diseases, reproduction or morality, the conduct of their daily lives, were of little concern to the sovereign. But with the gradual decline of feudal social and political relations, and the rise of mercantalism, the art of government came to centre on managing the health, wealth and morality of the population on which the new social and political arrangements depended. Thus, the growth of the human sciences was related to the provision of knowledge about populations and their characteristics, and the gathering of this information was itself a practice of regulatory control.

> The theory of the art of government was linked ... to the whole development of the administrative apparatus of the territorial monarchies, the emergence of governmental apparatuses; it was also connected to a set of analyses and forms of knowledge ... of the state, ... questions which were termed precisely 'statistics', meaning the science of the state.
>
> (Foucault, 1991a: 96)

The regulatory aspects of governmentality, that over two centuries contingently gathered about the state, involve two forms of 'bio-power': an anatomo-politics of the human body; and regulatory controls over the population (Foucault, 1978: 139).

The first form – the disciplinary anatomo-politics of the body – is 'centred on the body as a machine: its disciplining, the optimisation of its capabilities, the extortion of its forces, the parallel increase of its usefulness and its docility, its integration into systems of efficient and economic controls' (ibid.: 139). This is the disciplinary power and 'carceral society' described in such meticulous detail in *Discipline and Punish* (1979), which is most widely associated with Foucault. In the carceral institutions, the idealised exemplar of which is delineated in Bentham's treatise on the Panopticon, power is exercised through surveillance and bodily discipline, to produce 'docile bodies' with capabilities useful to, or at least, not threatening to, dominant groups. Disciplinary power shapes subjects who will come to do what is expected as a matter of course.

The disciplinary regimes of the carceral institutions, through the increasing power of experts – doctors, psychiatrists, prison officers, criminologists, teachers – in the nineteenth century, came to be diffused throughout the social body. Disciplining of individual bodies no longer focused solely on the classification, exclusion and normalisation of individual deviance on the model of Panoptical surveillance, but was concerned with normalising the population at large (Cohen, 1985; Burchell *et al.*, 1991). In this process, the gaze of the expert and the examination (medical, educational; Foucault, 1973), through their objectification of categories of normal (average) characteristics of the population, play a part in creating compliant subjectivities.

The second facet of governmentality – regulatory controls of the population:

> focussed on the species body, the body imbued with the mechanics of life and serving as the basis of the biological processes: propagation, births and mortality, the level of health, life expectancy and longevity, with all the conditions that can cause these to vary.
>
> (Foucault, 1978: 139)

That is, governmentality draws on the knowledge produced by statistics, demography, epidemiology, the mapping of poverty, concerns with reproduction and the health and morality of the population as it exists in a given territory and thus, are centrally concerned with relations of sexuality, gender and space.

So Booth's, and the multitude of other Victorian philanthropists', categorising, mapping, reporting and publicising of poverty, disease and depravity (both sexual and otherwise, but especially sexual: e.g. Walkowitz, 1992; Finch, 1993; Wilson, 1991; Hooper, 1998) in the industrial cities of the nineteenth century, at one and the same time, produced the city as an object of governmental knowledge, identified problems in need of solution, created categories of the population in terms of their contribution to these problems, and instituted modes of surveillance for monitoring and reforming the individuals who made up the created categories and the defined population (see Long, 1982; Stallybrass and White, 1986; Topalov, 1990, 1993; Soderstrom, 1996). Similarly, fifty or so years later, the Chicago School's mappings of population characteristics and ethnographies of the lives of the groups they identified contributed in no small part to the policies of social reform aimed at solving the problems and reforming the identities 'made up' in these studies (Fairfield, 1992; Jacobs and Fincher, 1998).

The self-surveillant and self-disciplining power attributed in idealised form by Bentham to his never-realised Panopticon is thus diffused throughout society in diverse and flexible ways. The emerging disciplines, both in the human sciences and in the dividing practices of the experts and institutions, generated systems that created deviance by classification against a norm, which in turn required more interventions, more classificatory schema, more expert personnel (Foucault, 1979; Cohen, 1985; Rabinow, 1989). The 'failure' of disciplines to achieve self-monitoring subjects and docile bodies is the success of disciplinary professions in perpetuating the conditions for their own existence and extension, bringing more classified subjects under their control.

> Bio-power spread under the banner of making people healthy and protecting them. When there was resistance, or failure to achieve its stated aims, this was construed as further proof of the need to reinforce and extend the power of experts. A technical matrix was established. By definition, there ought to be a way of solving any technical problem. Once this matrix was established, the spread of bio-power was assured, for there could be nothing else to appeal to: any other standards could be shown to be abnormal or to present merely technical problems. We are promised normalisation and happiness through science and the law. When they fail, this only justifies the need for more of the same.
>
> (Dreyfus and Rabinow, 1982: 196)

These practices for managing the population operate through flexible discourses of the 'normal' that construct as their 'benchmark' separately and simultaneously, sometimes the bourgeois as a measure of cultural normality, sometimes heterosexuality as the measure of reproductive morality, sometimes the professional as the source of scientific measures of deviance or disease, sometimes the masculine as the universalised subject, sometimes motherhood as the exemplar of the feminine (see Finch, 1993).

Normalising practices extend into what Rose (1999) calls contemporary 'advanced liberalism', in which social workers regulate the unemployed by promoting self-help and training schemes, efficiency experts and auditors monitor the workplace in which workers take responsibility for their conduct, and psychiatrists and fitness advisers assist the self-monitoring 'advanced liberal' subject to achieve his or her 'personal best'. In this development of Foucault's thought, which counterposes disciplinary control with productive aspects of power, liberalism is an assemblage of political technologies – a 'set of practices for the constitution of subjects' – that contribute to a 'social order that is compatible with individualism' (Simon, 1995: 58).

To see planning as a form of governmentality, then, is to trace its connections to various normalising discourses that seek to render subjects and the spaces constituted through them both manageable and free. So, for example, development controls and the classification and distribution of uses of land in space use normalising techniques to produce and reinforce taken-for-granted forms of environments, uses and users and their inter-relations (Huxley, 1994a, 1996; Lewi and Wickham, 1996). The most obvious of such social controls could be found in the socially exclusionary zoning of the United States which at times has regulated the size of families and the rights of unrelated people to share housing as well as being racially exclusive (e.g. Boyer, 1990; Silver, 1991). Similar ethnically-imbued and gendered planning practices can be identified in almost all planning regulations and are especially pertinent in racially-divided polities such as Israel (Yiftachel, 1992, 1996; Fenster, 1998, 1999) and South Africa (Robinson, 1990; Mabin, 1995).

But even apparently politically innocent systems are constructed around taken-for-granted conceptions of what is appropriate, which subjects should engage in what sort of activities, where and when (Huxley, 1996; Watson, 1996). For example, English policies to control urban sprawl, the identification of the need for urban containment, the creation of green belts and the preservation of the countryside are forms of management of a population in a territory, imbued with normalising assumptions about the 'Englishness' of the countryside and the inappropriate behaviours of certain sections of the urban population when 'out of place' (Matless, 1998).

However, the point is not that 'neutral' technical mechanisms are being used for dubious political ends – a state of affairs that suggests a solution in better-framed regulations, or which might be redressed by a more ethically informed, more self-reflective kind of planner – but that any form of classification and regulation and any reform or policy, no matter how progressive, is inescapably enmeshed in control and normalisation. Foucauldian analytics of these forms of power is not to attempt to correct the misuse of technical rationality, nor dissolve power in 'perfectly transparent communication' (Foucault, 1988a: 18), but to show the unwitting effects of regimes of practices, to break free of the common-sense acceptance of categories, to open up ways of thinking differently.

As Foucault famously said:

> My project ... is to give some assistance in wearing away certain self-evidences and commonplaces ...; to bring it about ... that certain phrases can no longer be spoken so lightly, certain acts no longer, or at least no longer so unhesitatingly, performed; to contribute to changing certain things in people's ways of perceiving and doing things.
>
> It's true that certain people ... are not likely to find advice or instructions in my books that tell them 'what is to be done'. But my project is precisely to bring it about that they no longer know what to do, so that the acts, gestures, discourses which up until then had seemed to go without saying, become problematic, difficult, dangerous.
>
> (1991b: 83–84)

Foucault's refusal to provide programmes for policy or prescriptions for action is part of what makes his work difficult for planners and feminists alike.

GENDERING GOVERNMENTALITY

Seeing planning as governmentality is indeed problematic for feminist positions presuming some configuration of continuity between sex/gender and identity. For if planning is the conduct of conduct and the shaping of identities through strategies of governmentality, these discourses are likely to perpetuate normalised, gendered, (racialised, 'etc.') hierarchies, regardless of the intentions of individual planners, no matter what their own gender. As Dreyfus and Rabinow (1982: 187) point out, even though a political analysis may be able to identify individuals who make decisions and groups who struggle for advantage, it does not follow that an overall subjectively-co-ordinated strategy is at work. In the ongoing operation of institutions, 'the logic is perfectly clear, the aims decipherable, and yet it is often the case that no one is there to have invented them and few who can be said to have formulated them' (Foucault, 1979: 95).

Thus, looking for the 'great women' of planning history can provide positive indications of the multiple subjects and voices that have contributed to forming the city (e.g. Greed, 1994; Freestone, 1995), but the search is not necessarily a transparently liberating project (Sandercock, 1998b; Moore-Milroy, 2000). Such women are more often than not deeply implicated in carrying out strategies for the 'normalisation' of other women. For example, the disciplinary power of Octavia Hill's methods of 'surveillance through friendship' for Victorian middle-class women's voluntary work in housing management of the poor aimed to install middle-class visions of appropriate working-class behaviours in the homes visited (Cruikshank, 1999; Robinson, 2000). A similar picture is painted by Reiger (1985) who traces the *Disenchantment of the Home* in the early 1900s, with the arrival of a host of professional and semi-professional experts (many of them female) who attempted to apply scientific methods to every aspect of domestic life. The limitations of feminist histories that unproblematically celebrate recovering women in planning are vividly illustrated by the 1928 text, *City Planning for Girls*, which aimed to control and regulate the unruly presence of adolescent girls in the spaces of the city (Wirka, 1998).

Women's implication in the regulatory and controlling aspects of planning poses difficult questions for projects of representation and equality based on notions of biological or psychological essential identities. Who knows where more ambivalent projects of genealogy might lead for challenges to the gendered nature of 'planning-as-governmentality'?

One direction is towards the question of who we are now, in the present, in which the possibility is opened up to see that subjectivity has a contingent and variable history. Foucault's works on disciplinary power and on governmentality are directed to examining how subjectivity is formed out of the conjunctions of networks of power, discourses and practices producing docile bodies, while at the same time creating liberal subjects who are constituted as free and who resist. For Foucault, the self is not fixed, pre-given, nor is it the autonomous author of intentional action, but a contingent product of powers, resistances and self-fashionings within the limits set by the taken-for-granted conditions of the present. In his work on the care of the self, based on studies of the ancient Greeks, Foucault (1986) explores the possibilities of thinking differently about what the self is and how it might be undertaken as a work of self-subjectification.

To use genealogy to question present forms of rationality is not to descend into relativism or nihilism, nor to deny the grounds for political action. On the contrary, such questions are 'the very precondition of a politically engaged critique' (Butler, 1992: 6–7). Undertaking a Foucauldian 'analytic of power' is a risky business and feminists have not unanimously found cause with Foucault's deracinated, degendered ways of posing the problem. Foucault's (1991b: 84) refusal of the blackmail of humanism – the demand that prescriptions for future action must accompany any critique of present arrangements – also makes his work difficult for professionals believing in the progressive possibilities of their practices. Nevertheless, feminists have made productive use of Foucault's insights in ways that have relevance for analysing planning.

Feminist post-structuralist approaches to politics and identity, together with radical reconceptualisations of the politics of race, postcoloniality and sexuality carried out by writers like bell hooks, Gayatri Spivak and Judith Butler, present the possibility of refiguring the traditional groundings and rationales of planning, by showing how identity politics contribute to reproducing identities that are normalised through taken-for-granted and consciously enacted repetition. In these theoretically active exchanges, feminist thinking about identity is central to the 'modern/postmodern' debate and its relevance for understanding the inter-relations of identity and space (e.g. Massey, 1994).

The relations between identity and space are of importance for understanding the effects of planning. For if identity is not fixed and can only provide a temporary base from which to make claims on the planning system, and if, at the same time, the system itself contributes to the regulation of identities through the regulation of spaces, then stories about 'women in planning' or the 'sexism' of city form are in need of radical extension. There is a growing literature about cities, spaces and subjectivities (e.g. Grosz, 1995; Watson and Gibson, 1995, especially Chapter 17; Donald, 1999), but, as Beth Moore-Milroy (2000) notes, the more radical positions of thinkers such as Judith Butler have not been taken up in any sustained way in the planning theory literature. Equally, post-structuralist theorists of identity have had little to say about governmentality as strategies through which subjects are produced and around which they struggle.

And indeed, there are difficulties with following a Foucauldian direction. Nancy Hartsock, in a much-quoted paragraph, sets out the problems that liberal, socialist and Marxist feminists have with Foucault's problematisations of the subject. She asks:

> Why is it that just at the moment when so many of us who have been silenced begin to demand the right to name ourselves, to act as subjects rather than objects of history, that just then the concept of subjecthood becomes problematic? Just when we are forming our own theories about the world, uncertainty emerges about whether the world can be theorized. Just when we are talking about the changes we want, ideas of progress and the possibility of systematically and rationally organizing human society become dubious and suspect? Why is it now that critiques are made of the will to power inherent in the effort to create theory?

(1990: 163–164)

Hartsock suggests that the answer to her questions lies in the continuation of Enlightenment thought which is inherently at odds with ideas of difference and multiplicity. She turns Foucault's criticism of universal rationality against him by arguing that he is still trapped within Enlightenment totalising, Western, masculinist modes of thought, characterising him as being caught in the dilemma of the 'coloniser who resists' (Hartsock, 1990: 166). However, other feminists such as Lois McNay (1992, 1994) and Jana Sawicki (1991) have found more positive sources of understanding of gender relations, sexuality and subjectivity in Foucault's work, while confronting what they see as the 'difficulties of assimilating a primarily philosophical form of critique into feminist theory which is rooted in the demands of an emancipatory politics' (McNay, 1992: 3). Both McNay and Sawicki are interested in exploring Foucault's formulations of the micro-politics of power, localised resistance, subjectivity and the body in terms of feminist engagements with questions of patriarchal domination, compulsory heterosexuality, motherhood and reproduction (see also Bartky, 1988; Bordo, 1997).

However, despite these important insights into gendered regimes of domination and the production of the female subject, in the end, most feminists drawing on Foucault have argued for the idea of an autonomous self, deriving their positions from Foucault's work on practices of self-subjectification in ancient Greece. Around this self, they envisage that a strategic, risky and provisional, yet committed and emancipatory politics might be created (Sawicki, 1991; McNay, 1992; see also Weedon, 1997). It is these forms of post-structuralist feminism that have most in common with, yet push the conceptual boundaries of, communicative planning theories that acknowledge difference and diversity and strive to empower marginalised groups and identities.

But such positions run into their limits with the constant expansion of plural varieties of the subject. 'The theories of feminist identity that elaborate predicates of color, sexuality, ethnicity, class, and able-bodiedness invariably close with an embarrassed "etc." at the end of the list' (Butler, 1990: 143). It is from the point of this 'etc.' that Butler argues for the understanding of identity, not as an epistemological centre of knowledge, nor as an ontological essence, but as a signifying *practice*, created through the repeated invocation of culturally-intelligible rule-bound discourses (ibid.: 144–145; 1993).

Butler does not accept that a version of stabilised identity is necessary for political action. She refuses the 'blackmail' that says *either* feminists engage in critiques of Cartesian rationality and logic on its own terms and, by demanding universalised rights, risk reproducing the very discourses of homogeneity and normative subjecthood which have marginalised 'difference' in the first place; *or*, in seeking to undo these forms of power by asserting their difference from it – by making positive claims to affective relations, motherhood, emotional sensitivity, ethics of care – feminists risk perpetuating the place of marginalised subjects 'outside the project' by assuming these discursively produced identities as foundational givens. For Butler, to uncritically perform identities created out of plays of domination, risks closing down the debate and cutting off possibilities for transformation at the very point where they might begin to take shape.

No appeal to the dangers of losing the grounds from which to speak as 'women' should be allowed to prevent the questioning of those grounds. 'To call a presupposition into question is not the same as doing away with it; rather, it is to free it up from its metaphysical lodgings in order to occupy [them] and to serve very different political aims' (Butler, 1992: 17). Butler proposes a politics of identity that dislodges and subverts dominant constructions and regulatory practices, calling them into question by tracing their multiple, complex and often contradictory genealogies. 'If the regulatory fictions of sex and gender are themselves multiple contested sites of meaning, then the very multiplicity of their constructions holds out the possibility of a disruption of their univocal posturing' (Butler, 1990: 32). Seeds of the disruption of the regulatory discourses of sex and gender can be found in the 'subversive bodily acts' that play with the possibilities of sexual difference (ibid.: Chapter 3). Identity, Butler (ibid.: 139) suggests, is performative – 'a dramatic and contingent construction of meaning' – and thus its very instability can serve as a base for local politics of resistance to dominant meanings and managed spaces (see, for example, Gregson and Rose, 2000).

This may seem to threaten, as Hartsock (1990) feels it does, the possibility of feminists/women engaging in politics of transformation of current relations of power, especially those constellations of theories, institutions and practices that produce masculine forms of domination. But by uncoupling sex and gender (and all other attributes around which identity politics have, or could be, formed) from the notion of a pre-given and immutable biological or psychological origin, however culturally modified, Butler opens up the possibility of showing how men, too, are enmeshed in regulatory and repetitive performances of masculinity, and thereby opens up new ways of thinking ourselves other than what we are, within fields of political action (see also Connell, 1987, 1995).

> If identities were no longer fixed as the premises of a political syllogism, and politics no longer understood as a set of practices derived from the alleged interests that belong to a set of ready-made subjects, a new configuration of politics would surely emerge from the ruins of the old.
>
> (Butler, 1990: 149)

Strategies and tactics that de-centre gendered identities also de-centre the performance of professional power. Unsettling planning and the figure of the autonomous 'liberal' planner expose to examination claims to the unique and privileged status of planning knowledge and expertise, in relation to both the object of the city, the empowerment of marginalised communities. Space, power, knowledge, bodies, subjects and cities (Foucault, 1984b; Grosz, 1995) can be thought and performed in a myriad ways that challenge the normalising underpinnings of planning and the given-ness of the built environment (Huxley, 1994b). Planning cannot be the 'politics of the right answer' (no matter how openly debated by a proliferating array of identities): rather, planning can be subjected to ongoing questioning through a politics of criticism that engages in a 'suspicious ethical reflection on the structures and styles of urban thought' (Donald, 1999: 124).

CONCLUSION

There are two main points I want to draw out of this discussion of the gender implications of planning as governmentality. The first is to use these ideas in juxtaposition to the communicative and multicultural planning literature, and the second is to think a little bit about the possibilities of subversive feminist acts in relation to the regulatory effects of planning.

State governmentality is expanded through the identification of 'problems' which reform and regulations are then deployed to solve: when these fail, or further problems result from the reforms, the solution is to provide new and more extensive forms of regulation (Dreyfus and Rabinow, 1982: 196). This is a problem for all projects of reform, and the nexus between beneficial change and social control can never be completely unravelled.

The turn to communicative, collaborative or 'multicultural' planning, empowerment, and community building might be seen to have a genealogy not inconsistent with such an analysis: as planning fails to solve the problems it has set itself, and thus produces resistance from those subjected to its failures, the problem increasingly becomes one of managing the subjects and the spaces of their inhabitation produced through liberal technologies of government. The strategy of including community building, feminist collectives, resident activism, local development initiatives in disadvantaged areas or self-help empowerment programmes in the ambit of 'planning' claims to counteract the stultifying and regulatory forms of state-based planning and produce self-directing independent subjects. To the extent that such projects offer different trajectories from those previously accepted, they do, indeed, contribute to possibilities for change. But 'empowering' communities still takes place through discourses of experts in 'mediation' and 'collaboration' and overcoming 'dependency' (Cruikshank, 1999). And community groups and experiments with alternative decision-making arrangements can just as easily become 'instruments of discipline and a rather unbearable group pressure' (Foucault, 1986: 247) or indeed, riots and violence (Mabin, 1995).

Planning theory, then, might be somewhat more constrained in its claims that, given the right forms of rationality – technical, communicative, multicultural – planning can fulfil the Enlightenment promise of progressive change and non-problematically act as a vehicle for democratic transformations. Planning practice has to confront the inescapable aspects of control that accompany liberal strategies of governmentality. If nothing else, a Foucauldian approach is alert to the paradox that unbalances the very idea of planning as 'future-oriented' activity: 'People know what they do; they frequently know why they do what they do; but what they don't know is what they do does' (Foucault, quoted in Dreyfus and Rabinow, 1982: 187). In other words, planning cannot guarantee its outcomes, but this does not mean giving up on short-term strategies for situated change: rather, it calls for planning to become 'action without determination' (Watson and Gibson, 1995: 259) – 'partial, temporary and contested' (ibid.: 262) – at once, optimistic and dangerous.

For feminists searching for ways to unsettle the uneasily dominant discourses of governmentality that create privileged masculine identities, the notion of performativity offers a sense of how fragile and fluid identity can be. Rather than a monolithic patriarchy that emerges from some separatist and psychoanalytical feminisms, the deconstruction of the notion of stable identities opens up localised possibilities for creative practices of difference. Feminists can challenge assumptions about normalised spaces and the normalised subjects presumed to inhabit them and explore ways in which spaces, bodies and identities are enmeshed. They can do this, not with the aim of bringing about linear progress or dramatic revolution, but, as Dean (1999: 7) says, with the more modest hope of offering their efforts toward the possibility of 'a collective project in making a small and still barely perceptible shift in our thinking'.

ACKNOWLEDGEMENTS

Many thanks to Jenny Robinson, John Allen and Beth Moore-Milroy who have all provided insightful comments at various stages in the production of this chapter.

NOTE

1   The term 'multiculturalism' covers a difficult and contested terrain. It can be seen as a 'homogenising strategy which has defined and created limits within which acceptable difference is permitted' (Watson, 1996: 208), especially in explicit government strategies for 'managing' ethnic spatial concentrations (see also Hage, 1998). However, other terms, such as 'cultural diversity' are in danger of being taken up in the same way. So, as 'multicultural' is a common term in planning literature, I use scare quotes to indicate its uneasy status.

Part III

Planning Movements and Trajectories

8

A Pragmatic Attitude to Planning

Philip Harrison

INTRODUCTION

In the post-positivist context of recent years, the expansive work of Jürgen Habermas has had a significant influence on the ways in which planning has been conceptualised (e.g. Forester, 1989; Sager, 1994; Healey and Hillier, 1996; Healey, 1997a). Planning theorists have, however, also found inspiration from other interrelated strands of non-positivist philosophy and social theory, including postmodernism (in its various forms), post-structuralism and pragmatism. This chapter is focused on the use of *pragmatism* within planning theory. It asks a 'pragmatic' question: what practical difference does it make whether planners draw on Habermas or on the work of the pragmatists? As will be shown, there is no clear-cut answer to this question as Habermas and the pragmatists share many common positions. There are, nevertheless, important – though not necessarily fundamental – differences. This chapter argues that pragmatism offers us a meaningful way to respond to *certain* of the theoretical and practical problems with the use of Habermas within planning theory (e.g. as identified by Tewdwr-Jones and Allmendinger, 1998).

Before proceeding to a discussion on the comparative outcome of 'Habermasian planning' and 'pragmatist planning', the chapter provides a brief outline of pragmatist thought, and of the extent to which pragmatism has influenced planning theory to date.

PRAGMATISM

The term 'pragmatism' was introduced to philosophy by Charles Sanders Peirce in 1878, and then used by a widening circle of mainly American thinkers to describe their often variant philosophical positions. This community of early pragmatists – which included William James, John Dewey, George Herbert Mead, George Santayana and Clarence Lewis – came to represent the most influential branch of philosophy, in America at least, during the first quarter of the twentieth century (Thayer, 1982). Pragmatism was, however, to be eclipsed by the rise of logical positivism. It was to resurface in the post-positivist context of the 1970s onwards within the work of theorists such as Richard Rorty, Hillary Putnam, Richard Bernstein, Hans Joas and Charlene Seigfried.

Pragmatism is a term that has both 'philosophical' and 'popular' meanings. The philosophers of pragmatism have generally taken care to differentiate their use of the term from suggestions of expediency and crude instrumentalism often associated with pragmatism (e.g. Dewey, 1931). Pragmatism, in its philosophical sense, resists easy definition. At an elementary level, pragmatism is, of course, concerned with the practical application of ideas and with what is evidently useful in an instrumental sense. However, philosophical pragmatists have used the term with far wider intent. Some of the key characteristics of early pragmatist writing include: a recognition of the fallibility of knowledge; an emphasis on the outcomes of knowledge rather than on the relationship of knowledge to the 'truth'; an emphasis on experience rather than on abstracted theory; a rejection of the dichotomies of modern science and philosophy, for example, belief/action, theory/practice, facts/values, intellect/emotion; the centrality of community and social relationships; and a recognition of the importance of language in creating realities and in shaping social practice (Thayer, 1968; Seigfried, 1996).

These aspects of pragmatism bring together a number of theoretical and practical influences of the nineteenth century including:

- Hegel's holism which rejected the Kantian distinction between pure and practical reasoning, and between facts and values;
- Darwinian theory which profoundly challenged the idea of fixed structures and essences and highlighted the importance of particular circumstances and contingencies in the evolution of life;
- English empiricism with its focus on concrete observation and its resistance to *a priori* assumptions and ideal systems of thought;
- Romanticism with its exploratory and creative spirit, and with the recognition it gave to human experience; and,
- the American Progressive Movement which was concerned with the creative transformation of society and the social purpose of knowledge.

American Pragmatism evolved as a loose doctrine or set of ideas that emphasised the importance of contextually located *human experience* in testing the validity or truthfulness of ideas. The pragmatist's orientation was towards the future and in Dewey's work, in particular, the focus was on a *creative experimentalism* that brought ideas and concrete experience together in the pursuit of social reconstruction. As Dewey put it, the concern of pragmatism is with the 'particular consequences of ideas for future practical experience' (1931: 27).

While pragmatism emerged in part from an empiricist tradition, which rejected Idealism and abstract theorising in general, it also moved beyond empiricism. In Dewey's words:

> when we take the point of view of pragmatism we see that general ideas have a very different role to play than that of reporting and registering past experiences. They are the basis for organizing *future* observations and experiences. Whereas, for empiricism, in a world already constructed and determined, reason or general thought has no other meaning that that of summing up particular cases, in a world where the future is not a mere word, where theories, general notions, rational ideas have consequences for action, reason necessarily has a constructive function.
>
> (1931: 33)

It was this focus on the use of past experience for a future purpose that led Dewey (1931) to define pragmatism as a *radical* empiricism. Joas (1998) echoes Dewey when he calls pragmatism 'a theory of the creative character of human action' (ibid.: 195). Another contemporary pragmatist, Kloppenberg, argues that 'pragmatism originates in reflection on experience and culminates in altered experience' (1998: 96). It is this future-directness that provides a direct link between pragmatism and planning. For the pragmatist, it is past experience that enables us to imaginatively project likely futures, and therefore to plan.

Although early pragmatism coalesced around general notions of the fallibility of knowledge, human experience, experimentalism and future consequences, there were significant differences between the leading proponents of pragmatism. Peirce, for example, remained a *realist*, believing that truth is independent of human experience, even if knowledge is inevitably flawed, whereas James and Dewey were *nominalist* or *anti-representationist*, insisting that there is no necessary connection between ideas and an objective reality, and that the 'truth' is what works for us, and what can be validated in our experience (Scheffler, 1974). Current differences within the broad school of pragmatism relate in part to these early divisions. Rorty, for example, emphasises the anti-representational aspects of early pragmatism, whereas Putnam leans more towards Peirce with his conception of 'pragmatic realism'.

However, more significant than this epistemological debate is the attempt by Rorty and others to remove the notion of human experience from pragmatism and replace it in its entirety with the idea of the linguistic construction of truth. Rorty's pragmatism has been described by Rosenfeld as 'a postmodern reformulation of the pragmatist project by means of a shift in focus from experience to language' (1998: 324). Kloppenberg joins Bernstein and Putnam in their unhappiness with the devaluing of experience when he reminds us that, 'thinking involves relating our choices and our actions to their consequences, which requires reflecting not merely on our words but on the experienced effects of our practical activity' (1998: 97).

The 'linguistic pragmatists', who have drawn heavily from Wittgenstein among others, have taken contemporary pragmatism away from the radical activism of early pragmatism towards a more politically conservative position. Kloppenberg writes that, 'the [radical] democratic convictions of James and Dewey have slipped out of focus because the political ideas of linguistic pragmatists such as Rorty have attracted so much attention' (1998: 103). Laclau reminds us, however, that:

> There is nothing in pragmatism that necessarily restricts it to the kind of piecemeal engineering advocated by Rorty. Pragmatism as an intellectual gesture liberates many more possibilities and courses of development than Rorty is actually prepared to recognize.
>
> (1996: 62).

An increasingly vocal band of contemporary pragmatists are reasserting pragmatism's progressive tradition (see, for example, the work of West, Putnam, Fraser, Seigfried and Mahowald). Feminist scholars, for example, have successfully appropriated pragmatism's conception of human experience in its attempts to direct attention to the value of the practical insights derived from the diverse life experiences of women (see Seigfried, 1996; Mahowald, 1997) whereas Cornell West has brought to pragmatism concerns with power, race, class and gender. These radical pragmatists go beyond early versions of pragmatism by asking the key question, '*whose* experience?' Planning theorists, including Forester (1993) and Sandercock (1998c), have been able to draw on this re-established tradition of radical or 'prophetic' pragmatism that directs attention to the possibilities for social change.

PRAGMATISM'S INFLUENCE ON PLANNING

Friedmann (1987) reminds us that planning has had a long involvement with pragmatism, and that the *social learning tradition* within planning was informed by the early American pragmatists. Pragmatism was not, however, to make the type of contribution to the development of planning thought that might have been expected given the stature and influence of early pragmatists such as James and Dewey. There is little reference to the work of the American pragmatists in the writings of the (mainly American) planning theorists in the 1950s through to the

1970s, despite the clear connections between planning and Dewey's concepts of reconstruction and goal-directed action. This can be explained by the dominance of logical positivism in the period in which planning theory emerged as an area of intellectual endeavour and in which planners were attempting to establish *scientific* legitimacy and status for their profession. In the post-war era the 'fuzziness' and open-ended experimentalism of pragmatism had little appeal when confronted with the certainties and logical clarity of positivism. In the post-war era, planning turned away from pragmatism's holism and creative experimentalism towards a procedural rationalism that was abstracted from the exigencies of context, and that separated human values from the 'scientific' endeavour of planning. This does not mean, however, that the pragmatic social learning tradition was entirely suppressed. An experimental pragmatism persisted within the everyday practice of planning, which was increasingly divorced from the abstract rationalism of planning theory.

With the broad shift away from positivism, from the early 1970s, there was a new opportunity for planning theorists to rediscover pragmatism. It is significant that the philosophers of planning turned first to philosophers such as Rawls and Habermas, rather than to Dewey or to contemporary pragmatists. Planners were seeking new certainties and universal principles even as the philosophical foundations for their old beliefs were disappearing. Gradually, however, a number of (mainly American) planning theorists have come to accept the conceptual openness and radical indeterminacy of pragmatist thought (e.g. Friedmann, 1987; Hoch 1992, 1996; Forester, 1993; Harper and Stein, 1995a; Muller, 1998; Sandercock, 1998c). Pragmatism has come to the attention of British planning academics but it has been received with less enthusiasm than in America (Campbell and Marshall, 2000a). The turn to pragmatism stems from a number of interrelated factors including: a search for a defensible post-positivist alternative to the perceived excesses of some postmodernist positions; a concern to rediscover community in the aftermath of a radical neo-liberalism; frustration at the lack of action in planning; and, a reaction to the emphasis on process rather than outcomes in contemporary planning theory. Kloppenberg suggests that some of the contemporary appeal of pragmatism lies in the perception that 'it is open to the critical insights of postmodernism but resistant to cynicism and nihilism because of its conception of experience and its commitment to democracy' (1998: 112).

COLLABORATIVE PLANNING AND PRAGMATISM

The ideas of classical and contemporary pragmatists, and those of Habermas, are closely inter-related, and have informed each other in their co-evolutionary development. Habermas, for example, draws heavily on the work of Peirce, Mead and Dewey in constructing his theory of communicative action (Koczanowicz, 1999). Kloppenberg even reports that 'Habermas now describes himself simply as "a good pragmatist" ' (1998: 97). However, Habermas's critical theory cannot be directly equated with pragmatism. At best, it represents a highly selective reconstruction of some parts of pragmatist theory (Joas, 1988). In the pages below there is an attempt to compare elements of Habermas's critical theory to aspects of pragmatist thought. A comprehensive comparison is not possible within the confines of this chapter as Habermas's work is a sprawling theoretical edifice (McCarthy, 1981) while pragmatism is a broad term for a collection of positions and attitudes that are often quite diverse.

The limited comparison provided below deals specifically with the following areas, which have a particular relevance to the theory and practice of planning:

- theoretical foundations;
- claims to a universal consensus;
- attitudes to instrumental reasoning;
- means–end relationships;
- conflict and power; and
- ethics.

Theoretical foundations

Habermas shares with the pragmatists the post-positivist denial that there are *a priori* foundations for knowledge that are waiting to be discovered through rational inquiry. Habermas sets out, however, to create a coherent theory of social action and communication. He may have abandoned the philosophical pretensions to comprehend the totality of what there is but he still believes that it is possible to construct a positive system of thought. McCarthy (1981) describes Habermas as having a 'quasi-transcendental theory' of knowledge that seeks to combine a pragmatic naturalism with an idealistic conception of the universal conditions for reasoning. He suggests that 'Habermas wants, paradoxically to hold onto both horns' (ibid.: 111).

Pragmatists, by contrast, have never attempted to ground their praxis in any systematic theory of rationality or social action. Rorty (1991), for example, writes of valuing 'undistorted communication' but feels no need to back this up with a theory of communicative action. For the pragmatists, individual value commitments and the norms of community are sufficient. Mouffe (1996) discusses the practical nature of the differences and similarities between Habermas and the pragmatists:

> Their disagreement with Habermas is not political but theoretical. They share his engagement with democratic politics but they consider that democracy does not need philosophical foundations and that it is not through rational grounding that its institutions could be made secure ... democratic action does not require a theory of truth and notions like unconditionality and universal validity but rather a variety of practices and pragmatic moves aimed at persuading people to broaden the range of commitments to others, to build a more inclusive community.
>
> (Mouffe, 1996: 1, 5)

The pragmatists put their faith in persuasion and the gradual extension of social solidarity rather than in the construction of a comprehensive theoretical argument to justify democratic action.

Claims to a universal consensus

Habermas's consensual theory of truth is an easy target for the postmodernists, with their celebration of diversity, and for the down-to-earth pragmatists. There is little point, however, in making too much of the claims to a universal consensus in a discussion on planning theory. Habermas, himself, recognises that his universal consensus – which requires an 'ideal speech situation' in which all participants have equal opportunity to participate in dialogue – cannot be realised in real life. At best, it remains a legitimate ideal and a critical standard to work towards. Healey (1993b, 1997a), who has drawn heavily on Habermas, recognises the potentially illiberal consequences of the consensual theory of truth when she warns that the consensus that emerges from communicative processes should not be allowed to consolidate into unified codes that would limit future discussion and innovation.

Given the accepted dangers of universalising consensus for planning, and the extent to which the ideal of consensus has already been diluted, it is not clear why the theoretical edifice of communicative action should be retained. Pragmatism would seem to offer a constructive and unpretentious alternative. The pragmatists share with Habermas a concern for creating sufficient common ground for collaborative social action, but they would consider Habermas's construct of transcendent rationality and universalising consensus to be a futile and utopian exercise that may even have oppressive consequences (Rorty, 1989). The early pragmatists, and Dewey especially, were concerned with directing individuals towards co-operative action rather than the pursuit of private interests, but they always balanced their 'philosophy of connectedness' with an appreciation for the importance of diversity. Bernstein points to this balance when he calls for 'practical judgement to balance the demands of individual liberty and communal active citizenship' (1998: 153).

Rorty (1989, 1991) offers the concept of *solidarity* as middle ground between the fragmented and incommensurable language games of Lyotard and other postmodernists, and Habermas's potentially stifling consensus. He writes of solidarity in terms of 'the desire for as much inter-subjective agreement as possible, the desire to extend the reference of "us" as far as we can' (1991: 23). However, for Rorty, solidarity is not something that is discovered in some common human nature or in the universal elements of human language (as Habermas would have it) but is to be gradually constructed from fragments of empathy, sentiment and common experience. This is an ungrounded communitarian solidarity that does not appeal to anything intrinsic or transcendental but rather to the loyalty of individuals who have found that they are better able to cope by clinging together. It is a deliberate process of relation building.

Rorty goes with Habermas only so far as an acceptance of a 'succession of consensuses' that would never foreclose possibilities for change. These shifting coalitions would provide the necessary basis for collective social action but their meaning would be limited in space and time, and they would be open to new voices and renegotiation.

Attitudes to instrumental reasoning

A discussion of Habermasian planning must inevitably address the question of the continued role of instrumental or technical reasoning. The 'new planning direction' outlined by Healey (1997a: 242) presents planning as 'an interactive and interpretative process' and thus presents a powerful challenge to conceptions of planning as technical or instrumental rationality.

Following from the Frankfurt School of Critical Theory, Habermas has taken as his primary theoretical objective the critique of instrumental reasoning, and it is therefore not surprising that planning theorists drawing on Habermas have made the shift from instrumental to communicative reasoning the central objective of their endeavours. However, it is debatable whether planning theorists have made correct use of Habermas in this regard. Habermas clearly understands the necessity of instrumental reasoning within spheres of human activity requiring purposive–rational action, even while he fears the intrusion of this form of reasoning into all areas of life. As McCarthy points out, 'the real problem [for Habermas] is not technical reason but its universalisation' (1981: 22). Planning theorists working within the Habermasian framework have not adequately addressed the question of why planning is the appropriate domain of a communicative rationality. Healey's concern with the dominance of instrumental reasoning within planning could be turned on its head; what about the problems caused by the intrusion of a communicative rationality into a domain that might be better organised in terms of an instrumental rationality? Are all aspects of urban planning and management best handled through processes of democratic argumentation? Berger (1991) asks the question of how far life-world principles should be permitted into the 'monetary-bureaucratic complex' before serious problems of functionality arise.

The either-or choices suggested by the questions posed above can, however, be avoided by resisting Habermas's dualistic distinction between purposive–rational action (which includes goal-directed instrumental action and strategic action) and norm-directed communicative action. As Berger argues, these supposedly distinct forms of action 'cannot be disentangled as easily as Habermas imagines' (1991: 172). Purposive–rational action is always embedded within a communicative context while communicative action generally has instrumental expectations. Processes of reasoning are matters of degree and not type and transitions between different forms of reasoning are frequent and fluid (McCarthy, 1981: 27). Following from pragmatism's rejection of dualism, we could better understand planning as an area of social endeavour in which different forms of reasoning and action combine and interact. The appropriate mix is contingent upon the circumstances and would require the type of practical and experientially based judgement that has been referred to by Dewey. Pragmatism offers the resources for developing a contingency theory of planning, as it avoids the analytical dualism used by Habermas. As Wolfe writes, 'a suspicion of demarcations is part of pragmatism's appeal' (1998: 203). It offers a *mediating philosophy* that brings oppositions together in a constructive engagement (Scheffler, 1974).

Attitudes towards scientific knowledge provide another example of how the holistic perspective offered by pragmatism leads to a more satisfying outcome than the dualism that characterises much of modern thought. Unlike Nietzsche and a number of twentieth-century critics of modernism, pragmatists saw in science and technology a positive and creative tool rather than a malevolent and destructive force. They were attracted to the methodology of science, with its focus on practical experimentation and creative intelligence, and yet never fell prey to a narrow *scientism*:

> Dewey valued the scientific method because it embodied an ethical commitment to open-ended inquiry wherein human values shaped the selection of questions, the formulation of hypotheses, and the evaluation of results. Dewey conceived of the ideal scientific community as a democratically organized, truth-seeking group of independent thinkers who tested their results against pragmatic standards, but those standards always reflected moral rather than narrowly technical, considerations.
>
> (Kloppenberg, 1998: 101)

Contemporary pragmatists have also expressed a non-scientistic appreciation of the achievements of science:

> Reaction against scientism led to attacks on natural science as a sort of false god. But there is nothing wrong with science, there is only something wrong with the attempt to divinize it, the attempt characteristic of realism.
>
> (Rorty, 1991: 34)

In the final event, pragmatism was able to incorporate modern science and instrumental reasoning without being reduced to a narrow positivism, and without sacrificing its primary focus on inter-subjective communication and social solidarity. As Scheffler (1974) pointed out, pragmatism was able to take seriously other modes of human experience including morality, art, poetry, history and even religion. In this sense, pragmatism is not far removed from Habermas's critical theory – which also recognised science as one category of knowledge and technical control as one mode of action – but pragmatism's avoidance of dualism has meant that it is better able to conceive of an integrated experience of different modes of knowledge and action.

Means–end relationships

Habermas's dualism 'distinguishes the teleological or strategic models of action from norm-regulated, dramaturgical and communicative action' (Joas, 1991: 100). In other words, Habermas makes a quite rigid separation between those forms of action for which the goals are set in advance and those for which the goals emerge only through the process. Pragmatists have shown the problems with this typology of means–end relationships, and have pointed to the complex interactions between means and ends within concrete decision situations:

> [Pragmatism's theory of action] does not conceive of action as the pursuit of ends that the contemplative subject established a priori and then resolves to accomplish; the world is not held to be mere material at the disposal of human intentionality. Quite to the contrary, pragmatism maintains that we find our ends in the world, and that prior to any setting of ends we are already, through our praxis, embedded in various situations. There is an interplay between the manifold impulses of the actor and the possibilities of a given situation. Between impulses and possibilities of action, the actor experimentally establishes connections, of which, in any given circumstance, only one is realised.
>
> (Joas, 1991: 101–102)

In Dewey's conception, the experience we derive from concretely situated praxis allows us to project future possibilities, and thus develop *ends-in-view* to guide our current action. The ends-in-view are the fallible hypotheses that provide direction at any point in time.

Dewey insisted that they are always being open to reformulation as they are linked to an ongoing experimental process. There is thus an interactive relationship between the identified ends and the unfolding process; the ends provide direction to the process but the experience gained through the process lead to the reconstitution of the ends.

Dewey never reduced his methodology of creative experimentalism to any particular set of procedures. His idea of rational deliberation involved the imaginative rehearsal of the likely consequences of different courses of action directed by particular ends-in-view, but was not tied to a specific methodology (Scheffler, 1974). Rorty is even more hostile to the idea that rationality can be linked to prescribed methodology. He writes of a fundamental distrust of 'the positivistic idea that rationality is a matter of applying criteria' (1991: 25) and refers to a 'pragmatism without method' (1991). For Rorty, there are many possible procedures of justification for rationality, for to be rational is simply to be persuasive or reasonable in argument in 'a way that eschews dogmatism, defensiveness, and righteous indignation' (1991: 37). While Habermas provides a new set of criteria for what a rational outcome requires, the pragmatists retain a broad conception of rationality that provides no methodological principles that can be laid down in advance of decision-making processes. The pragmatist is results oriented and is focused on methodology or procedure only to the extent that it will bring the desired future consequences. As Thayer wrote, 'the end conclusion is what the process is *good* for' (1985: 83).

Conflict and Power

A contemporary discussion on planning theory cannot avoid the issues of conflict and power. Planning theorists who have drawn on Foucault (e.g. Flyvbjerg) have brought into sharp focus the question of power relations within the practice of planning. Habermasian theorists have been criticised by 'Foucauldians' for their naïve understanding of the exercise of power. Habermas does not ignore power but he does treat power as something that is somehow external to communicative processes and that can be eliminated if the conditions of the ideal free speech situation are met. While Habermas is concerned with removing the distorting effects of power within the communicative process, the Foucauldians emphasise the ubiquity of power relations and the inescapable relationship between knowledge and power and between rationality and power. Habermas attempts to separate discourse and power, whereas for Foucault, the discursive is always an exercise of power. In a similar way, Habermas has been criticised for downplaying conflict, with his theory of universal pragmatics and his concern with the consensual foundations for action.

These criticisms of Habermas are now well established, even within planning theory. The question here is whether pragmatism offers a better take on power and conflict. Here there must be ambivalence. Dewey has himself been criticised for his lack of attention to power relations: 'If Dewey is to be faulted, it is because, at times, in his reliance on metaphors of harmony and organic unity, Dewey underestimates the conflict, dissonance, and asymmetrical power relations that disrupt the "harmonious whole" ' (Bernstein, 1998: 149). Yet, pragmatism is arguably better able to incorporate the role of power and of conflict than Habermas's consensus-focused critical theory, and it is able to do so in a responsible way that does not threaten us with social disorder. As Bernstein writes:

> At a time when we seem to be threatened by opposing extremes – bland homogenization and standardization or a politics of separatist identity and difference – it is worthwhile to recall what is best in our [pragmatist] tradition – a recognition of plurality and unity, of difference and commonness, of agonistic conflict combined with more universal solidarity with our fellow human beings.
>
> (ibid.: 155)

The writings of the pragmatists offer far fewer insights into power than does the work of Foucault. However, pragmatism may offer something of an antidote to the depressing repercussions of the Foucauldian critique of modernity (and of planning as an instrument of modernity). Dewey wrote with a sense of social hope that sometimes appears to be lacking in the work of Foucault. Rorty comments that, 'Dewey seems to me to have done it better, simply because his vocabulary allows room for unjustifiable hope, and an ungroundable but vital sense of human solidarity' (1982: 208). In the spirit of constructive pragmatism he suggests that a critical awareness of power relations could be used for positive effect. Instead of focusing on the disturbing ubiquity of power relations we should explore 'who [is] currently getting and using power for what purposes, and then (unlike Foucault) suggest how some other people might get it and use it for other purposes' (Rorty, 1991: 175). Rorty is probably unfair in suggesting that Foucault never considered the positive uses of power, but he does identify a particular orientation in Foucauldian thought that is undermining of constructive action.

Ethics

The final area of comparison is that of ethics. Here the major difference relates to Habermas's presumption that the norms arrived at through properly constituted communicative action can be considered as being universally valid. Habermas's *discourse ethics* deal with the necessary conditions for arriving at these universally valid rationally-grounded norms. The most important of these is the 'general symmetry requirement' that gives all those who may be affected by the norm equal opportunity to participate in a dialogue that is free from coercion of any kind.

The pragmatists share with Habermas the view that normative claims and moral action must be grounded in community and must be derived through a process of practical reasoning, and that there can be no appeal to some a priori foundational truth. They have little interest, however, in an idealised conception of universal norms that can never be attained in practice. As Seigfried writes, 'pragmatist ethics is naturalistic, pluralistic, developmental and experimental . . . [it] situates moral judgements within problematic situations that are irreducibly individual and social' (1996: 7).

Pragmatism requires ethical deliberation in relation to each problem situation. It does not allow for the simple transfer of ethical principles from one context to another, notwithstanding the process through which these principles were constructed.

Contextualist ethics of this nature are open to the charge of relativism. However, pragmatism does not leave ethical decisions simply to the whim of the individual. Dewey, for example, insisted that normative claims had to be rigorously tested by a 'community of inquiry', and that democracy provides the means of adjudicating normative claims.

Dewey's democratic discourse ethics located moral reasoning firmly within the context of community but nevertheless required that the norms of community should be intelligently questioned in relation to the exigencies of context. A contemporary pragmatist, Henry Richardson (1995), has also attempted to reconcile individual ethical deliberation with the social nature of moral behaviour. He refers to community values as the 'generally speaking norms' that provide us with strong guidance, but also recognises that contextually located ethical deliberation may require constant re-evaluation of these norms. Pragmatism thus offers a degree of moral firmness but there is also the flexibility to revise what is considered to be the good and the right.

CONCLUSION

The contemporary pragmatist, Richard Bernstein, is mindful that pragmatism does not offer an easy way out:

> Long ago the pragmatists argued that we never escape from contingency, uncertainty, and ambiguity. But the pragmatists also passionately argued that the response to contingency and uncertainty should not be despair, wild relativism, or the flight to new absolutes. Our task – and it is a difficult, never-ending task – is to live with this contingency, to respond as intelligently as we can to the new conflicts and crises that arise in our everyday life.
>
> (1998: 154)

We should be careful not to claim too much for pragmatism or to suggest that it offers substantive solutions to the theoretical and practical dilemmas of planning. In the final event, pragmatism does not tell us what to do or even what values or ends to adopt. It does, however, suggest a particular 'attitude' that would allow us to think creatively and act experimentally within our particular field. I suggest that this attitude has the following inter-related characteristics:

- an orientation towards a productive social purpose;
- a goal directedness but with the flexibility to reconsider the 'ends-in-view';
- an orientation towards consequences and outcomes rather than to first principles or to methodology in its own right;
- an aversion to any form of dogmatism;
- an openness to the lessons of experience;
- attention to the concreteness of context and particular circumstances;
- a concern with building and extending social solidarity while also respecting difference;
- a respect for the norms of community (including those of the 'community of planners') but also a readiness to diverge from the norm where required by context;
- an appreciation for the place that both rational argumentation and instrumental reasoning have within planning processes;
- a concern with the productive use of power;
- a bearing that is creative and imaginative rather than scientistic;
- an attitude that is intelligently experimental in the way that it relates ideas to action.

It would certainly be unfair to suggest that planners who have drawn on Habermas, rather than on the pragmatists, do not evidence these characteristics. The Habermasian orientation is pragmatic in many respects. However, there are a number of respects in which Habermas's critical theory is different in tone and emphasis from the orientation(s) of the pragmatists. It is arguable that a leaning towards Habermas rather than towards Dewey, for example, leads towards: more emphasis on method than outcome; more emphasis on general principle than on contextual deliberation; less openness to the use of instrumental reasoning when required by context; less space for the role of the individual planner; less sensitivity to the ways in which power can be used for productive purposes; and, a less goal-directed approach to planning.

Does pragmatism take us beyond collaborative planning? The answer cannot be clear-cut for both the pragmatist and the Habermasian planner would adopt a collaborative and discursive approach to planning that would be based on varying degrees of consensus or social solidarity. The pragmatist would, however, not adopt an 'ideological' position in this regard, and would therefore be open to the use of instrumental reasoning in certain contexts. Also, the pragmatist would not necessarily seek the validation of wide-ranging consensus but would be content with a sufficient level of social solidarity for successful collaborative action. In general, the pragmatist would adopt an open-ended experimental approach and would not be overly concerned with meeting any formal requirements of rationality, whether in its instrumentalist or communicative form. The pragmatist would work within the framework of community but would also be free to inject individual creativity into the process. Finally, pragmatism, with its ends-in-view, offers planners a middle way between a procedural rationalism, where goals are clearly stated prior to planning processes, and the indeterminacy of a purely inter-subjective process where ends are only clear once consensus has been reached.

9

Planning and the Postmodern Turn
Mark Oranje

INTRODUCTION

The last two decades have witnessed a growing awareness and engagement by a number of planning theorists[1] with what has, for lack of a better word, been called 'postmodernity' and 'postmodernism'.[2] These textual excursions, in what can accordingly be termed a 'postmodern turn', have taken a variety of forms, largely as a result of different readings of 'the postmodern' and of planning. In this chapter an attempt is made to provide an overview and a reading of the state of this turn, including both the texts of those authors that have engaged postmodernity head-on and those that have acted within its ambit. In addition to this, some avenues for further exploration and enlightenment are also highlighted. As a prelude to these texts brief definitions of the terms 'postmodernism' and 'postmodernity' are provided.

DEFINITIONS

One of the things that many postmodernists detest is that of providing definitions for postmodernism and postmodernity as this entails categorising, caging and closing-down, instead of freeing/opening up, and does not recognise the instability of meaning (Parker, 1993; Lewis, 1998: 129–131; Sim, 1998: 5–6). The brief definitions that follow are thus not meant to be exhaustive in any way, but merely to provide a backdrop/setting for the stories that are to follow.

'Postmodernity/the postmodern condition' can be regarded as a collective name for a set of phenomena, an epoch, or a condition that is distinguishable in form, content and intent from modernity/the modern condition. One of the key areas of difference is the postmodern opposition to the privileging of reason as the only route to knowledge and the modernist belief that there is a universal, absolute, unchanging 'Truth'[3] that can be uncovered through application of the universal scientific method (Habermas, 1981; Lyotard, 1984; Rosenau, 1992; Hollinger, 1994; Westman, 1996). A major outcome of this has been a declining faith in the idea of progress and 'a better tomorrow' made possible by the application of reason, as well as nihilism, relativism, a preoccupation with the here and now and immediate gratification. Another has been the focusing of attention on 'modernity's Others', marginalised groups/voices in society, spirituality and 'the planet' (Connor, 1994; Dear, 1994; Sancar, 1994; Sayer, 1994).

'Postmodernism' on the other hand refers to the consciousness and critique of the condition, and the styles/methods in which this is expressed/done, while 'postmodern' simply is a word that is used to describe/label something as belonging to, or being a manifestation or a symptom of, the condition.

Despite their differences, postmodernity is not the direct, binary opposite of modernity, and in many ways a continuation, or radicalisation of some modern ideas, such as an intensification in the drive to extend human rights to all people and an even stronger craving for individuality (Giddens, 1990; Simonsen, 1990). In some ways postmodernity can also be regarded as a wake-up call to modernity, informing it that Reason did not slay all the pre-modern 'demons' it had set its sights on and that these survivors 'have now returned' in a sequel to h/taunt it. It is this 'oozing of some of its traits and tendencies through time' that has made it difficult for authors to locate the starting point of the condition/epoch, as is evident in the divergence in opinion as to this date.[4] It does, however, seem that there is general agreement that its mass penetration and global manifestation only began during the 1980s,[5] roughly about the time in which planning theorists began narrating their perceptions and experiences of it.

'PLANNING THEORY' AND POSTMODERNITY/ISM

In this section some engagements of planning theorists with postmodernity and postmodernism are related. Using the postmodern treatment of theories as narratives/stories, the various types of narrative responses are labelled as genres (see Mandelbaum, 1991; Throgmorton, 1992; Harper and Stein, 1993: 6; de Souza Briggs, 1998: 1). Before retelling the tales in these genres, which include a group of theorists who have not explicitly engaged the postmodern–planning debate, but who have narrated planning from what can be termed a postmodern angle, a recount of some of what can be seen as early, *petite* postmodern stabs at planning.

BEFORE THE GENRES

Long before the words postmodernity and postmodernism had entered the planning discourse, the first jabs at a set of planning practices built on a strange mix of utopianism, evangelism, bourgeois fears, middle-class values and a belief in rationality, 'professional male expertise' and comprehensiveness, were already made.

These stabs, in no particular order, while still firmly located in a modernist container, but displaying a postmodern twist,[6] were *inter alia*:

- the attacks by Jacobs (1961) and Sennett (1973) on the expertise and wisdom of the expert planner and the planning practice of the day,[7] and Jacobs' advocacy of her own blend of celebratory/paranoid urbanism (see Sudjic, 1993: 22), which laid the groundwork for much of the postmodern New Urbanism of the 1980s and 1990s;
- the critiques by Lindblom (1959), Etzioni (1973) and Davidoff (1965) of the single rational comprehensive planning process and their alternative 'incrementalist', 'mixed scanning' and 'recognition of pluralism in planning/ plurality of plans' approaches, which not only dented the hegemony of the comprehensive model, but also the idea(l) of a single, universal planning process;
- the 'advocacy' and 'equity planning' approaches of Davidoff (1965) and Krumholz (1982) in which planning's focus/gaze on functionality, technical issues and land use concerns was shifted to include the reality of difference and the political questions of who gets what, when and where and by whom and how these issues are decided on;
- the 'transactive planning' model of Friedmann (1973) in which a starter pack-version of the expert listening and learning from 'the people' and vice versa, was sketched; and
- the attack by the (then) Marxists, like Castells (1978), Scott and Roweis (1977) and Fainstein and Fainstein (1982) on planning for being hand in glove with the powers that be, which placed an early question mark over the view of planning as a technocratic, value-free process in service to 'society/the public interest'.

Genre 1: First contact/blood

From the second half of the 1980s onwards a number of exploratory stories appeared in which their authors (see Beauregard, 1989, 1991; Friedmann, 1989, 1991, 1994; Moore-Milroy, 1989, 1991; Cooke, 1990a, 1990b; Goodchild, 1990; Hemmens, 1992; Hoch, 1992; Taylor, 1998: 162–167) were doing three things. First, becoming acquainted with, describing, creating an awareness of and/or trying to make sense of the postmodern condition and the 'isms' it had spawned. Second, (anxiously) pondering the implications of the condition and its 'isms' for planning and planners and, third, making some, often incoherent, fragmented, tentative, small and reactive suggestions for adaptation/change.

In these texts postmodernity/ism was introduced to the reader as a schizophrenic, amoeba-like character, that was *both* a Beauty and a Beast. The *Beast* was portrayed as a character with a dark, dangerous and even a deadly side that rejected/gobbled up all grand narratives and displayed a tendency towards fragmentation, slicing (in the *Scream 1–3* mould) and 'anything goes'-relativism. This side of the creature, it was feared, could spell disaster for emancipatory projects grounded in rationality/reason and requiring collective action towards the attainment of shared goals. As a *Beauty* the character was lauded for emphasising the importance of local context, the Environment and 'the Other' and for celebrating diversity and plurality, which would make it possible for local communities to develop their own, unique brands of modernity.

In order for planning, which was presented as one of the most modern of modernity's many children, to (in SWOT-speak) survive the threat and exploit the opportunities, it was suggested, in what can be termed an uneasy postmodern response, that planning find a position somewhere between modernity and postmodernity. In so doing, it was held, planning's commitment to social justice and the realisation of 'a better future' could be retained, and even deepened by letting 'other voices' be heard and by allowing for different ways of seeing, knowing and making sense. On a practical level many of these stories contained the mundane, maybe naïve, but potentially very powerful proposal that 'communities' should be granted far more voice/power in determining the course of their future/s. What distinguishes these stories from Genres 5 and 6 is that none of them spoke of, or proposed, full-scale paradigmatic change.

Genre 2: Rereading the first Genre

After the initial shock/awareness of postmodernity/ism, a few authors (Allmendinger, 1998; Filion, 1999) have, in what can be termed a 'second order' engagement with the postmodernity/ism–planning debate. In their stories they began questioning whether things were really all that different/new, and if so, what was different/new and how different/new it all was. Also, whether (all) planning was really all that modern, whether planners should be buying everything that postmodernists were preaching and whether there was/is a need for radical adjustment. Making use of case studies both authors in this group were able to paint a far more nuanced picture of postmodernity/ism and of planning under postmodern conditions than what the authors in the first genre had done.

Genre 3: Southern s(l)ides

Two types of tales have been told from the South. First, those by Leontidou (1993, 1996), Simon (1998) and Andresen and Castel-Branco (1993) in which they called for the recognition of the different kinds of postmodernism and the different blends of modernity and postmodernity in the South, as well as the accompanying unique challenges and opportunities this situation poses. These authors also argued that certain strands of what have been read in the North as being part of the postmodern condition were part of Southern practices long before the Northern word 'postmodernism' was invented. In these stories a common theme was that many planning practices have always been conducted in a postmodern way and that local Southern communities have managed to eclectically invent/carve out creative ways of ensuring a better life for themselves.

A second version of this genre are stories that were told by South African planners such as Harrison (1995, 1996), Mabin (1995), Bond (1992) and Oranje (1995, 1996) who were grappling with the difficulties of realising the developmental needs of a previously excluded majority of diverse 'Others' under postmodern conditions. In these texts a common theme was the fear that postmodernism would lead to further fragmentation and polarisation of the already highly segregated 'South African City', as well as slow down the huge reconstruction and modernisation project underway in that country.[8] As can be expected, the proposed planning responses have been of a very 'middle of the road' nature, in most cases suggesting the accommodation of diversity without relinquishing the drive towards 'a better tomorrow'.

Genre 4: Strike back

Since the arrival of the word postmodernism in the social sciences many prominent Leftist authors have treated it with outright hostility (see *inter alia* Eagleton, 1985, 1997; Callinicos, 1990; O'Neill, 1995).

In the case of planning, the stories in which such a response to postmodernity/ism was adopted were primarily the product of David Harvey (1987, 1989a, 1990, 1992, 1993a, 1993b, 1996). In his stories Harvey expressed two major concerns with postmodernism. First, that postmodernism's loathing of meta-narratives/theory and normative foundations (especially the question of social justice) and its favouring of local/small narratives were a recipe for implosion into infinite relativism. Second, that by shifting the focus/gaze of social theory to difference and local, small-scale struggles, postmodernism was really preparing the road/making the world safe for a globally prowling Late Capitalism. Hence, in Harvey's stories, especially an article published in 1987, postmodernism was presented as a spectre haunting the emancipatory promise of a Leftist/Radical Geography and Planning that had to be resisted/slain. Even though he adopted a far less harsh treatment in his later writings (i.e. post-1989), even suggesting that there are lessons to be learnt from it, and in so doing, taking on a somewhat postmodern response himself, he maintained a critical/sceptical distance from it.

Genre 5: Walking into the postmodern sunrise

In the stories told by the two prime orators of this genre, Michael Dear (1986, 1989, 1994, 1995a, 1995b, 2000) and Leonie Sandercock (1995, 1998b, 1998c), it was proclaimed that modernity is dead or dying, that postmodernity is the new condition/epoch planning finds, or will be finding itself in, and that planning needed to adapt to this. A key characteristic of Dear's texts was that, true to the postmodern ethos (were such a thing to exist), no concrete proposals for the shape of a postmodern planning were made, not even in his most recent book *The Postmodern Urban Condition* (Dear, 2000). Instead, he opted for broad suggestions such as that new ways of looking at cities are required and that the out-dated notions of urban governance and planning built up under modernity had to change. In the case of Sandercock, it was different. Here there always was the clear (modernist?) desire to find a more satisfying, constructive and progressive conclusion to the modern–postmodern impasse, the development of which can be traced through her engagement with postmodernism beginning in 1995 and culminating in her, destined-for-seminal-status, 'Towards Cosmopolis' in 1998.[9] In this story, still infused with a strong sense of justice, she not only made a very passionate case for a postmodern planning practice, but also for a 'postmodern Utopia' in which different ways of knowing and living are understood, respected and cherished.

example, model.

Genre 6: How to live happily [ever] after postmodernism

Over the last decade a number of planning theorists have toyed with the notion of a paradigm switch, in the process ensuring that planning adapt to the postmodern condition without becoming (too) postmodern in the process. Two alternative paradigms have been proposed, the one, pragmatism, sharing many characteristics with postmodernism, the other, collaborative/communicative planning, in many ways staunchly opposed to many of the postmodern tenets. Despite these differences, the planning practices they propose are, however, in many ways very similar. As these two paradigms are dealt with at length in other chapters in this book they are only dealt with very briefly here.

treating things from practical p.o.view.

In those stories calling for a switch to pragmatism (see Harper and Stein, 1995b; Hoch, 1996; Verma, 1996; Harrison, 1998), the allure seems to lie in the pragmatist belief that there are no foundational truths, but that ideas, which are community-derived, acquire truth status for a community only when they prove their worth/use in practice, i.e. in solving a problem. Furthermore, these truths being temporal, they are/can be incrementally updated by communities. What these stories tried to achieve is to steer planning away from a nihilist postmodernism that would argue that there is 'no truth', to keep it focused on

Rejection of all moral + religious principles.

outcomes and to avoid the strait-jackets imposed by modernist metaphysical, universal truths and values.

In the communicative/collaborative planning stories (see Healey, 1992a, 1993a, 1996c, 1996b, 1997a; Innes, 1995, 1996, 1998b; Sager, 1994),[10] the neo-modernist narrators, like postmodernists, recognised diversity, but believed that this could be reconciled by setting up structures in which stakeholders can through open, honest and respectful debate make sense together, learn to live together and reach consensus on 'a future together'. In proposing the switch to communicative planning, the proponents of this paradigm believed that this would enable planning to move not only within, but also through and beyond postmodernity by making use of its positive aspects and steering clear of its negative tendencies.

Genre 7: Doing the postmodern thing

Whereas the previous genres contained tales of direct engagements with postmodernity/ism a number of storytellers began telling (horror) stories of planners and planning practices and documents, strongly influenced by authors who have been branded with the postmodern label, such as Derrida, Foucault, Nietzsche, Lyotard and the later Wittgenstein. While not making any direct suggestions on how planning c/should respond to the postmodern condition, these stories do represent a certain genre of stories that are part of the postmodern turn in planning.

One group of stories in this genre includes texts in which authors (Forester, 1989; Hoch, 1992; Yiftachel, 1995a, 1995b, 1998; Flyvbjerg, 1998b, 2000), much like the Marxists a decade or two before them, explored the role/s and abuse/s of power in planning practices and exposed the dark side of (modern) planning. The major difference between these stories and the earlier Marxist works being that of scale. In the more recent texts the analysis and arena for change/struggle (if any) was primarily on a micro-level, whereas the level of analysis and arena for change/struggle in the Marxist stories was typically on the macro-level.

A second group includes stories in which a postmodern and poststructural turn to textual analysis and deconstruction was made (see *inter alia* Boyer, 1983; Mandelbaum, 1990, 1991, 1993; Tett and Wolfe, 1991; Throgmorton, 1992; Myerson and Rydin, 1994; Hillier, 1996a; Lauria and Soll, 1996; Oranje, 1997; Sharp and Richardson, 1999). In these stories planners were presented/portrayed as persuasive, future-oriented storytellers and planning texts as stories/narratives told within the rules of a particular language game. As for the reader-researcher of these texts, s/he becomes a textual stalker, searching out the hidden rules, indiscretions, distortions, inconsistencies, fantasies, fetishes and stereotypes of the particular language game and its players.

READING THE GENRES: ASSESSING THE STATE OF THE POSTMODERN TURN AND SOME SUGGESTIONS FOR FURTHER TURNS (AND SOME RETURNS)

In the introduction to his latest offering Dear (2000: 7) argues that:

> Postmodern thought is not going away, even though no-one can be sure of its ultimate legacy. In the meantime, I believe that there is an acute intellectual imperative to meet its challenge. Whether one decides ultimately to be for or against postmodernism may be less important than the obligation to engage its discourse.

Later on, after having weighed planning, Dear (ibid.: 303) comes to the conclusion that the engagement of planners with postmodernity/ism has been very limited and as a result 'the impact of postmodernism in urban planning theory and practice has been minuscule'.[11]

While my reading of the theory-tales to date concurs in broad terms with that of Dear,[12] I would argue that the seven genres discussed in this chapter indicate that there has been more than just a passing engagement and exploration of the postmodern–planning interface. In addition to that, 'other' ways of practising planning under postmodern conditions have been proposed, and planning practices have been interrogated by making use of the words and the tools of postmodern thinkers. But, at the same time there are silences, strange readings and practices contained in the stories that are worrying and that deserve more attention and/or that could be improved upon. It is to these and the proposed improvements that I now turn.

On readings

There is a tendency, if not explicitly, but implicitly, especially in some of the stories in Genre 1, to treat modernity/ism and postmodernity/ism in a modern binary-coded way as clearly demarcated, opposing entities with no shared characteristics. In many cases the 'post' in postmodernity/ism is also interpreted as *only* meaning 'non- and anti-modernity/ism', which does not adequately reflect the nature of the condition. As Eagleton (1997: viii) observes, ' "postmodernism" itself means not just that you have left modernism definitely behind, but that you have worked your way through it to a position still deeply marked by it'. Furthermore, very few storytellers, other than those in Genre 2 and maybe some in 3, have tried to establish in their readings of the present just how postmodern different localities have actually become, or what postmodernity entails in different localities. In the absence of such readings this could lead to the blanket suggestion that everyone, everything and every place has moved in every way from a modern to a postmodern condition.

Along with this tendency has gone another totalising reading, namely, that planning is a single, uniform entity and that this entity is a distinctly modern phenomenon. Such a reading does not recognise that planning includes a wide variety of practices displaying many different kinds of modernism, as well as practices that are anything but modern.[13] Nor does it recognise that already in some of its earliest versions planning was a pastiche of traditionalist, anti-modernist and modernist fears and hopes, giving it a distinctly postmodern character. (This does of course not deny the fact that in many cases/places planning did develop into an iron-caged, legalistically constrained activity, a version of modernity that Marshall Berman refers to as 'modernisation as routine'.[14])

What is particularly worrying about these two sets of totalising readings is that their combined outcome is a situation where the interaction of planning with postmodernism becomes a very simple affair.[15] It becomes 'modernism versus or threatened by postmodernism and hence planning versus or threatened by postmodernism'.[16] Even worse, it leads to a 'binary-loaded' situation where modern planning is equated with 'all that is good' and postmodern planning with 'all that is bad/evil' or vice versa. This reduces the chance of a far more interesting and productive engagement taking place between the two, including the kind of responses planners come up with for planning practices under and informed by postmodern conditions. It is the lack of such an engagement which is especially worrying in the case of 'postmodernism and professionalism and the organised profession'[17] and 'the how and what of planning education under postmodern conditions'[18] and where far more work is urgently required.

On theory and theorising

I have seven areas of concern in this regard. First, that important questions about planning theory under postmodern conditions have not been asked. These are questions such as whether there can be something like '(planning) theory' under postmodern conditions, and if so, what the nature of such theory could/should be.[19] In many of the stories it would seem that there has not been a 'stop-stare-and-think'-phase. Planning theorists have simply continued writing (modern) planning theory, albeit from a different angle and with different intents, but without these questions being asked. In some cases postmodernism has also been treated as a hurdle/wall that has to, and can be, crossed, in a once-off jump into the (terror-filled) world of 'the solution'. A number of authors (Huxley and Yiftachel, 1998: 13; see also McLoughlin, 1994; Leontidou, 1996: 179, 193; Muller, 1998) have, however, made the refreshing suggestion that in postmodern times, instead of trying to produce theory, planners should 'theorise planning'.[20]

Second, that the potentially dark side of a postmodern planning theory has not been fully investigated. In dabbling with texts and moving deeper and deeper into textual analysis there is the very real danger that planning theory can reach a point where 'there is nothing but the text',[21] that it does not refer back to material realities, but in an intertextual[22] way, to other texts only. While textual analysis is very powerful in exposing excesses, distortions and abuses of power in the production and use of planning texts, planning, even under postmodern conditions, must still ensure 'improved outcomes' in the real world[23] and keep the hope for the speedy arrival of those outcomes alive. If it cannot do that it has no reason to live and may just as well become the subject of history only.

Third, the limited number of stories dealing with the future, or seeking to imagine/provide maps of possible futures, like Sandercock has so ably done in *Towards Cosmopolis* (1998c). In trying to come to grips with the present postmodern condition, planners have neglected the telling of stories of the 'planning of the future' and what the contribution of that 'future planning' will be to the communities and the places in which it will be practised.[24] Some planners, in particular those in Genre 7, seem to also have become fixated on exposing the past and present 'evils that planners do', without providing (some) guidance as to 'the ways of the good planner' in the future. This does of course not suggest that a single once-off future must be provided, but that questions as to the why, how and where of a future planning must be asked and answers sought. Hopefully this will also bring some balance to, and some movement beyond, the far-too-easy stories featuring 'bad/mad/evil/malicious planners'.

Fourth, that despite the postmodern desire to break down, or at least soften boundaries, planning theorists, especially those in Genre 6, have largely remained concerned with 'procedure', stuck within the artificial boundaries separating planning process/procedure and substantive issues/outcomes and neglecting the context in which they tell their stories (see Huxley, 1997). As argued by Neuman (1998: 68), 'The divorce of knowledge from action, of content from process, is nearly complete in planning theory. The primacy of process is held firm under the grip of theories of communicative action.'[25] It seems that planners are still heeding Faludi's (1984: 3) call that 'planning theory should be concerned with this (procedural theory) rather than with substantive theory'.[26] On the same score, the notion that there are two distinct activities, planning practice and planning theory, and hence two distinct groups, planning theorists and planning practitioners, has remained untouched. It would be useful if the nature, meaning and value of these two terms, as well as their continued use in their current format could become the topic of investigation.

Fifth, the persistence of the notion that there can be a single paradigm in postmodern times, as is especially the case in the collaborative planning genre.

This proposal has of course come in for severe critique (see *inter alia* Muller, 1998; Huxley and Yiftachel, 1998; Oranje, 1999), with most of those opposed to the idea of a single paradigm, proposing a multiplicity of small narratives in which planning practices are theorised. Telling endless little tales is of course not 'the solution' as the endeavour of only writing up the local, the different and the unique may lead to a neglect of the similarities/sameness and the areas of mutual concern, and might lead to the equally totalising statement that 'there are no similarities'. It would be just another (binary-coded) case of switching one set of privileged discourses for another (see Young, 1993: 126; Haber, 1994: 5, 114; Huxley, 1997). As Short (1993: 171) observes, 'To only look at universals was the blindness of modernism. To only consider the places of the local is the silence of postmodernism.'[27] In much the same vein Harvey (1993a: 118) argues that:

> the mere pursuit of identity politics as an end in itself (rather than as a fundamental struggle to break with an identity which internalises oppression) may serve to perpetuate rather than to challenge the persistence of those processes which gave rise to those identities in the first place.

The postmodern challenge is hence not to produce small stories describing difference, but stories in which authors highlight *both* those things that are novel/different and those that are similar to other parts of other small stories. In this process authors will not only enable a respect for difference, but also provide the opportunity for readers in other places to identify with other actors and to learn from their/other practices (see Innes, 1998a: viii for a similar perspective). The ultimate aim should not be to find/establish difference, but to find ways of making life better for 'all of us', whatever that means and to seek ways in which this is more, rather than less, likely to happen.

Sixth, the persistence of a discourse in particularly the stories of the communicative action-genre in which certain concepts are privileged over others, or in which a certain reading of discourse ethics is treated as a given/the universal norm.[28] Stating it differently, many of the *a priori* positions on which collaborative planning is built would actually first have to be negotiated/agreed upon in a communicative way if it were to be true to its essence – they cannot be generated in/from an armchair.[29] By the same token storytellers in this genre use words as if their meanings were a given, stable and unproblematic, including words open for many interpretations, such as 'community', 'consensus', 'mutual learning' and 'stakeholder' (see Healey, 1997a).[30]

Finally, that despite postmodernism also having a playful side and a populist and democratic intent, which has for instance found expression in architecture and the arts in pastiche and 'double-coding', most planning theory, like this chapter, is still written in a very stale way, for a very small group. (Definite exceptions being the latest books by Dear (2000) and Sandercock (1998c).) This goes for the way it is written, how it is presented and what the chosen topic/theme is. It would seem that while many planners (like Hillier, 1998b) now recognise the need to read 'other texts' and listen and learn from 'others', many do not yet see the need to enable 'others' to do likewise.

CONCLUSION

It is no easy task to conclude a chapter dealing with postmodernity/ism. As indicated earlier on, postmodernism is not so much about closure as it is about opening up and exposing what is, or wants to stay, hidden.[31] Furthermore, as texts are also viewed by many postmodernists as 'only a picnic where the author brings the words and the readers bring the sense' (Todorov, as quoted in Eco, 1992: 24), this entails that readers become authors of their own stories/texts during their engagement with a story/text (see Collini, 1992: 8; Caputo, 1997: 1). Conclusions are thus partial and temporary as they only bring a (forced) closure to the thoughts of the author of a text at a specific point in time and space – 'right here, right now' – and not those of the hopefully many reader-authors at various other points in time and space. So, for now, my conclusion is this: while there definitely has been an engagement with postmodernity, there are many avenues/openings for taking it further and deepening our sense/s of it. There sadly still are far too many vestiges of a modernity in planning theory that favours/privileges sameness and *even* the closing down of the progressive possibilities and opportunities that some of the other strands of modernity in postmodernity still offer. There is no safe haven/paradigm in which to 'hide from postmodernity', and to search for such a place/point is a futile and a distinctly anti-modern exercise.[32] What would be far more productive for now would be, along the lines of Sandercock (1998c), to engage more, learn more, feel more, listen more and also *do more* to/in 'the local and beyond', than to enslave/tie our-and-everybody-else's-many-selves down more. While doing that, ceaselessly reflecting on our actions and seeking ways of doing things better in and for the futures of the communities we live/work in/with, and that we, as planners, are supposedly so passionate about.

NOTES

1   This includes urban geographers who have engaged planning theory.

2   The use of the words 'postmodernity' and 'postmodernism' actually reinforce the binary-coded notion of modernity and modernism as being 'the norms' in terms of which all else, past and present, must be measured/described.

3   'Truth' in postmodernity is treated as a relative, subjective 'opinion' that is time and space-specific (Young, 1991: 300; Dear, 1994: 298).

4   Best and Kellner (1991: 5) trace the foundations of the condition back to as long ago as 'around 1870' when an English painter, John Watkins Chapman, spoke of 'post-modern painting'. Lodge (1977) locates its first dawn in 1916 in the revolt of the Dadaists during the First World War and Jencks (1986) and Wickham (1991) pin-point it in 1934 in the work of the Spanish writer, Frederic de Onis. Madsen (1995) in a bibliography of Postmodernism in which she only tracked texts that had post-modernism in their bibliographical description or cataloguing data, cites the first text to a collection of essays published in 1926.

5   There is agreement that its actual rise to prominence only began in the 1960s in the USA (Bürger, 1984), the late 1970s in Europe (Kellner, 1988) and in the international arena during the 1980s (Best and Kellner, 1991, see also Dear and Wassmansdorf, 1993).

6   The idea that there could be such a precursor to the responses to postmodernism was born during a reading of Sandercock (1998c).

7   According to Sudjic (1993: 19) Jane Jacobs's 'tract was one of the first attacks in the onslaught on professionals of all kinds that characterised the political climate of the late 1960s and early 1970s'.

8   In a number of texts the authors pointed to the tensions in the Reconstruction and Development Programme – a strong modernist text with postmodern subtexts. These tensions they believed, while making it possible for local communities to invent their own brand of modernity, were making it very difficult for mass (modernist) delivery to take place (see Mabin, 1995; Harrison, 1996: 32; Oranje, 1996, 1997: Chapter 8).

9   See Sandercock (1995, 1998b, 1998c) and see also Beauregard (1998: 95–96) for a discussion of Sandercock's engagement with postmodernism.

10   While Forester has also been associated with this group, his work (1982, 1987, 1989, 1990, 1996a) has been more on the use of critical theory in planning, distorted communication and the role and abuse of power in planning practice, and not on the progression to a new paradigm.

11   The reason for this, he believes is 'clientism', that planning is a profession and that as professionals planners sell their expertise and cannot come across as being insecure about what they are selling (Dear, 2000: 303–304).

12   Planning practice is of course not covered in this chapter.

13   Allmendinger (1998: 228) and Hague (1995a, 1995b) provide a similar reading.

14   This type of modernity is one in which reason/intellect is used to create something new, but once this has been done, is then used to control the world so created to keep it 'as it is' (see Berman, 1982: 242–243).

15   See Allmendinger (1998: 231) for a move in the same direction.

16   See Short (1993), Pile and Rose (1992) and Harrison (1996) for a similar concern.

17   The closest to such an engagement are the attacks by Evans (1993) and Evans and Rydin (1997) on the notion of a planning profession and a paper by Hague (1996) in which some reference is made to the postmodern condition as part of the changed environment in which the planning profession functions.

18   Friedmann (1996) and Feldman (1994) have produced useful texts in this regard.

19   According to Ward (1996: 32), 'For postmodernists, the concept of "theory" is a product of the modern episteme. It is part of the modern epistemic idea that an accurate account of phenomena can be found, conceptualized, and brought to light.'

20   According to Huxley and Yiftachel (1998: 13) 'theorising planning' entails, 'on the one hand to ask questions about the genealogy of the practices and the power/knowledge discourses combined under the heading of "planning"; and on the other hand, to understand the role of planning as a state-related strategy for the creation and regulation of space and populations'.

21   Derrida as quoted in Gottdiener (1995: 19) and see Neuman (1998) for a similar concern about planning. Baudrillard's text (1995) suggesting that the Gulf War did not take place is a very chilling example of what this can lead to.

22   Intertextuality is 'derived from the poststructuralist claim that signifiers refer always and only to other signifiers' (Sim, 1998: 285).

23   In a way the communicative rationalists have tried to prevent this from happening by making texts serviceable to agreed upon communicative action/s and outcomes.

24   Warren et al. (1998) express a similar concern.

25   Huxley and Yiftachel (1998: 3) also support this view, arguing that the communicative paradigm is removed from the spatial and political context in which it is located.

26   Back in 1959 John Friedmann, in a very similar reductionist-mode wrote that: 'The problem of planning has become a problem of procedure and method.'

27   See also Eagleton (1997: 120) for a similar reading with regards to the goals of socialism.

28   Examples of such cases include the idea that consensus is inherently 'good' and must and can always be attained (Huxley, 1997: 12 and see Haber 1994: 22) and that the 'power of the better argument' will win the day (Healey, 1997a: 54). See also Tewdwr-Jones and Allmendinger (1998) for a far more detailed critique of communicative/collaborative planning. Healey (1997a: 63–64) acknowledges many

of these problems, but does not provide a way around them other than communicative rationality.

29 In the unlikely event that you have not yet read Innes's reference to 'armchair theorising' see Innes (1995: 183).

30 For a similar critique see Huxley (1997: 12).

31 For an excellent piece on the problems of closure and authorship see Parker (1993).

32 See Berman (1982) and also Bauman (1998) in which the 'forever-searching/creating' nature of modernity is brilliantly illuminated.

10

A Hayekian Liberal Critique of Collaborative Planning
Mark Pennington

INTRODUCTION

Patsy Healey's *Collaborative Planning* draws on wider movements within social science, which advocate the extension of Habermasian deliberative models of democracy in public decision-making. Collaborative planning offers a critique of bureaucratic decision procedures and a reassertion of the case for radical forms of social democratic planning as an alternative to the market models put forward by the 'New Right'. This chapter welcomes Healey's Habermasian critique of techno-cratic planning, but argues that the sceptical attitude towards competitive market institutions is based on a misreading of the intellectual case for private markets. This is shown most clearly by the lack of attention paid to the work of leading clas-sical liberal thinkers such as Hayek and others in the so-called 'Austrian School'.

Having outlined the basic features of the collaborative approach and its critique of rationalist planning methods, the chapter outlines the Hayekian advo-cacy of competitive markets. The analysis suggests that the epistemological approach adopted by Hayek is not dissimilar to that put forward by authors such as Healey. Where the Hayekian analysis parts company with collaborative planning, however, is in its normative account of the institutional arrangements that are com-patible with these epistemological foundations. Within this context, the chapter argues that if the goals of collaborative planning are actually to be achieved, then, far from extending the range of state intervention, there should be a reduction in the role of social democratic planning and the extension of private markets. The concluding part moves on to consider how property rights and market approaches might fruitfully be extended into areas of environmental and land use planning, which it is often assumed should be the preserve of the social democratic state.

COLLABORATIVE PLANNING

'Rationalist' models of land use planning are often based on a technocratic con-ception of decision-making, whereby public managers in possession of objective knowledge, make decisions on the basis of 'maximising' social welfare (Faludi, 1973; Harrison, 1977). If the market economy and the price system are thought not to respond effectively to pre-given individual preferences through the inter-action of supply and demand, then land use planners, appropriately trained in the best scientific methods of preference assessment, are required to step in to perform this co-ordinating role. Theoretically, this rationalist approach draws heavily on neo-classical welfare economics with its focus on the 'correction' of 'market fail-ures'. Due to the existence of externality and collective goods problems, market institutions are thought to 'fail' in the environmental sphere (Pigou, 1920). The task of the environmental planner, therefore, is to deploy a range of neutral evaluation techniques such as social/cost benefit analysis in order to objectively identify and measure individual preferences for the relevant environmental goods (Harrison, 1977; Pearce, 1989; Turner *et al.*, 1994). These preferences can then be aggre-gated in order to maximise public welfare and a similar set of evaluation techniques deployed so as to identify the appropriate means to implement the chosen policy goals.

Collaborative planning represents a theoretical reaction to this technocratic approach to public policy-making and land use planning in particular. According to authors such as Healey (1997a), the emphasis on objective, scientific conceptions of knowledge in the rationalist approach acts to exclude other forms of knowledge, including tacit knowledge or practical 'common-sense reason' and appeals to moral or ethical claims, that are *not* open to scientific measurement and quantifica-tion. That these forms of value are not taken sufficiently into account by rationalist planning methods leads, it is argued, not only to poor policy outcomes but to a pro-found sense of citizen disempowerment and growing distrust of the political appar-atus of the modern state.

From the perspective of collaborative planning, the claims made for the objectivity of science are subject to serious limits. Science itself has limited poten-tial for objectivity and is shaped by complex cultural processes of social interaction. It is, for example, well accepted (even by their adherents) that the results of sup-posedly objective techniques, such as social/cost benefit analysis are in large part a reflection of subjective value judgements made by the planners concerned (For-maini, 1991). Collaborative planning, therefore, is more modest in its assumptions about the availability of the knowledge base for engaging in planning activities. Technocratic forms of planning are held incapable on their own, of understanding the complexity inherent in social and ecological systems. Similarly, knowledge itself is not something that exists in an objective sense, but is actively produced through a social process of interaction and inter-subjective learning.

According to this Habermasian model, the ideal institutional environment for policy-making requires the rejection of centralised bureaucratic models towards a more inclusionary or participatory form of planning, where all the relevant 'stakeholders' are given a chance to have their say. Correspondingly, this requires the imposition of a greater array of social democratic controls on private markets in order to facilitate the questioning of individual goals and values so that preferences can actively be shaped and a social consensus built as part of an ongoing process of open public discourse. Such measures are considered necessary in order to shift the emphasis away from a narrowly instrumental conception of rationality and the notion of the individual as 'consumer', towards the socially more 'empowering' notion of 'citizenship' and reflect the long-standing social democratic desire to subject the 'anarchy of the market' to conscious social control.

HAYEK AND THE AUSTRIAN CRITIQUE OF PLANNING

Given the failures of technocratic planning demonstrated most clearly by the experience of East European socialism, the critique of such procedures by Habermasian approaches seems well placed. What is perplexing about collaborative planning from a classical liberal perspective, however, is its generally critical attitude towards market institutions. Healey (1997a), for example, argues that collaborative planning represents a theoretical foil against the advocacy of competitive markets by the 'neo-liberal' right (ibid.: 28). The focus on non-quantifiable, tacit and subjective forms of knowledge in collaborative planning, however, also constitutes the very heart of the critique of planning and the advocacy of markets put forward by the most influential of all modern liberal thinkers – Hayek.

It is disappointing that Healey's seminal book makes no reference to the works of Hayek – or any other members of the so-called 'Austrian school'.[1] This is especially surprising because, as will be shown below, key elements of the Hayekian critique of central/bureaucratic planning can be turned against the case for a collaborative planning approach. The problem appears to be that Healey (1997a), along with other deliberative democrats (see Jacobs, 1992) tends to equate the intellectual case for markets with neo-classical economics. The most forceful and influential advocacy of market competition, however, comes *not* from this direction, but from an intellectual tradition that explicitly rejects most of the positivist neo-classical apparatus. Hayek's liberalism does not rest on a rationalist defence of the market but instead offers a radical, epistemological alternative to neo-classical economics as a means for illuminating the primary merits of the market system.

Hayekians oppose neo-classical conceptions of markets, arguing that these models present individuals as atomistic automatons, responding to objective price signals in the manner of robots. If the world of neo-classical economics existed, then there would be no scope for individual choice – people would, in fact, have no option than to respond to the objective stimuli before them and to speak of 'choice' in such a context would be meaningless (Buchanan, 1969; Shackle, 1972; Buchanan and Vanberg, 1991; Boettke, 1998). Similarly, if objective knowledge of means–ends relationships could be made available in 'scientific' form then there would be no case for a decentralised market economy. If objective knowledge of preferences and relative scarcities could be made known, then it would be possible to dispense with the market in favour of central planning and to have the allocation of resources supervised by government officials employing the techniques of cost/benefit analysis. To the extent that neo-classical economists advocate a market economy, therefore, this normative policy stance is often at odds with their substantive methodological position (Lavoie, 1985; Kirzner, 1997; Boettke, 1998).

From a Hayekian perspective it is precisely *because* values and knowledge are to a significant extent subjective, that central planning is unlikely to succeed. The 'Austrian' advocacy of markets views individual choice as a creative act, which takes place under conditions of imperfect information, chronic uncertainty and with the distinct possibility of error (O'Driscoll and Rizzo, 1985). Individuals are *not* conceived as atomistic 'rational actors', because such action would require the pursuit of some optimal course, given objective knowledge of economic opportunity. Rather, people should be viewed as purposeful actors who base their plans and decisions on subjective perceptions of the opportunities before them. Within this context, the market economy is seen as a profoundly social process of inter-subjective trial and error, in which people learn about and at the same time shape one another's plans and preferences.

To the extent that collaborative planning and the Hayekians conceive of social interaction as a process of inter-subjective learning, then these two approaches appear to be treading similar ground. Where the Hayekians part company with collaborative planning, however, is in their account of the institutional processes that are most likely to bring this inter-subjective learning about. Collaborative planning emphasises the importance of face-to-face communication and the conveyance of information via public discourse and debate. For the Hayekians, by contrast, markets are required to facilitate inter-subjective learning and co-ordination in situations where conscious deliberation and face-to-face communication are simply not possible. In order to understand the basis of a Hayekian critique of collaborative planning, which flows from this analysis it is necessary to flesh out in a little more detail the communicative role of markets as emphasised by Hayek.

At the core of Hayek's advocacy of markets and his critique of government planning is the notion of dispersed, subjective information and tacit knowledge. In neo-classical economics, data such as knowledge of technology and under perfect competition, market prices themselves, are conceived as objectively given facts.

For the Austrian School, however, economic knowledge is to a large extent subjective and far from being *given*, must be produced through a process of trial and error learning (Hayek, 1948c, 1978). This is not to say that no objective, information may be obtained in a centralised form – such as historical data on land use patterns and past prices – but that even in the presence of such information, different individuals will interpret the implications to be derived from the same data in different ways (Hayek, 1948c). Prices formed by the interaction of market participants, therefore, are not a reflection of objective underlying relative scarcities, but are formed through the interplay of subjective beliefs about these scarcities. Human action takes place in a world of uncertainty where the outcomes of choices are to a significant extent imagined (Shackle, 1972; Buchanan and Vanberg, 1991).

The market system, therefore, is seen as a process of inter-subjective learning where people discover the compatibility of their own subjective expectations and plans with those of others through an open-ended process of entrepreneurial trial and error, i.e. not the equilibrium end state of neo-classical theory (O'Driscoll and Rizzo, 1985). When entrepreneurs undertake production and investment decisions, their subjective perceptions of profit opportunities – their readings of the market 'text' – are tested for compatibility with those of consumers through the account of profit and loss. Market actors are, to use Gadamer's terminology, attempting to 'fuse their horizons' with those of others so as to discover which goods to produce. Given the uncertainty and possibility of error, individual actors require a feedback mechanism that can help them learn reflexively about the quality of their decisions. For Hayek and the Austrian School, the price system and the account of profit and loss generated by the free exchange of property titles provide such a mechanism. Prescient entrepreneurship is rewarded with profits, whereas losses penalise error. While markets themselves may result in many erroneous decisions, it may be better to rely on the diverse expectations of diverse market participants, at least some of whom may prove to be correct, than to rely on the more monistic decisions of government planning and regulation (Hayek, 1948c, 1978; Kirzner, 1985, 1992, 1997).

From an Austrian perspective, it is the lack of an effective equivalent to the constant feedback provided by the profit and loss account that provides an insurmountable barrier to effective attempts at central economic planning. Still more important, however, planners (democratically elected or otherwise) can never perceive and respond to as many instances of dis-co-ordination as can individuals who have the freedom to exchange property titles in the market (Hayek, 1948c, 1978; Lavoie, 1985). Knowledge of means and ends is scattered *in the minds* of many dispersed actors, each of whom may possess subjective information that no one else discerns. Each entrepreneurial act, such as the offering of a new price/product or changing the organisational form of production, actively creates new knowledge that might otherwise have gone unnoticed and may act to per-suade other individuals to change their plans.[2] Entrepreneurial successes (and fail-ures) may then be noticed by actors who imitate the behaviour of the successful and learn *not* to make the same errors as the unsuccessful. This process provides a way for people to discover what goods are more or less saleable, without ever having explicitly to ask or to articulate reasons why this is the case. As the behavi-our of the successful is imitated, more knowledge is produced and spreads throughout the market in a snowballing process, the results of which could never have been given to a group of minds attempting to simulate this process in advance (Hayek, 1948c, 1978; Kirzner, 1985, 1992, 1997).

It should be noted that the existence of large, bureaucratically managed cor-porations, which might themselves be said to engage in a form of 'central planning' does not refute the case for private markets. Not all transactions are best con-ducted through individual contracts – there may be important gains in terms of reducing transaction costs and the benefits of scale economies to be made from centralisation and the operation of a hierarchical management system. As Coase (1937) famously pointed out, this is, after all, why firms exist. What is at issue, from a Hayekian perspective, is that the optimum scale of economic organisations (i.e. the optimum scale at which planning can take place) cannot be known in advance but is itself something that must be discovered and rediscovered through an open-ended process of trial and error (Hayek, 1978; Kirzner, 1985, 1992, 1997). It is for precisely this reason that the size and number of firms in different industrial sectors are subject to dynamic change and vary so markedly from decade to decade (see Brozen, 1982; Steele, 1992 for empirical evidence on these trends). Again, while far from 'perfect', markets may offer a better mechanism to determine the appropri-ate scale of planning organisations than administration by government bureaucra-cies, which are not themselves subject to an equivalent competitive discovery procedure.

In concluding this outline of the Hayekian critique of planning, it is of para-mount importance to emphasise that none of these arguments make any assump-tions about the motivations of individual decision-makers. They do not, for example, assume that individuals are self-interested utility maximisers as is the case in ortho-dox neo-classical economics or in those versions of classical liberalism influenced by the tradition of public choice theory. The latter perspective (which the present author has used at length elsewhere – see Pennington, 2000) argues against plan-ning on the grounds that incentive structures in a social democratic setting lead to a system which is relatively less accountable than market competition. As a consequence, planning is prone to a process of special interest capture and bureaucratic expansionism, as the empirical evidence from Britain and many other countries would seem to confirm (see also Evans, 1991; Pennington, 1997, 2000). The Hayekian case against planning, by contrast, does not rest on such controversial assumptions. Put simply, even in a world of perfect altruism, public-spirited planners may lack the information to engage in a process of conscious social planning due to the cognitive limits of the human mind.[3]

HAYEK AND THE INFORMATIONAL LIMITS OF COLLABORATIVE PLANNING

The Hayekian critique is of course most forceful when explaining the failure of attempts to plan the entire economy. Its conclusions also apply, however, to less comprehensive attempts at planning, which seek to 'correct' various 'market failures'. The account can, for example, throw considerable light on the repeated failure of planners in Britain, and elsewhere, to successfully engage in the kind of strategic approach to land use planning so frequently advocated in the environmental policy literature. Evidence suggests that attempts to develop integrated land use policies to reduce car dependence have often not had the desired effect because planners have repeatedly been unable to anticipate the effects of technological innovation and changing lifestyle patterns (Gordon and Richardson, 1997; Hall, 1999). From a Hayekian perspective, it may be a mistake to suggest that planning can improve on the apparently haphazard operation of markets in order to arrive at an integrated land use policy because planners may not be able to know what they are supposed to be integrating. The failure of land use planning to deliver effective strategic policies may not, as is often suggested, reflect a lack of power and resources, but may be due to the informational impossibility of strategic planning as an ideal. In Britain, for example, it is not clear what the case for more strategic planning can actually be when existing structure plans are already years out of date by the time of their completion (Cherry, 1996). What is significant for the purposes of this chapter is that many elements of the Hayekian critique are equally relevant when applied to Healey's (1997a) model of collaborative planning. Consider first the fundamental issue of social and ecological complexity.

Advocates of deliberative democracy stress the inter-relatedness of socio-economic and environmental systems. Seen from this perspective, society needs to move beyond the reductionist focus of instrumental rationality and to adopt new forms of discourse which are reflective of the systemic and symbiotic character of the relevant social and environmental processes. This is said to require a more holistic understanding of social and environmental problems and correspondingly a more holistic and integrated set of policy responses to them. It would appear, therefore, that active stakeholder deliberation and democratic community participation are to render more transparent what must remain obscure to technocratic planners. If technocratic planning is held incapable of producing appropriately 'integrated' and 'holistic' land use policies, comparatively fewer doubts are held as to the capacity of deliberative democracy to deliver such objectives. While it must surely be accepted that greater community participation can provide information that might otherwise be neglected by purely 'expert' driven procedures, there are a number of problems with this approach.

First, if it is accepted that the knowledge base necessary for effective decision-making is diffused throughout the minds and actions of many dispersed individuals, then collaborative planning, while appearing to recognise the theme of complexity, may be subject to many of the same epistemological problems as its more technocratic counterparts. To suggest that *because* social and ecological systems are complexly related entities they *must* be managed on a similarly holistic basis is a *non sequitur.* The normative conclusion that deliberative democratic control is required does not follow from the premise that social and ecological systems are holistically related. On the contrary, from a Hayekian perspective, it is precisely because these systems are complexly related wholes that conscious social control is a problematic concept (Hayek, 1973, 1988). The communicative rationality approach appears to be suggesting that epistemological problems of this sort could somehow be solved if only all the relevant stakeholders (in their multiple social and economic roles) could be gathered together in some sort of grand committee meeting to discuss the issues in hand (a logistical impossibility in itself). It is, however, because of the magnitude of the inter-relations between the many components that make up complex systems that they may not be grasped by a group of minds engaged in such a discussion (Hayek, 1973, 1988).

The logistical problems of collaborative planning are revealed, when one examines the 'deliberative designs' that are advocated. It is never suggested that all or even a majority of the relevant populations will be involved in the requisite plan-making. Instead, the devices proposed include 'citizens' juries', 'community workshops' or 'focus groups' – small groups of citizens randomly selected from the populations concerned. When involved in the making of strategic plans and other 'integrated land use policies', such groups are to make more comprehensible the complex inter-community relationships which permeate urban and regional economies and environmental systems, that are held beyond the comprehension of professional technocracy. For the reasons outlined in the previous paragraph, such claims seem questionable. How, for example, are the members of citizens' juries to learn reflexively about the quality of their decisions when there is no equivalent of the profit and loss account and the constant feedback provided by prices which can 'test' the quality of the choices made? Similarly, how are voters to make meaningful judgements on the performance of such processes if the actors concerned may be attempting to engage in a process that may be beyond everybody's comprehension?

One might also ask why the population in general should feel the sense of empowerment that is often claimed. It is far from clear why the multitude of people, who cannot for logistical reasons be involved, should feel any more 'empowered' than they might under the rule of technocratic procedures.

From a Hayekian perspective, by contrast, rather than seeking to manage social and environmental systems according to some holistic plan, it may be better to rely on impersonal, self-organising mechanisms to bring about the necessary co-ordination. As both Hayek's work (1973, 1988) and recent developments in chaos theory suggest (see, for example, Parker and Stacey, 1994), self-organisation is a conceptual idea that may be more appropriate to complex orders whose particular characteristics are *not* the intended outcome of the actors who make up the relevant order. As Di-Zerega (1993) points out, self-organisation refers to those non-reductionist processes wherein relatively simple reactions by the components of a system result in complex patterns of order far beyond the capacity of each of the component parts to construct mechanically. Eco-systems exemplify self-organisation, for the principles generating ecological order are completely unknown to most beings following them. Such orders arise where the individual participants are involved in co-ordinative process, the patterns of which are far too complex for them to grasp.

Seen in this context, the impersonal, price-guided market is much more akin to complex social and environmental orders than the consciously directed model of deliberative governance put forward by collaborative planning. The constant feedback signals provided by the prices, profits and losses generated in the market bring together dispersed knowledge that facilitate a degree of co-ordination between a multitude of actors that may be greater than could be achieved if all those concerned had sought to plan the outcome in advance. The most that can be understood about such spontaneous orders are the general principles (such as the tendency for prices to rise when demand exceeds supply, or the process of ecological succession), which connect the multitude of component parts. How specific individual acts of co-ordination will come about, however, may never be known in sufficient detail (Hayek, 1957, 1973, 1988).

It is of course, the largely impersonal character of the price system that enthusiasts for deliberative democracy dislike most about markets. From a Hayekian perspective, however, this impersonality should not be seen as purely a product of market capitalism but is an inevitable feature of an advanced mass society. It may, therefore, be misplaced to attack supposedly 'abstract', 'disempowering' systems such as the market, as Habermasian theorists are prone to do, and to suggest that we can rely on discursive face-to-face contacts as a significant co-ordinating mechanism in other than a context of very small groups.

Moreover, even if it is accepted that discursive co-ordination may be possible in small group settings, the epistemological problems raised by the Hayekian critique are raised again when the thorny issue of inter-community co-ordination is confronted. The economies and environments of different local communities are inter-linked in a myriad of flows, which may be far too complex to enable co-ordination through conscious means. This problem is clearly evident in Healey's work, which for all the emphasis on local participation remains wedded to the notion of 'strategic planning' to 'integrate' what might otherwise be a disparate and inconsistent set of local agendas. If complex inter-community relations are not to be co-ordinated through impersonal market forces, then at some point recourse must be made to some central political authority to perform a co-ordinating role – a position that would seem radically at odds with the goal of 'empowering' local communities. It is precisely this sort of planning, which the Hayekian account and the actual experience of attempts at 'integrated land use policies' suggest are prone to the severe epistemological difficulties discussed above.

None of this is to suggest that *no* information can successfully be communicated via public discourse and debate. As Hayek himself repeatedly emphasised, language and discourse are also a form of spontaneous order, which evolve without conscious social control (Hayek, 1973, 1988). Moreover, Healey and those writers in the 'industrial districts' literature (e.g. Amin and Thrift, 1995b) are correct to emphasise the importance of verbal communication, for example, in business networks, as a means of transmitting valuable economic information and disseminating innovation. Gossip, for example, is often an important source of knowledge about new techniques, prices and production processes as well as about the plans of competitors. These processes have not been lost on Austrian School theorists. Desroches (1998) has argued that it is precisely because of the advantages of accessing such localised verbal knowledge that firms in a given industry often have a propensity to locate in close proximity to one another, in order to tap into knowledge of this sort. What is at issue from a Hayekian perspective, however, is that there are important limits to the amount and type of information that can successfully be communicated in this way.

Verbal knowledge communication in contexts such as business networks and in others such as the process of academic debate is effective in so far as it is focused on a relatively narrow and circumscribed set of issues. In academia, for example, discursive knowledge transmission is possible because the terms of debate tend to be confined within what are fairly tight theoretical and disciplinary boundaries (Shearmur, 1996). Severe problems arise, however, when attempts to communicate knowledge and to co-ordinate decision-making through discursive means are extended to much wider, more complex sets of issues. This is, however precisely what collaborative planning, in terms of the strategic planning of urban/regional economies, attempts to achieve. The range, complexity and inter-relatedness of the issues and co-ordinative processes in hand are of a magnitude far too extensive to rely on conscious deliberation. In the context of land use plan-ning, this problem appears particularly evident with regard to the ongoing debate over 'optimal urban form'. The planning literature is polarised between those advo-cating 'compact settlement' approaches as the best way to tackle problems of urban pollution and congestion (Report of the Urban Taskforce, 1999) and those who favour a more low-density alternative (Gordon and Richardson, 1997). From a Hayekian, point of view none of the relevant planners may genuinely be in a posi-tion to judge the 'optimal' policy response, because the range of inter-connected variables that contribute to the quality of urban life may be far too complex to rely on conscious co-ordination.

Seen through a Hayekian lens, collaborative planning over-estimates the extent to which social co-ordination can be brought about by deliberative means, a problem that is perhaps reflected by the vague and often contradictory usage of the 'sustainable development' discourse in much planning documentation. In turn, it is because of these epistemological limits that we may need to rely more on impersonal markets. The constant process of positive and negative feedback embodied in prices facilitates a process of mutual self-adjustment between people who never actually meet *and cannot* know in sufficient detail the precise circum-stances of others. What is still more serious, however, from a Hayekian point of view, is that the institutional arrangements advocated in collaborative planning may actually *reduce* information flows and hence thwart the desired process of inter-subjective social learning.

At the core of Hayek's critique of planning is his emphasis on the signific-ance of *tacit knowledge*. This refers to time- and place-specific information that cannot be articulated in verbal form. Certain varieties of tacit knowledge may be contained within social institutions such as tradition or custom and may be regarded in some sense as a collective social asset. There is, however, a larger body of such information, which is inherently private in character – knowledge of the phenomenal pictures that exist within the individual mind and which no one else discerns. This species of tacit knowledge is epitomised in a person or group of persons 'being in the right place at the right time', exhibiting 'flair and intuition', 'knowing a particular market' and constitutes the essence of creative entrepreneur-ship (Hayek, 1948c; Polanyi, 1951). Faced with the same set of 'facts' some indi-viduals will perceive creative opportunities, where others see nothing.

According to Hayek, individuals are most likely to be able to deploy their per-sonal fund of tacit knowledge for social good, when they are the least constrained by collective decision procedures in which this knowledge is likely to be diluted or lost. If tacit knowledge is to be put to effective social use, then people need a private sphere, institutionalised through property rights and market competition in which they can make decisions solely on their own judgement, at their own risk and to succeed or fail accordingly. This is not to suggest that none of the relevant knowledge can be articulated in a group context. Collective forms of decision abound in all aspects of life, such as in company boardrooms, for example. What is crucial, however, is that there are clear lines of responsibility linking decisions and the relevant knowledge to specific individuals/groups, so that people have a clear feedback mechanism to learn about the quality of their own decisions and know-ledge. Private property rights and the account of profit and loss provide such a link and hence facilitate social learning. In addition, property rights provide people with the space to try out eccentric and innovative ideas the merits/demerits of which people occupying other phenomenal spaces cannot discern but which, once put into practice may prove successful. Knowledge of this sort cannot be communi-cated by verbal means, but is only revealed through *action* (Hayek, 1948c; Polanyi, 1951). It is only when private projects are put into practice that the relevant information is revealed. A learning process may then be set in motion as previously indiscernible successes are imitated and previously indiscernible errors can be avoided (Hayek, 1978; Kirzner, 1985).

From a Hayekian perspective, attempts to 'expand the scope of the public sphere' through the extension of further social democratic controls over private property rights may act to dilute tacit knowledge. Seen in this context, references to the significance of such knowledge by Healey in defence of discursive democracy are surprising, since by definition much of the relevant knowledge cannot be com-municated via linguistic means. If individuals are consistently allowed to veto the exercise of private property rights through majoritarian democracy then the relevant discovery process may be thwarted as the range of possible plans that may be implemented is reduced. Equally, the extension of third party decision rights to actors who are not themselves held financially responsible for their actions, blurs the lines of responsibility linking the use of knowledge to outcomes and hence may inhibit social learning. The greater the extension of social democratic controls over property rights, the more difficult it becomes for people to judge which particular bits of knowledge are most appropriate to the tasks in hand. This is, from a

Hayekian perspective, part of a more general deficiency caused by the over-extension of social democratic mechanisms. In general, it is much easier to generate clear feedback signals and to assess cause and effect relationships in a market context, such as the link between product quality and a particular producer, than it is to link the quality of complex social outcomes to public policy decisions.

The repeated emphasis on the importance of consensus building in collaborative planning is also problematic from a Hayekian point of view. If no new actions are to be allowed to proceed until there is a majoritarian consensus (a major feat in itself given the difficulties of securing consensus even in small group settings such as the running of academic departments or company boardrooms), then innovation and entrepreneurship are likely to be thwarted. The essence of creative entrepreneurship in the economy and other contexts such as science is to break with the consensus position. Learning and innovation, therefore, may be more likely to occur in a situation of ongoing dissensus.[4] For all the emphasis on the importance of diversity by collaborative planning advocates, it is hard to see how such diversity would be possible if majoritarian consensus is to be the primary decision rule. In the case of British land use planning, for example, there is already evidence that the nationalisation of development rights may have thwarted experimentation in such fields as building and architectural design. It is difficult for innovative and radical new designs to receive planning permission since these must first be approved by an array of planners and political committees that are inclined towards conservatism and preservation of the status quo (Evans, 1988, 1991). A similar lack of experimentation has also been evident with respect to the question of urban form. The often blanket emphasis on 'urban containment' appears to have prevented experimentation with a range of competing urban forms, that might have delivered as yet unforeseen environmental benefits (Pennington, 1999, 2000). There comes a point, therefore, where the use of the 'voice' mechanisms that characterise collective decision procedures needs to be backed up by the 'exit' mechanisms that are more evident in private markets (Hirschman, 1970).

It is this emphasis on experimentation that ultimately constitutes the core of the Hayekian case in favour of markets and competition and against the advocacy of consensus building in Habermasian thought. The Hayekian case for the market does not rest on a narrowly instrumental conception of rationality where knowledge of ends and means is given. On the contrary, it is based on the need for an open-ended process of experimentation to discover both ends and means in an uncertain world, where it is difficult enough for people to comprehend their own interests, let alone the 'public interest'. As Hayek (1948d: 101) puts it, to participate in a market economy is to participate in 'a voyage of exploration of the unknown, an attempt to discover new ways of doing things better than they have been done before'. Preferences in this sense are not given but are constantly shaped and reshaped as the process of experimentation in the market unwinds. Each new product/mode of organisation is an attempt to challenge existing preferences and to alert people to new opportunities and ways of living. In turn, it is the process of market competition that allows for a wider variety of options to be presented to people, from which they may then choose. The market economy does not act to maximise or optimise any thing or to fulfil a single hierarchy of ends (Hayek, 1978; Buchanan and Vanberg, 1991). Rather, it provides a forum for experimentation and enables a degree of co-ordination between people with disparate and perhaps inconsistent plans. The market process, therefore, acts as a form of 'surrogate debate', that for the epistemological reasons outlined previously, facilitates a wider range of options to be tried and tested than might ever be achieved through the processes of formal political communication (Shearmur, 1996).

In the light of this analysis, the traditional concerns of the Left over excessive inequality and unequal 'power relations' may, from a Hayekian point of view, be better addressed through redistributive taxation rather than attempts to restrict private property rights and to transform the process of decision-making itself along social democratic lines. In this way, greater equality in material resources would allow the subjective values of those individuals with previously low incomes to be given greater weight in an otherwise free market. Hayek was not opposed to a measure of income redistribution so long as the purpose of this was not to deliver aggregate, rationalist concepts such as 'social justice', which are subject to many of the same epistemological problems as central economic planning.

A PROPERTY RIGHTS ALTERNATIVE TO COLLABORATIVE PLANNING

Unlike collaborative planning, the Hayekian arguments sketched in this chapter suggest a case for minimising the scope of conscious deliberation and planning in land use and other social affairs. The important question remains, however, to what extent can markets be relied upon to deliver those goods and in particular those environmental goods that are often considered susceptible to 'market failure'? From a Hayekian liberal perspective, while there is likely to remain an important category of such goods, these are not as extensive as is often thought and there is much more potential to rely on property rights approaches than is commonly recognised. Just as collaborative planning tends to over-estimate the potential of discursive political communication, so it under-estimates the range of areas where markets might operate successfully.

The key to understanding the potential of property rights approaches is to recognise that the market process continually offers opportunities for institutional/property rights entrepreneurs to find ways of overcoming the high transaction costs and to internalise the externalities that are the principal causes of market failure. As Anderson and Leal (1991) have argued, any case of external benefits/costs may provide fertile ground for an entrepreneur who can devise new ways of defining property rights and of converting what are currently collective/public goods into private marketable commodities. Seen from this perspective, the role of the state should be confined to facilitative functions, to the enforcement of private contractual bargains and to the provision of a legal system, which adjudicates disputed property rights in courts.

One example of this property rights approach in a land use context is the use of private covenants and deed restrictions. Such privatised/contractual forms of planning had a long history of use in Britain before the advent of statutory land use regulation. Many of the urban developments in Westminster, Hampstead and Oxford, for example, were created through the use of private restrictive covenants (West, 1969). In these cases, developers specify in contracts the activities to be permitted with respect to a particular set of properties for sale, in order to inter-nalise external effects and to capture the returns through higher asset prices. These contractual devices included restrictions on the use of open spaces, noise, chimney smoke and permitted alterations to exterior design. Such approaches facilitate the creation of markets in amenity values and may allow a creative discov-ery process to unfold, as individuals choose between competing developments, which offer different bundles of contractual restrictions and their associated exter-nalities.

In a more recent innovation, Foldvary (1994) has advanced the idea of the proprietary community as a way for markets to deal with land use externalities and collective goods. Foldvary argues that many collective goods are in practice 'terri-torial goods' and are excludable by definition. The benefits of a scenic view or open space, for example, can often be 'tied in' to the provision of other goods, such as leisure or the purchase of residential environments. So long as the relevant area is privately owned by an individual or group/co-operative, people must reveal their preferences to gain access to such goods and the 'free rider problem' can be resolved (see also Buchanan and Stubblebine, 1962, for a similar approach).

The collective facilities provided by private shopping malls provide a small-scale example of this 'tie-in' concept. Shopping centre merchants provide an array of collective goods through the market, such as malls, security forces, parking lots and a pleasant shopping environment, 'tied in' to the purchase of private merchan-dise. While competitors could, in theory, enter the market offering comparable private goods at a lower price by not 'tying in' a surcharge for the collective goods

(Varian, 1994), there are many goods whose value is *contingent* on being provided as part of a package deal (Buchanan and Stubblebine, 1962; Demsetz, 1964; Foldvary, 1994; Schmidtz, 1994). Thus, shopping centre merchants who do not provide car parking or a litter collection service, might well be able to charge less for food, but they will also lose the custom of those who value these services (witness the trend from town centre to out of town shopping in Britain). Likewise, a housing developer who fails to provide a package of restrictive covenants to protect amenity values may lose custom to those competitors who do so. As Schmidtz (1994: 535) put it:

> One does not have to be a visionary to realise that market forces can in theory provide shopping malls, but the point is that there is no a priori reason why similar structural tie-ins could not lead to the provision of a variety of other public goods as well.

The property rights approach set out above is not dissimilar to the proposals for 'common property regimes' outlined by authors such as Ostrom (1990). In the proprietary community model individuals are, in effect, contracting into a set of collective or shared private property rights offered for profit by institutional entrepreneurs (Nelson, 1977; Foldvary, 1994).[5] In the proprietary community model people enter into a voluntary contract to sacrifice complete control over decisions relating to their property to the principles of governance laid down in the proprietary contract. The communities examined by Foldvary (1994), for example, marketed 'constitutional provisions' for the settlement of neighbourhood disputes and laid down a set of rules and procedures (voting rules, etc.), by which the members of the community could change the terms of collective control.[6]

The great advantage of the proprietary community model, therefore, is that it may facilitate competition and experimentation between different communities and lifestyles offering various bundles of collective and individual private property rights and different rules for community management on a range of territorial scales. Which particular mix of individual and common property rights works best cannot be known in advance, but may be discovered over time through a process of entrepreneurial trial and error in the market. In addition, while allowing an element of collective control, the property rights approach provides a clear feedback link to the knowledge and decisions of institutional/property rights entrepreneurs through the account of profit and loss, facilitates consumer choice between an array of property rights structures and hence enables the conditions for social learning.

The proprietary community model may also offer advantages over local authority-based forms of governance. Local authority boundaries have, in many cases, been imposed on communities for reasons which have little to do with their efficacy in delivering services and improving environmental quality (Foldvary, 1994). One advantage of a property rights approach, therefore, would be to facilitate the formation of proprietary communities on a voluntary, contractual basis, with competition allowing a process of entrepreneurial discovery to reveal the scale of community governance best suited to the management of land use externalities. Just as the optimum size of a firm is not something that can be known in advance of competition, so the optimum scale of a proprietary community or common property regime must be discovered and rediscovered through a process of organisational trial and error within the market.

From a Hayekian perspective property rights approaches such as those above (for a more detailed analysis, see Pennington, 1999, 2000), may help to internalise externalities and facilitate trade in environmental goods by bringing environmental values within the market system. In doing so, they may allow for a high degree of institutional experimentation and enable a degree of co-ordination that might not be possible via deliberate social planning. Rather than seeking consciously to 'integrate' the actions of a range of diverse actors into a holistic strategic plan, the property rights approach may facilitate a wider variety of plans on a range of territorial scales. These plans may then be co-ordinated through a process of mutual self-adjustment in the market as the prices paid for differing bundles of property rights indicate, at least to some extent, the relative value placed on environmental assets by dispersed individuals who may never actually meet. As such, the property rights approach may be more in tune with the principles of self-organisation that characterise complex social and environmental systems, than the conscious model of deliberative democracy advocated by collaborative planning.

Notwithstanding the untapped potential for property rights approaches, it must be recognised that there is likely to remain an important category of goods where market failure may indeed remain pervasive. Prime candidates would appear to be those large-scale trans-boundary goods such as air quality management and bio-diversity preservation, where prohibitive transaction costs seem likely to be the norm. In these circumstances, the Hayekian perspective is *not* opposed to a role for the state in laying down a set of environmental standards within which the market can be allowed to operate. Moreover, the forms of deliberative democracy advocated by collaborative planning may well provide the most appropriate decision-making mechanism to decide what these minimal standards should be. For the epistemological reasons outlined in this chapter, deliberative approaches are more likely to be effective if they are pared back to such narrowly defined functions. What is crucial, however, is that beyond laying down such basic regulatory rules, no attempt should be made to co-ordinate land uses according to some holistic plan. Rather, from a Hayekian point of view, the maximum scope should be allowed for experimentation and innovative property rights solutions to facilitate co-ordination via the spontaneous forces of markets.

CONCLUSION

The previous pages have sought to analyse the contribution of Habermasian col-laborative planning to contemporary land use and environmental problems, from the perspective of Hayekian Liberalism. The resulting critique suggests that the model of deliberative democracy advocated by authors such as Healey, while rep-resenting an improvement on purely technocratic forms of decision-making, is neglectful of the informational and co-ordinative limits of discursive political processes. In addition, the analysis suggests that many of the normative institu-tional arrangements advocated by collaborative planning may be at odds with much of its epistemological basis. More specifically, recognition of the holistic and systemic nature of economic and environmental problems does not imply support for attempts to manage such problems on a similarly holistic basis. On the con-trary, the inherent complexity and inter-relatedness of these issues may mean that they are often beyond the effective scope of conscious social control. In order to facilitate the process of inter-subjective learning that is desired in Habermasian thought, therefore, it may be more appropriate to rely as far as is possible on impersonal, self-regulating markets. These markets are, of course, far from perfect institutions and will always rely on an institutional framework of rules, which must predominantly be provided by the state. What precisely the ideal institutional framework is within which markets can function most effectively is a matter for ongoing empirical inquiry. What is apparent from the analysis presented in this chapter, however, is that proposals to subject markets to a still greater array of social democratic controls are unlikely to be appropriate to the task.

NOTES

1   This would appear to reflect a tendency for many academic planners to regard Hayek as a free market polemicist and to associate him with the case for cruder versions of 'Thatcherism' – see Thornley (1991). In so far as analysts are acquainted with Hayek, this knowledge seems confined to well-known polemics such as *The Road to Serfdom* (1944) and to a lesser extent *The Constitution of Liberty* (1960). As a con-sequence, the vast bulk of Hayek's work on the philosophy of social science, evolu-tionary psychology, the methodology of economics and the theory of the market process remain lost on the majority of the planning community – though they are much better known within economics and political science. This is an unfortunate

state of affairs, especially when one considers that in works such as 'Individualism: True and False' (1948b), *The Sensory Order* (1952) and *The Counter-Revolution of Science* (1957), Hayek was advocating the rejection of positivist neo-classical economics in favour of a hermeneutic and even 'post-modern' approach (Burczak, 1994) decades before the surge of interest in such approaches within the wider social sciences.

2   In the Austrian account of markets – *all* individuals, whether manager/entrepreneurs, workers or consumers are considered to act *entrepreneurially* – i.e. that they exhibit a sensitivity or alertness to new opportunities and instances of dis-co-ordination such as spotting the potential demand for a new product, or the existence of alternative job opportunities or sources of cheaper products, etc.

3   While epistemologically and conceptually distinct, there is an important link to be made from a classical liberal perspective between Hayekian arguments against planning and those of the public choice theorists – it is because of the epistemic difficulties of knowing what the 'public interest' actually is that individuals tend to act according to the interests that they are *more likely* to know, i.e. *their own* interests and those of their immediate circle.

4   The Hayekian perspective is in this sense notably closer to a postmodern analysis than the Habermasian approach of collaborative planning.

5   As is now widely recognised in the property rights literature, 'common property' regimes are radically different from the 'open access' regimes that are associated with the 'Tragedy of the Commons'. The latter refers to a situation where a resource or asset lacks any form of organisational structure to manage the resource in question (Ostrom, 1990). 'Common property' regimes, however, refer to a position where a resource is managed by some form of co-operative organisation. McKean and Ostrom (1995) have described 'common property' regimes as approximating a model of shared private ownership.

6   There is, of course, a possibility that such rules could be used for purposes, such as the creation of racist or homophobic communities, the worst excesses of which might not wish to be tolerated by a liberal state.

11

Conclusion

Communicative Planning, Collaborative Planning and the Post-Positivist Planning Theory Landscape
Mark Tewdwr-Jones and Philip Allmendinger

since 1980's

The emerging paradigm of communicative or collaborative planning has dominated theoretical discourse since the early 1980s. Rather than one coherent position there are a variety of schools that vary in their emphasis on different aspects of social and critical theory and their mixture of analyses and prescription. Critiques of communicative planning have been scarce and have largely challenged or questioned specific aspects rather than critiquing the paradigm as a whole. In the conclusion to this book, we identify broad themes that have emerged from a variety of sources and explore their relationship to collaborative planning theory. These themes do not, in our opinion, threaten to undermine collaborative planning but present questions that need to be addressed. In undertaking a dialectical engagement with such critiques, collaborative planning theory will be strengthened and made more attractive to practitioners – an audience that has expressed an interest in taking up such ideas.

INTRODUCTION

According to a number of authors there is an emerging consensus that the communicative or collaborative turn is now the paradigm that dominates urban planning theory (e.g. Innes, 1995; Mandelbaum, 1996; Alexander, 1997). The communicative turn has certainly dominated theoretical discourse since the late 1980s and has begun to spurn a number of interpretations and investigations beyond the original core proponents. But it has also undergone a number of mutations as 'planning through debate' (Healey, 1992a), 'communicative planning' (Healey, 1993a; Innes, 1995), 'argumentative planning' (Fischer and Forester, 1993), 'collaborative planning' (Healey, 1997a) and 'deliberative planning' (Forester, 1999d). It has also developed in different directions as a consequence of stemming from various intellectual schools of thought that have intertwined with the communicative approach, including neo-pragmatics (Harper and Stein, 1995a), critical theory (Forester, 1993), Foucauldian perspectives (Flyvbjerg, 1998b), and planning practice (Hoch,

1992). It has also overlapped academic concern relating to governance processes and policy ideas and institutional structures that have attempted to pin down, after Giddens, a 'new institutionalism' (Amin and Thrift, 1995a; Amin and Hausner, 1997; Painter and Goodwin, 1995).

In its latest manifestations, the communicative turn has been referred to as 'collaborative planning' in the UK literature (Healey, 1997a) and 'deliberative planning' in the US literature (Forester, 1999c). In a UK context, the collaborative planning approach is seen as fitting in with the *Zeitgeist* of global economic restructuring and local responses – a method for deepening institutional capacity and helping communities to compete for foreign direct investment (Healey, 1998b). It has also overlapped with notions of a 'third way', trumpeted as the ideological underpinnings in the UK of the New Labour government (Giddens, 1998, 2000), echoing concerns over participation, empowerment and partnership. This is occurring as part of 'a wave of intellectual reformulation which is sweeping across the social sciences in general' (Healey, 1999b). This wave has moved on from earlier views that saw it viewed explicitly as a means of assessing the personal dilemmas of the individual in day-to-day urban planning contexts by promoting debate (Forester, 1989; Healey, 1992a, 1992b; Innes, 1992; but cf. Tewdwr-Jones and Thomas, 1998) and as a way of promoting social justice and environmental sustainability (Healey, 1992b). What we today refer to as the communicative or collaborative turn in urban planning is in actuality a range of different theoretical pulses allied together by Habermasian and/or Giddensian thinking.

Differences in interpretation of the collaborative approach highlight one of a number of problems in trying to make any assessment of the communicative turn, as the contributions to this book have proved. That it is to say, there is not one turn but a multitude of approaches that focus on such a level of generality as to preclude detailed analysis and practical application. But questions over interpretation have been largely bypassed (often quite unintentionally) in the rush to fill the conceptual gap in urban planning left by the instrumental rational basis to theory and the New Right philosophical questioning of planning during the 1980s and 1990s.

The largely enthusiastic reception that has greeted the communicative and collaborative turn in urban planning has started to be accompanied by attempts to both question the theory and develop it further through fine tuning (Huxley, 1998a; Huxley and Yiftachel, 1998; Tewdwr-Jones and Allmendinger, 1998; Hillier, 2000; Phelps and Tewdwr-Jones, 2000). These attempts have not sought to undermine the rationale for a theory of collaborative planning (as has been suggested in some quarters), but rather have attempted to continually question the approach, justifications utilised and models presented in an attempt to progress debate.

In a paper published in 1998 (Tewdwr-Jones and Allmendinger, 1998), we highlighted some concerns with the development of the paradigm and called on protagonists of the theories to clarify their position in relation to, essentially, three issues: the power component; the problem of application to a governmental context; and the problems of individualism and the multitude of social actions that can occur within or beneath collaborative planning ideas. Healey (1999b) responded to her critics on many of these issues and provided some useful explanations of the uncertainties. The debate has moved forward, but some of these uncertainties are nevertheless still apparent, and various themes are continually being explored by academics. This chapter attempts to categorise the present uncertainties with the collaborative turn by bringing together and reviewing the work of the contributors to this volume. The rationale of this chapter is to assist students and practitioners of urban planning to make sense of these difficulties, to debate the possibilities, and to move forward by developing collaborative theory and other planning movements through further fine tuning.

ENCES BETWEEN COMMUNICATIVE PLANNING AND BORATIVE PLANNING

The first issue to consider is the idea that there is just one paradigm known as the 'communicative turn' in urban planning. Various names have been used to describe the communicative turn over the past twenty years as we mentioned in the Introduction. This diversity in part represents a normal evolution of theoretical thinking but it is also due to significant differences between the theoretical bases of different forms of the communicative turn. The mixture of these two components – evolution and difference – makes pinning down the idea of communicative planning problematic, as Harris discussed in Chapter 2. Indeed, any exegesis is almost impossible given a third ingredient: the use of vague and amorphous terms across the theoretical pulses. For example, Norris defines the basis to communicative rationality as a situation where 'communication will no longer be distorted by the effects of power, self-interest or ignorance' (1985: 149) while Healey (1992b) talks of collaborative planning as involving an 'interactive and interpretative process undertaken among diverse and fluid discourse communities'. At this level of generality, it is difficult to disagree with the sentiments expressed but their meaning and implications remain obscure and contentious (Hooper, 1982). As Ball (1998: 1512) has noted in relation to Healey's work, for example, 'the emphasis is on structure and agency, yet no precise definition is given of what constitutes a "structure", an "agency" or an "institution" '.

This ambiguity concerning structure and agency is particularly problematic

Discourse- Communication, debate

as some of the theoretical pulses draw heavily upon structuration theory. Following Giddens (1984) in particular, some forms of collaborative planning theory focus attention on the idea of structural and individual influences upon outcomes in planning. As Tewdwr-Jones discussed in Chapter 4, planning is a constraint upon individual action though individual action may alter the form of constraint. Healey emphasises this when she comments that Giddens' structuration, 'offers a social theory which helps to interpret individual ways of being in the context of social constraints' (1997a: 44). This ambiguity in the institutional foundations to the collaborative planning approach is also not assisted by the existence of two broad collaborative schools that each place different emphasis on aspects of the institutional framework. Both Healey and Forester draw heavily upon Habermas's idea that democracy should revolve around the transformation rather than the simple aggregation of preferences (Elster, 1998: 1). However, Forester combines these ideas with neo-pragmatic philosophical foundations while Healey remains firmly rooted in Habermas's concern to finish the 'unfinished project of modernity'. This has implications on the outlook of the two approaches.

Forester's earlier work (for example, Forester, 1989) is more concerned with analysing the systematic distortions in communication from the abstract reference point of ideal speech as developed by Habermas. Distortions reflect structural influences (e.g. inequalities of income and wealth) as well as more individual factors (e.g. the personal pursuit of power). Thus, although Forester is concerned with structural influences upon daily action, it is the day-to-day cut and thrust of communication that forms the basis of his analysis. Healey, on the other hand, takes a less critical theory position and uses Giddens' structuration as a basis for her analysis of social reproduction and uses Habermas's ideal speech as both abstract benchmark and a guide for planners to follow.

This difference between the two approaches not only reflects different personal understandings but also reflects the different experiences and focus of each – Forester's emphasis is on the USA with its fragmented federal planning framework reliant on more informal negotiation while Healey's experience is of more formal institutional arenas for mediation typical of the UK system which have often constrained the development of participatory processes (Healey, 1998, 1999b). Consequently, Healey's collaborative planning is more concerned with the transformative influence upon existing structures (in the institutional sense) while Forester's communicative planning focuses more on agency and the mechanisms and direct outcomes of inter-personal relations.

Notwithstanding these differences, what is important to note here are the different aspects of the communicative turn that are inherent in the theoretical pulses to date: communicative planning as *analysis* (comparing discursive distortion with an abstract ideal situation), communicative planning as _prescription_ (how we should 'go about' planning so as to challenge and avoid such distortions) and communicative planning as _normative theory_ (the values that underpin deliberation as a form of collective decision-making over, for example, aggregate methods). While these aspects of the communicative turn make pinning down the various pulses of the paradigm problematic, it is possible to map a general landscape and some common features, relating to:

> collective decision making with the participation of all those who will be affected by the decision or their representatives [and] decision making by arguments offered _by_ and _to_ participants who are committed to the values of rationality and impartiality.
>
> (Elster, 1998: 8).

GUIDES AND IMPEDIMENTS TO COLLABORATIVE ACTION IN PLANNING

The basis for any attempt to translate the ideas of the collaborative turn into practice (i.e. the practical application of the approach through prescription) must rest on locally contingent and generated processes as there can be no _a priori_ imposition or model (Healey, 1997a: 268–269). However, Healey suggests that process invention and communication or collaboration can be aided by the use of and reflection upon four 'guides'. These are: the process of 'getting started'; routines and discussions; making policy discourses; and maintaining consensus. We now turn to briefly address each of these 'guides'.

Getting started: initiators, stakeholders and arenas

Urban planners do not seem to figure here but 'initiators' can be taken to be an amorphous group of actors who take the responsibility to launch any process including those who might have a stake in decision-making and the issue of where discussion might take place. Existing political and administrative procedures may be part of the communication problem through their masking of power relations and distorted communication. They can be changed, however, when an 'opportunity' arises and participants start to agitate and organise for a different structure or goals. Once this has commenced, then the 'initiators' can begin to decide who to include in the discourse of the new or emerging arena and how to proceed. How this is carried out varies depending on the situation but there is a lot of discretion left to the 'initiator' particularly in enforcing a form of rules early on in the process before established powers and interests shape it to suit them. This links to the teleological action in social relations that might be inherent within communicative action debated elsewhere (see Phelps and Tewdwr-Jones, 2000). The matter to take into consideration here is that there remains the possibility for initiator-led distortion through the design of communicative processes and by 'nesting' all other types of social action, even if the initiator as openly signed up to the process of undistorted forms of communicative action.

Routines and styles of discussion

'Opening out' discussions to explore their boundaries as they are perceived by different actors is important as is questioning 'accepted' assumptions and 'truths' and learning about each other's interests, hopes and fears. Healey identifies three particular aspects of this process that require attention: style; language and representation. The *style* of discussion that ensures everyone has a voice and is heard through sensitivity to cultural differences, room arrangements, who speaks and when. *Representation* refers to the different ways in which participants are 'called up' to speak and to prevent those 'not present' from being 'absent' from the discussion (1997a: 275). The *language* that each participant uses gives respect to each other while avoiding ambiguous imagery or misleading statements. The Habermasian-inspired communicative turn rests on the notion of undistorted communication, of course. But we wish to broaden this notion in the development of the communicative turn in urban planning to recognise the possible incorporation of communicative *action*, as well as language, in the style of discussion. This reflects the potential for the fact that action may not always be in conformity to language utilised, the opinions expressed and decisions made. The communicative turn is founded on the principle of truth and honesty and openness. Healey's (1999b) notion that the theory is rooted in power recognition and politics and is intended to counteract existing power relations is accepted. But decision-making processes rest on political (with a small 'p') will, whether they are part of existing institutional processes or new processes intended to facilitate openness and inclusiveness in participation. Essentially, we are considering to what extent the communicative turn in planning becomes, by its very nature, a political process accompanied by the trappings of political strategic behaviour. The communicative turn, in attempting to create consensus-building strategies, will develop an inherent politicisation and could even transfigure into the sort of effort the new system was designed to counteract as Pennington discussed in Chapter 10.

Making policy discourses

A more 'open' approach will undoubtedly throw up a lot of information, opinions, facts, views, etc. which need to be organised somehow. Normally this is filtered through the technical planning arena into a planning biased point which 'smooths out' or blunts the different discourses. This process needs to be less technical and more richly textured to allow for different views to be maintained. This can be achieved through a mutual sifting exercise. But, as Healey points out, how can a strategy emerge from such an open process? The answer is not clear but it appears to rely on a collective decision-making process that does not 'close off' options but works through different scenarios and their consequences. From this will emerge a 'preferred' policy discourse which will have been collaboratively chosen.

Maintaining the consensus

Ownership of the strategy should have emerged through the collaborative and open process described above even though it may disadvantage some. However, as new participants emerge and situations change, then the more formalised institutional arrangements become useful in enforcing the consensus. Courts provide an arena for arbitration if required though their operation and remit will need to be agreed by the participants.

Following on from this brief review of the four guide components to the collaborative turn in urban planning, we wish to discuss the critiques of the paradigm as they have developed to date. These critiques can be distinguished into several broad camps covering a number of schools of thought and stem from the previously discussed contributions to this volume. We concentrate here on two salient issues: paradigmatic and praxis dimensions. We feel each of these dimensions need to be dissected and debated further in order to move forward with planning theorising.

PARADIGMATIC RELATIONSHIPS BETWEEN COLLABORATIVE PLANNING AND POST-POSITIVIST THEORIES

Harris outlined the broad landscape of the communicative and collaborative turn in planning in Chapter 2 and we attempted to explain both the differences and features of the collaborative approach earlier in this chapter. We now wish to turn to a number of themes that have emerged from a deeper study of the approach before trying to show how these could be addressed through a different interpretation of the structure–agency foundations. We have tried to steer away from purely normative critiques and, instead, we have focused on two more substantive issues as well as some implications of the collaborative turn for theory and practice.

The paradigmatic dimension

There is a longing for urban planning and urban planning theorists to provide an overarching theoretical understanding and prescription for planning – a desire that has been ridiculed for some time (Reade, 1987) and, according to some postmodern critiques, should not be attempted at all (see Oranje, Chapter 9). Following the collapse of the comprehensive–rational approach in urban planning theory, championed by Faludi (1973, 1987) and others, and its criticisms by neo-Marxists (e.g. Scott and Roweis, 1977), it is not surprising to hear the claim at the present time that there is a new paradigm emerging around which both academics and practitioners can unite (e.g. Innes, 1995). The various chapters in this book undermine this notion. Margo Huxley in Chapter 7 also argues that this claim goes too far and disputes the existence of such a paradigm in the light of evidence to the contrary (see also Huxley and Yiftachel, 1998). Huxley and Yiftachel's argument is that, if we were to think in terms of paradigms in the Kuhnian sense, the dominant paradigm would still be instrumental rationality that pervades practice. As one of us has argued elsewhere, there is a complex accretion of different rationalities that pervades planning practice in the UK (Allmendinger, 1998; 2001). However, it could be the case that the collaborative turn is a dominant *theoretical* paradigm. It seems that there has been a great deal written about the collaborative approach and from a number of influential and productive sources. However, there are also healthy debates occurring around other urban planning theories that have been overshadowed by the collaborative turn, including neo-liberal and project-led planning, discussed by Mark Pennington in Chapter 10 (Evans, 1988, 1991; Ehrman, 1990; Lewis, 1992; Pennington, 1996), postmodern planning, discussed by Mark Oranje in Chapter 9 and (to a lesser extent) Flyvbjerg and Richardson in Chapter 3 (Beauregard, 1989; Sandercock, 1998c; Allmendinger, 1998, 2001), neo-pragmatism, discussed by Phil Harrison in Chapter 8 (Hoch, 1984, 1996, 1997a; Harrison, 1998), in addition to critical realist/political economy approaches (e.g. Ambrose, 1994; Feldman, 1995, 1997). We would also argue that the term 'paradigm' is one that urban planning needs to understand better and one that can help cast some more light on the collaborative turn.

It was by no means clear what Kuhn (1970) actually meant by the term paradigm and there needs to be leniency in interpreting an approach that was aimed more at the natural as opposed to social sciences. Many of the claims of Kuhn, in particular his emphasis on subjective rather than objective bases to knowledge, will be familiar to social scientists steeped in two decades of postmodern and poststructural critique. But the central idea of the paradigmatic understanding of theory is one that seemingly captures the spirit of urban planning theory generally as well as the growth and position of collaborative planning.

Kuhn's paradigms are broadly a dominant common understanding of a field that shapes concepts, perceptions and styles of reasoning to create a community of research. The dominant paradigm remains so until it can no longer provide answers to certain questions when alternative challenging paradigms emerge. Competing paradigms are often incommensurable because of their opposing world views, leading to ruptures in scientific knowledge that are only resolved once one paradigm gains ascendancy through gaining wider community support. The image of a left-leaning substantive explanatory and prescriptive theory emerging out of the neo-liberal, anti-planning morass of the 1980s certainly appears attractive.

In addition to the existence of a plethora of competing theories identified above, there are some important other critiques of the idea and image of paradigm. Most prominently Feyerabend (1961, 1970, 1978, 1988), Lakatos (1978), Longino (1990) and Barnes and Bloor (1982) have all provided important perspectives and developments on the broad Kuhnian theme of paradigms. First, there is the question of the implicit normative assumptions within much of scientific knowledge and the extent to which researchers never depend solely upon empirical data but are swayed both in their choice of theory, interpretation and presentation of facts by external factors such as values. This is perpetuated by the existence of what Barnes and Bloor (1982) term a 'strong programme' – similar to Kuhn's paradigms but emphasising the normative underpinnings of theory – that inculcates students into regurgitating theories to pass exams and academics into publishing academic work. The communicative and collaborative turn in planning is not simply a theory but a 'world view' based on a participatory perspective of democracy and either a suspicion of or a more balanced attempt to situate free-market economies: 'Its context [is] planning as a democratic enterprise aimed at promoting social justice and environmental sustainability' (Healey, 1997a: 233).

The turn's normative elements are embedded within this perspective to the level that, 'Adoption or rejection of Habermas' theory depends more on holistic judgements at the level of social theory than a piecemeal acceptance of successive philosophical arguments' (Outhwaite, 1994: 109). This is the position which both the analytical and prescriptive aspects of communicative planning are now reaching – a 'strong programme' comprised of seemingly empirically based and rational arguments. The danger here is that this strong programme could start to mask deep-seated normative values and 'crowd out' other ways of thinking and acting.

Second, Feyerabend criticises Kuhn's conception of paradigms as focusing exclusively on 'dominant' paradigms and 'emerging' paradigms, whereas – given the argument above – there are likely to be many competing and overlapping paradigms that are incommensurable in certain respects and share common understanding in others. This can be seen within the communicative canon itself where proponents employ different aspects of social theory or understanding in their approaches. Third, Feyerabend rightly points out that competing paradigms do not necessarily emerge through a crisis in the dominant paradigm; they can emerge for a multitude of reasons.

This book has demonstrated that there is not one dominant paradigm in planning theory today, even if we could be mistaken for thinking that the current popularity of the communicative and collaborative turn has masked a great deal of debate centred on other planning movements and trajectories. Although there remain some deep-rooted differences between collaborative planning and the proponents of these other approaches, there are nevertheless a number of important similarities that are worthy of consideration in themselves.

Praxis concerns

Concern has also been expressed about the position of power within the collaborative approach particularly in relation to one of the main concentrations of power within planning: the individual planner. Both Tewdwr-Jones in Chapter 4 and Campbell and Marshall in Chapter 5 discuss individualism within the planning arena from the point of view of personal dynamics and ethical judgements, and both chapters question the motivation and perception of planners expected to perform a wider democratic role. It is not at all clear why the narrow conception of the public should be privileged over other demands or interests particularly when they could well be (and are) prejudiced in favour of distinct interests (Healey *et al.*, 1988). Second, there is evidence to suggest that planners do not believe that they should act more democratically (Allmendinger, 1996; Kaufman and Escuin, 1996; Flyvbjerg, 1998b). This perspective has often coloured the attitude of public sector planners and made them suspicious about increasing the degree of participation that often tends to favour narrow sectional interests.

Finally, as Campbell and Marshall (1999) have argued elsewhere, the institutional context within which planners work is not necessarily or even ordinarily democratically friendly Hillier discusses aspects of this in Chapter 6. The pressures for increased accountability and participation from a more highly politicised and motivated public which echo the thrust of collaborative or communicative planning cannot assume a neutral or conducive institutional context. Recent shifts in local governance in many parts of the world have broadly and in part been characterised by a fragmented landscape of public, semi-public and private bodies. This is what Luhmann terms a plethora of governments that government cannot steer – a centreless society (1982: xv, 253–255).

In the UK, compulsory competitive tendering of public services (a crude method of privatisation) in local government has led to an increasingly privatised planning service as local planning authorities have to deal with parts of the planning service run by arm's-length bodies or even private companies (Tewdwr-Jones and Harris, 1998; Higgins and Allmendinger, 1999). Not only does this introduce a more juridical relationship between, for example, forward planning and economic development functions built upon service level agreements but it also commodifies the outlook and practice of planners including their attitude towards the public. The public interest is placed alongside commercial pressures to deliver a service of specified standard within a specified time.

CONCLUSION

Collaborative or communicative planning is an important direction for planning theory with significant potential for practice that will continue to dominate academic debate. This situation arises because of a confluence over favourable factors; its fitting in with the *Zeitgeist* of Third Way thinking, and the broad support of the planning theory community. As such, there needs to be a willingness on behalf of its proponents to engage with emerging critiques and encourage debate with other ideas and schools of thought.

The critiques that have been assembled here from a collection of disparate sources are the first step in that direction. Such critiques do not undermine collaborative planning but merely ask to be addressed. Ultimately, a more dialectical engagement between collaborative planning and these critiques will serve to strengthen the former and further embed it as a democratic and progressive basis for planning. There seems to be a recent willingness on the part of collaborative or communicative theorists to engage with their critics (Forester, 2000; Healey, 2000; Yiftachel and Huxley, 2000). While this debate should be welcomed for its very presence it is clear that it is still less of an engagement of ideas and more of another example of academics talking past each other. There is a basic normative difference between the different positions that, we suspect, comes down to ontological as well as epistemological differences. Perhaps, then, we await a debate that will never occur as the different perspectives are based upon different *Weltanschauungen*. A position that, according to the proponents of the collaborative or communicative school, can be overcome by open discourse.

Bibliography

Albrechts, L. (1991) 'Changing roles and positions of planners', *Urban Studies* 28(1): 123–137.

Albrechts, L. (1997) 'The difficult art of getting public support', paper presented at ACSP conference, Fort Lauderdale, November. Copy available from author.

Albrechts, L. (1999) 'Planners as catalysts and initiators of change: the new Structure Plan for Flanders', *International Planning Studies* 7(5): 587–603.

Alexander, E.R. (1984) 'After rationality, what? A review of responses to paradigm breakdown', *Journal of the American Planning Association* 50(1): 62–69.

Alexander, E.R. (1992) *Approaches to Planning: Introducing Current Planning Theories, Concepts and Issues*, 2nd edn, Luxembourg: Gordon and Breach.

Alexander, E.R. (1996) 'After rationality: towards a contingency theory of planning', in S.J. Mandelbaum, L. Mazza and R.W. Burchell (eds) *Explorations in Planning Theory*, New Jersey: Center for Urban Policy Research, pp. 45–64.

Alexander, E.R. (1997) 'A mile or a millimetre? Measuring the "planning theory-practice gap" ', *Environment and Planning B: Planning and Design* 24: 3–6.

Alexander, E.R. (1999a) 'The planner-prince: interdependence, rationalities and post-communicative practice', paper presented at the ACSP conference 1999, Chicago.

Alexander, E.R. (1999b) 'Response to commentaries: planning theory and practice – mixing them or minding the gap?', *Environment and Planning B: Planning and Design*, 26: 1–4.

Alexander, E.R. and Faludi, A. (1996) 'Planning doctrine: its uses and implications', *Planning Theory Newsletter*, 16: 11.

Allen, J. (1996) 'Our town: Foucault and knowledge-based politics in London', in S.J. Mandelbaum, L. Mazza and R.W. Burchell (eds) *Explorations in Planning Theory*, New Jersey: Center for Urban Policy Research, pp. 328–344.

Allmendinger, P. (1996) 'Development control and the legitimacy of planning decisions: a comment', *Town Planning Review* 67(2): 229–234.

Allmendinger, P. (1998) 'Planning practice and the postmodern debate', *International Planning Studies* 3(2), 227–248.

Allmendinger, P. (1999) 'Beyond collaborative planning', paper presented at AESOP conference, Bergen, 7–11 July. Copy available from author.

Allmendinger, P. (2001) *Planning in Postmodern Times*, London: Routledge.

Allmendinger, P. and Tewdwr-Jones, M. (1997) 'Mind the gap: planning theory – practice and the translation of knowledge into action; a comment on Alexander (1997)', *Environment and Planning B: Planning and Design* 24: 802–806.

Ambrose, P. (1984) *Urban Processes and Power*, London: Routledge.

Amin, A. (1996) 'Beyond associative democracy', *New Political Economy* 1(3): 309–333.

Amin, A. and Graham, S. (1997) 'The ordinary city', *Transactions of the Institute of British Geographers* NS 22: 411–429.

Amin, A. and Hausner, J. (1997) 'Interactive governance and social complexity', in A. Amin and J. Hausner (eds) *Beyond Market and Hierarchy*, Cheltenham: Edward Elgar, pp. 1–31.

Amin, A. and Thrift, N. (eds) (1994) *Globalisation, Institutions and Regional Development*, Oxford: Oxford University Press.

Amin, A. and Thrift, N. (1995a) 'Institutional issues for the European regions: from markets and plans to socioeconomics and powers of association', *Economy and Society* 24(1): 41–66.

Amin, A. and Thrift, N. (1995b) 'Globalisation, institutional "thickness" and the local economy', in P. Healey, S. Cameron, S, Davoudi, S. Graham and A. Mandani-Pour (eds) *Managing Cities*, Chichester: John Wiley and Sons.

Anderson, T. and Leal, D. (1991) *Free Market Environmentalism*, San Francisco: Pacific Research Institute for Public Policy.

Andresen, M.T. and Castel-Branco, C. (1993) 'Heading for a post-modern landscape – Portuguese trends in the reconciliation of environmental quality and landscape with economic development', *Landscape and Urban Planning* 23: 183–194.

Argyris, C. and Schön, D. (1974) *Theory in Practice*, San Francisco: Jossey-Bass.

Baert, P. (1998) *Social Theory in the Twentieth Century*, Cambridge: Polity Press.

Ball, M. (1998) 'Institutions in British property research: a review', *Urban Studies* 35, 9: 1501–1517.

Barsalou, L.W. (1992) *Cognitive Psychology: An Overview for Cognitive Sciences*, Hillsdale, NJ: Erlbaum.

Barnes, B. and Bloor, D. (1982) Rationality, relativism and the sociology of knowledge', in M. Hollis and Luke, S. (eds) *Rationality and Relativism*, Oxford: Oxford University Press.

Bartky, S. (1988) 'Foucault, femininity and the modernization of patriarchal power', in I. Diamond and L. Quinby (eds) *Feminism and Foucault: Reflections and Resistance*, Boston: Northeastern University Press, 61–86.

Baudrillard, J. (1968) *Le Système des objets*, Paris: Gallimard.

Baudrillard, J. (1970) *La Société de consommation*, Paris: Gallimard.

Baudrillard, J. (1975) *The Mirror of Production*, St Louis: Telos.

Baudrillard, J. (1976) *L'échange symbolique et la mort*, Paris: Gallimard.

Baudrillard, J. (1995) *The Gulf War Did Not Take Place*, Bloomington: Indiana Press.

Baum, H. (1996) 'Practising planning theory in a political world', in S. Mandelbaum, L. Mazza and R. Burchell (eds) *Explorations in Planning Theory*, New Brunswick: State University of New York Press.

Bauman, Z. (1991) *Modernity and Ambivalence,* Cambridge: Polity Press.

Bauman, Z. (1998) 'Parvenu and pariah: heroes and victims of modernity', in J. Good and I. Velody (eds), *The Politics of Postmodernity,* Cambridge: Cambridge University Press.

Beauregard, R.A. (1989) 'Between modernity and postmodernity: the ambiguous position of US planning', *Environment and Planning D* 7: 381–395.

Beauregard, R.A. (1991) 'Without a net: modernist planning and the postmodern abyss', *Journal of Planning Education and Research* 10(3): 189–193.

Beauregard, R.A. (1995) 'Edge critics', *Journal of Planning Education and Research* 14(3): 163–166.

Beauregard, R.A. (1996) 'Between modernity and postmodernity: the ambiguous position of US planning', in S. Campbell and S. Fainstein (eds) *Readings in Planning Theory*, Oxford: Blackwell.

Beauregard, R.A. (1998) 'Writing the planner', *Journal of Planning Education and Research* 18: 93–101.

Bell, D. (1973) *The Coming of Post-Industrial Society*, New York: Basic Books

Benhabib, S. (1992) 'Models of public space: Hannah Arendt, the liberal tradition and Jürgen Habermas', in C. Calhoun (ed.) *Habermas and the Public Sphere*, Cambridge, MA: MIT Press, pp. 73–98.

Benhabib, S. (1996a) 'Toward a deliberative model of democratic legitimacy', in S. Benhabib (ed.) *Democracy and Difference*, Princeton, NJ: Princeton University Press, pp. 67–94.

Benhabib, S. (1996b) *The Reluctant Modernism of Hannah Arendt*, Newbury Park, CA: Sage.

Benhabib, S. (1996c) 'Introduction', in S. Benhabib (ed.) *Democracy and Difference*, Princeton, NJ: Princeton University Press, pp. 1–8.

Benhabib, S. and Cornell, D. (eds) (1987) *Feminism as Critique: Essays on the Politics of Gender in Late Capitalist Societies*, Cambridge: Polity Press.

Berger, J. (1991) 'The linguistification of the sacred and delinguistification of the economy', in A. Honneth and H. Joas (eds) *Communicative Action,* Cambridge: Polity Press.

Berman, M. ([1982] 1989) *All That is Solid Melts into Air: The Experience of Modernity*, London: Verso.

Bernstein, R.J. (ed.) (1983a) *Beyond Objectivism and Relativism: Science, Hermeneutics and Praxis*, Oxford: Basil Blackwell.

Bernstein, R.J. (1983b) *Habermas and Modernity*, Cambridge, MA: The MIT Press.

Bernstein, R.J. (1985) 'Introduction', in R.J. Bernstein (ed.) *Habermas and Modernity*, Cambridge: Polity Press, in association with Basil Blackwell, London, pp. 1–32.

Bernstein, R.J. (1992) *The New Constellation: The Ethical-Political Horizons of Modernity/Postmodernity*, Cambridge, MA: The MIT Press.

Bernstein, R.J. (1998) 'Community in the pragmatic tradition', in M. Dickstein (ed.) *The Revival of Pragmatism: New Essays on Social Thought, Law and Culture*, Durham, NC and London: Duke University Press.

Best, S. and Kellner, D. (1991) *Postmodern Theory: Critical Interrogations*, New York: The Guilford Press.

Blowers, A. (1980) *The Limits of Power*, Oxford: Pergamon Press.

Boettke, P. (1998) 'What went wrong with economics?', *Critical Review* 11: 10–64.

Bohman, J. (1991) *New Philosophy of Social Science*, Cambridge: Polity Press.

Bohman, J. and Rehg, W. (1997) 'Introduction', in J. Bohman and W. Rehg (eds) *Deliberative Democracy,* Cambridge, MA: The MIT Press, pp. ix–xxx.

Bond, P. (1992) 'Re-using the spaces of confinement: from urban apartheid to post-apartheid without post-modernism', *Urban Forum* 3(1): 39–55.

Bordo, S. (1997) 'Anglo-American feminism: "Women's Liberation" and the politics of the body', in L. McDowell and J. Sharp (eds) *Space, Gender, Knowledge: Feminist Readings*, London: Arnold, pp. 232–236.

Bordo, S. and Jaggar, A. (eds) (1990) *Gender/Body/Knowledge*, New Brunswick: Rutgers University Press.

Bourdieu, P. (1990) *In Other Worlds: Essays Towards a Reflexive Sociology*, Oxford: Polity Press.

Boyer, M.C. (1983) *Dreaming the Rational City: The Myth of American City Planning*, Cambridge, MA: The MIT Press.

Boyer, M.C. (1990) *Dreaming the Rational City: The Myth of American City Planning*, 2nd edn, Cambridge, MA: The MIT Press.

Brand, A. (1990) *The Force of Reason: An Introduction to Habermas' Theory of Communicative Action*, London: Allen & Unwin.

Breheny, M. and Hooper, A. (1985) (eds) *Rationality in Planning: Critical Essays on the Role of Rationality in Urban and Regional Planning*, London: Pion.

Brown, W. (1995) *States of Injury: Power and Freedom in Late Modernity*, Princeton, NJ: Princeton University Press.

Brozen, Y. (1982) *Concentration, Mergers and Public Policy*, New York: Macmillan.

Buchanan, J.M. (1969) *Cost and Choice*, Chicago: Chicago University Press.

Buchanan, J. and Vanberg, V. (1991) 'The market as a creative discovery process', *Economics and Philosophy* 7: 167–186.

Buchanan, J.M. and Stubblebine, W.C. (1962) 'Externality', *Economica* 29: 371–384.

Burchell, G., Gordon, C. and Miller, P. (eds) (1991) *The Foucault Effect: Studies in Governmentality*, London: Harvester Wheatsheaf.

Burczak, T. (1994) 'The post-modern moments in F.A. Hayek's economics', *Economics and Philosophy* 10: 31–58.

Bürger, P. (1984) 'The decline of the modern age', *Telos* Winter, 62: 117–130.

Burns, D. and Taylor, M. (1997) *Mutual Aid and Self Help: Coping Strategies for Excluded Communities*, York: Joseph Rowntree Foundation.

Butler, J. (1990) *Gender Trouble: Feminism and the Subversion of Identity*, New York: Routledge.

Butler, J. (1992) 'Contingent foundations: feminism and the question of "Postmodernism" ', in J. Butler and J. Scott (eds) *Feminists Theorize the Political*, New York: Routledge, pp. 3–21.

Butler, J. (1993) *Bodies that Matter: On the Discursive Limits of Sex*, New York: Routledge.

Callinicos, A. (1990) *Against Post-Modernism: A Marxist Perspective.* Cambridge: Polity Press.

Campbell, H. and Marshall, R. (1998) 'Acting on principle: dilemmas in planning practice', *Planning Practice and Research* 13(2): 117–128.

Campbell, H. and Marshall, R. (1999) 'Ethical frameworks and planning theory', *International Journal of Urban and Regional Research* 23(3): 464–478.

Campbell, H. and Marshall, R. (2000a) 'Instrumental rationality, intelligent action and planning: American pragmatism revisited', a paper presented at the Planning Research 2000 Conference, The London School of Economics and Political Science, 27–29 March.

Campbell, H. and Marshall, R. (2000b) 'Moral obligations, planning and the public interest: a commentary on British planning practice', *Environment and Planning B: Planning and Design* 27: 297–312.

Campbell, H., Ellis, H., Henneberry, J. and Gladwell, C. (2000) 'Planning obligations, planning practice, and land-use outcomes', *Environment and Planning B: Planning and Design* 27(4): 759–775.

Campbell, H. and Tait, M. (2000) 'The politics of communication between planning officers and politicians: the exercise of power through discourse', *Environment and Planning A* 32: 489–506.

Campbell, S. and Fainstein, S. (eds) (1996) *Readings in Planning Theory*, Oxford: Blackwell.

Caputo, J.D. (1997) *Deconstruction in a Nutshell: A Conversation with Jacques Derrida*, New York: Fordham University Press.

Carleheden, M. and Rene, G. (1996) 'An interview with Jürgen Habermas', *Theory, Culture and Society* 13(3): 1–18.

Casey, E.S. (1996) *The Fate of Place: A Philosophical History*, London: University of California Press.

Castells, M. (1978) *City, Class, and Power*, New York: Macmillan.

Catanese, A. (1974) *Planners and Local Politics: Impossible Dreams*, London: Sage.

Chambers, S. (1995) 'Discourse and democratic practices', in S. White (ed.) *The Cambridge Companion to Habermas*, Cambridge: Cambridge University Press, pp. 233–259.

Cherry, G. (1996) *Town Planning in Britain since 1900*, Oxford: Blackwell.

Chomsky, N. and Foucault, M. (1974) 'Human nature: justice versus power', in F. Elders (ed.) *Reflexive Water: The Basic Concerns of Mankind*, London: Souvenir.

Chriss, J.C. (1995) 'Habermas, Goffman, and communicative action: implications for professional practice', *American Sociological Review* 60: 545–565.

Christensen, K.S. (1993) 'Teaching Savvy', *Journal of Planning Education and Research* 12(3): 202–212.

Coase, R.H. (1937) 'The nature of the firm', *Economica* 4: 386–405.

Coase, R.H. (1960) 'The problem of social cost', *Journal of Law and Economics* 3: 1–44.

Cockburn, C. (1977) *The Local State*, London: Pluto Press.

Cohen, J. and Arato, A. (1992) *Civil Society and Political Theory*, Cambridge, MA: The MIT Press.

Cohen, J. and Rogers, J. (1995) 'Secondary associations and democratic governance', in E. Wright (ed.) *Associations and Democracy*, London: Verso, pp. 7–98.

Cohen, S. (1985) *Visions of Social Control: Crime, Punishment and Classification*, Cambridge: Polity Press.

Coles, R. (1995) 'Identity and difference in the ethical positions of Adorno and Habermas', in S. White (ed.) *The Cambridge Companion to Habermas*, Cambridge: Cambridge University Press, pp. 19–45.

Collini, S. (1992) 'Introduction: interpretation terminable and interminable', in S. Collini (ed.) *Interpretation and Overinterpretation*, Cambridge: Cambridge University Press.

Committee on Public Participation in Planning (1969) *People and Plans*, London: HMSO.

Committee on Spatial Development (1999) *European Spatial Development Perspective: Towards Balanced and Sustainable Development of the Territory of the European Union*, Luxembourg: European Commission.

Committee on Standards in Public Life (1997) *Third Report: Standards of Conduct in Local Government in England, Scotland and Wales,* London: The Stationery Office.

Connell, R. (1987) *Gender and Power: Society, the Person and Sexual Politics*, Sydney: Allen & Unwin.

Connell, R. (1995) *Masculinities*, Cambridge: Polity Press.

Connolly, W. (1991) *Identity/Difference*, Ithaca, NY: Cornell University Press.

Connolly, W. (1998) 'Beyond good and evil: the ethical sensibility of Michel Foucault', in J. Moss (ed.) *The Later Foucault*, London: Sage, pp. 108–128.

Connor, S. (1994) *Postmodernist Culture: An Introduction to Theories of the Contemporary*, Oxford: Blackwell.

Cooke, M. (1994) *Language and Reason: A Study of Habermas's Pragmatics*, Cambridge, MA and London: The MIT Press.

Cooke, P.N. (1983) *Theories of Planning and Spatial Development*, London: Hutchinson.

Cooke, P.N. (1990a) *Back to the Future: Modernity, Postmodernity and Locality*, London: Unwin Hyman.

Cooke, P.N. (1990b) 'Modern urban theory in question', *Transactions of the Institute of British Geographers* 15: 331–343.

Cooke, P.N. and Kemp, R.V. (1980) 'Normative structures: their role in the analysis of communicative content in public policy making', *Papers in Planning Research*, 3, Department of Town Planning, Cardiff: UWIST.

Cruikshank, B. (1999) *The Will to Empower: Democratic Citizens and Other Subjects*, Ithaca, NY: Cornell University Press.

Crush, J. (1994) 'Scripting the compound: power and space in the South African mining industry', *Environment and Planning D: Society and Space* 12: 301–324.

Cullingworth, J.B. (1999) *British Planning: Fifty Years of Urban and Regional Policy*, London: Athlone Press.

Dalton, L. (1986) 'Why the rational paradigm persists – the resistance of professional education and practice to alternative forms of planning', *Journal of Planning Education and Research* 5(3): 147–153.

Dalton, T. (1996) 'Participation: influencing policy in troubled times', in A. Farrar and J. Inglis (eds) *Keeping it Together*, London: Pluto, pp. 182–206.

Darke, R. (1985) 'Rationality planning and the state', in M. Breheny and A. Hooper (eds) *Rationality in Planning: Critical Essays on the Role of Rationality in Urban and Regional Planning*, London: Pion, pp. 15–26.

Davidoff, P. (1965) 'Advocacy and pluralism in planning', *AIP Journal* November: 331–338.

Davies, H.W.E. (1999) 'Development control', in J.B. Cullingworth (ed.) *British Planning: Fifty Years of Urban and Regional Policy*, London: Athlone Press.

Dean, M. (1994) *Critical and Effective Histories: Foucault's Methods and Historical Sociology*, London: Routledge.

Dean, M. (1998) 'Questions of method', in I. Velody and R. Williams (eds) *The Politics of Constructionism*, London: Sage Publications, pp. 182–199.

Dean, M. (1999) *Governmentality: Power and Rule in Modern Society*, London: Sage.

Dear, M.J. (1986) 'Postmodernism and planning', *Environment and Planning D* 4: 367–384.

Dear, M.J. (1989) 'Survey 16: privatisation and the rhetoric of planning practice', *Environment and Planning D* 7: 449–462.

Dear, M.J. (1994) 'Who's afraid of postmodernism? Reflections on Symanksi and Cosgrove', *Annals of the Association of American Geographers* 84(2): 295–300.

Dear, M.J. (1995a) 'Prolegomena to a postmodern urbanism', in P. Healey, S. Cameron, S. Davoudi, S. Graham and A. Madani-Pour (eds) *Managing Cities. The New Urban Context*, Chichester: Wiley, pp. 27–44.

Dear, M.J. (1995b) 'Beyond the post-fordist city', *Contention* Fall, 5(1): 67–76.

Dear, M.J. (2000) *The Postmodern Urban Condition*, Oxford: Blackwell Publishers.

Dear, M.J. and Wassmansdorf, G. (1993) 'Postmodern consequences', *Geographical Record* 83: 321–325.

Demsetz, H. (1964) 'The exchange and enforcement of property rights', *Journal of Law and Economics* 7, October: 127–146.

Dennis, N. (1972) *Public Participation and Planners' Blight*, London: Faber and Faber.

De Sousa Briggs, X. (1998) 'Doing democracy up-close: culture, power, and communication in community building', *Journal of Planning Education and Research* 18(1): 1–13.

Desroches, P. (1998) 'Austrian insights on economic geography', *Quarterly Review of Austrian Economics* 2: 34–51.

Dewey, J. (1920) *Democracy and Education*, New York: Macmillan Co.

Dewey, J. (1931) *Philosophy and Civilisation*, New York: G.P. Putnams Sons.

Dickstein, M. (1998) 'Pragmatism then and now', in M. Dickstein (ed.) *The Revival of Pragmatism: New Essays on Social Thought, Law and Culture,* Durham, NC and London: Duke University Press.

Diggins, J. (1998) 'Pragmatism and its limits', in M. Dickstein (ed.) *The Revival of Pragmatism: New Essays on Social Thought, Law and Culture*, Durham, NC and London: Duke University Press.

Dillon, M. (1980) 'Conversation with Michel Foucault', *The Threepenny Review* Winter/Spring: 4–5.

Di-Zerega, G. (1993) 'Social ecology, deep ecology and liberalism', *Critical Review* 6(2–3): 305–370.

Donald, J. (1999) *Imagining the Modern City*, London: The Athlone Press.

Dorfman, J., Shames, V.A. and Kihlstrom, J.F. (1996) 'Intuition, incubation, and insight: implicit cognition in problem solving', in G. Underwood (ed.) *Implicit Cognition*, Oxford: Oxford University Press.

Dreyfus, H. and Rabinow, P. (1982) *Michel Foucault: Beyond Structuralism and Hermeneutics*, New York: Harvester Wheatsheaf.

Dreyfus, H. and Rabinow, P. (1986) 'What is maturity?', in D.C. Hoy (ed.) *Foucault: A Critical Reader*, Oxford: Blackwell.

Dryzek, J.S. (1990) *Discursive Democracy: Politics, Policy and Political Science*, Cambridge: Cambridge University Press.

Dryzek, J.S. (1993) 'Policy analysis and planning: from science to argument', in F. Fischer and J. Forester (eds) *The Argumentative Turn in Policy Analysis and Planning*, London: UCL Press, pp. 213–232.

Dunn, W.N. (1993) 'Policy reforms as arguments', in F. Fischer and J. Forester (eds) *The Argumentative Turn in Policy Analysis and Planning*, London: UCL Press, pp. 254–290.

Dyrberg, T. (1997) *The Circular Structure of Power*, London: Verso.

Eagleton, T. (1985) 'Capitalism, modernism and postmodernism', *New Left Review* 152, July/August: 60–73.

Eagleton, T. (1997) *The Illusions of Postmodernism*, Oxford: Blackwell Publishers.

Eco, U. (1992) 'Interpretation and history', in S. Collini (ed.) *Interpretation and Overinterpretation*, Cambridge: Cambridge University Press.

Ehrman, R. (1990) *Nimbyism: The Disease and the Cure*, London: Centre for Policy Studies.

Elster, J. (1998) 'Introduction', in J. Elster (ed.) *Deliberative Democracy*, Cambridge: Cambridge University Press, pp. 1–18.

Etzioni, A. (1973) 'Mixed scanning: a third approach to decision-making', in A. Faludi (ed.) *A Reader in Planning Theory*, New York: Pergamon Press.

Evans, A.W. (1988) *No Room! No Room!*, Occasional Paper 79, London: Institute of Economic Affairs.

Evans, A.W. (1991) 'Rabbit hutches on postage stamps: planning, development and political economy', *Urban Studies* 28: 853–870.

Evans, B. (1993) 'Why we no longer require a planning profession', *Planning Practice and Research* 8(1): 9–15.

Evans, B. (1995) *Experts and Environmental Planning*, Aldershot: Avebury.

Evans, B. and Rydin, Y. (1997) 'Planning, professionalism and sustainability', in A. Blowers and B. Evans (eds) *Town Planning in the 21st Century*, London: Routledge.

Ezine, J.L. (1985) 'An interview with Michel Foucault', in *History of the Present I*: 2–3, 14. First published in *Les Nouvelles littéraires* 17 March 1975: 3.

Fainstein, N. and Fainstein, S. (1982) 'New debates in urban planning: the impact of Marxist theory within the United States', in C. Paris (ed.) *Critical Readings in Planning Theory*, Oxford: Pergamon Press.

Fainstein, S. (1995) 'Politics, economics and planning: why urban regimes matter', *Planning Theory* 14: 34–41.

Fainstein, S. (1999) 'New directions in planning theory', paper presented at the Planning Research Conference, the University of Sheffield, April.

Fairfield, J. (1992) 'Alienation of social control: the Chicago sociologists and the origins of urban planning', *Planning Perspectives* 7: 418–434.

Faludi, A. (1973) *A Reader in Planning Theory*, Oxford: Pergamon.

Faludi, A. (1984, original published in 1973) *Planning Theory*, Oxford: Pergamon Press.

Faludi, A. (1987) *A Decision-Centred View of Environmental Planning*, Oxford: Pergamon Press.

Faludi, A. and Korthals Altes, W.K. (1994) 'Evaluating communicative planning: a revised design for performance research', *European Planning Studies* 2(4): 403–418.

Farthing, S. (2000) 'Town planning theory and the "paradigm wars" in the social sciences', paper presented to the Planning Research Conference at the LSE, March.

Feldman, M.M.A. (1994) 'Perloff revisited: reassessing planning education in postmodern times', *Journal of Planning Education and Research* 13: 89–103.

Feldman, M.M.A. (1995) 'Regime and regulation in substantive planning theory', *Planning Theory* 14: 65–95

Feldman, M.M.A. (1997) 'Can we talk? Interpretive planning theory as comedy', *Planning Theory* 17: 43–64.

Fenster, T. (1998) 'Ethnicity, citizenship, planning and gender: the case of Ethiopian immigrant women in Israel', *Gender, Place and Culture* 5(2): 177–189.

Fenster, T. (ed.) (1999) *Gender, Planning and Human Rights*, London: Routledge.

Festenstein, M. (1997) *Pragmatism and Political Theory*, Cambridge: Polity Press.

Feyerabend, P. (1961) *Knowledge Without Foundations*, Oberlin: Oberlin College.

Feyerabend, P. (1978) *Science in a Free Society*, London: New Left Books.

Feyerabend, P. (1980) *Realism, Rationalism and Scientific Method, Philosophical Papers*, vol. 1, Cambridge: Cambridge University Press.

Feyerabend, P. (1988) *Against Method*, 2nd edn, London: Verso.

Filion, P. (1996) 'Metropolitan planning objectives and implementation constraints: planning in a post-Fordist and postmodern age', *Environment and Planning A* 28: 1637–1660.

Filion, P. (1999) 'Rupture or continuity? Modern and postmodern planning in Toronto', *International Journal of Urban and Regional Research* 23(3): 421–444.

Finch, J. (1993) *The Classing Gaze: Sexuality, Class and Surveillance*, Sydney: Allen & Unwin.

Fischer, F. and Forester, J. (eds) (1993) *The Argumentative Turn in Policy Analysis and Planning*, London: UCL Press.

Fischler, R. (1995) 'Strategy and history in professional practice: planning as world making', in H. Liggett and D. Perry (eds) *Spatial Practices: Critical Explorations in Social/Spatial Theory*, Thousand Oaks, CA: Sage, pp. 13–58.

Fischler, R. (1998) 'Health, safety and the general welfare: markets, politics and social science in early land-use regulation and community design', *Journal of Urban History* 24(6): 675–719.

Fischler, R. (2000) 'Linking planning theory and history: the case of development control', *Journal of Planning Education and Research* 19: 233–241.

Flynn, T. (1993) 'Foucault's mapping of history', in G. Gutting (ed.) *The Cambridge Companion to Foucault*, Cambridge: Cambridge University Press.

Flyvbjerg, B. (1996) 'The dark side of planning: rationality and "*Realrationalität*" ', in S. Mandelbaum, L. Mazza and R. Burchell (eds) *Explorations in Planning Theory*, New Jersey: Center for Urban Policy Research, Rutgers University, pp. 383–394.

Flyvbjerg, B. (1998a) 'Empowering civil society: Habermas, Foucault and the question of conflict', in M. Douglass and J. Friedmann (eds) *Cities for Citizens*, Chichester: Wiley, pp. 185–211.

Flyvbjerg, B. (1998b) *Rationality and Power: Democracy in Practice*, Chicago: University of Chicago Press.

Flyvbjerg, B. (2000) 'Bringing power to planning research: One researcher's story', plenary paper read at the Planning Research 2000 conference, London School of Economics and Political Science, 27–29 March.

Flyvbjerg, B. and Richardson, T. (1998) 'In search of the dark side of planning theory', paper presented at the Oxford Planning Theory conference, 2–4 April.

Foldvary, F. (1994) *Public Goods and Private Communities*, Aldershot: Edward Elgar.

Forester, J. (1980) 'Critical theory and planning practice', *Journal of the American Planning Association* 46(3): 275–286.

Forester, J. (1982) 'Planning in the face of power', *Journal of the American Planning Association* Winter: 67–80.

Forester, J. (1985a) 'Practical rationality in planmaking', in M. Breheny and A. Hooper (eds) *Rationality in Planning: Critical Essays on the Role of Rationality in Urban and Regional Planning*, London: Pion, pp. 48–59.

Forester, J. (1985b) 'Introduction: the applied turn in contemporary critical theory', in J. Forester (ed.) *Critical Theory and Public Life*, Cambridge, MA and London: The MIT Press, pp. ix–xix.

Forester, J. (1987) 'Planning in the face of conflict', *Journal of the American Planning Association* Summer: 303–314.

Forester, J. (1989) *Planning in the Face of Power*, Berkeley, CA: University of California Press.

Forester, J. (1990) 'Reply to my critics . . .', *Planning Theory Newsletter* Winter, 4: 43–60.

Forester, J. (1993) *Critical Theory, Public Policy and Planning Practice: Toward a Critical Pragmatism*, Albany, NY: State University of New York Press.

Forester, J. (1996a) 'Argument, power and passion in planning practice', in S. Mandelbaum, L. Mazza and R.W. Burchell (eds) *Explorations in Planning Theory*, New Jersey: Center for Urban Policy Research.

Forester, J. (1996b) 'Beyond dialogue to transformative learning: how deliberative rituals encourage political judgement in community planning processes', in S. Esquith (ed.) *Democratic Dialogues: Theories and Practices*, Poznan: University of Poznan.

Forester, J. (1999a) 'An instructive case study hampered by theoretical puzzles: critical comments on Bent Flyvbjerg's "Rationality and Power" ', http://www.crp.cornell.edu/forester/Bentcritical.htm (accessed: October 1999).

Forester, J. (1999b) 'Dealing with deep value differences: how can consensus building make a difference?', in L. Susskind, S. McKearnon and J. Thomas-Larmer (eds) *Consensus-Building Handbook*, Thousand Oaks, CA: Sage, pp. 463–493.

Forester, J. (1999c) 'Reflections on the future understanding of planning practice', *International Planning Studies* 4(2): 175–194.

Forester, J. (1999d) *The Deliberative Practitioner: Encouraging Participatory Planning Processes*, Cambridge, MA: The MIT Press.

Forester, J. (2000) 'Conservative epistemology, reductive ethics, far too narrow politics:

some clarifications in response to Yiftachel and Huxley', *International Journal of Urban and Regional Research* 24(4): 914–916.

Formaini, R. (1991) *The Myth of Scientific Public Policy*, New York: Transaction Books.

Foucault, M. (1965) *Madness and Civilisation: A History of Insanity in the Age of Reason*, London: Tavistock.

Foucault, M. (1970) *The Order of Things: An Archaeology of the Human Sciences*, London: Routledge.

Foucault, M. (1972) *The Archaeology of Knowledge*, London: Tavistock.

Foucault, M. (1973) *The Birth of the Clinic: An Archaeology of Medical Perception*, London: Routledge.

Foucault, M. (1979) *Discipline and Punish: The Birth of the Prison*, New York: Vintage Books.

Foucault, M. (1980) 'Postface', in M. Perrot (ed.) *L'impossible Prison*, Paris: Seuil.

Foucault, M. (1981) *Colloqui con Foucault*, Salerno.

Foucault, M. (1983) 'On the genealogy of ethics', in H. Dreyfus and P. Rabinow (eds) *Michel Foucault*, Chicago: University of Chicago Press.

Foucault, M. (1984a) 'What is Enlightenment?', in P. Rabinow (ed.) *The Foucault Reader*, Harmondsworth: Penguin, pp. 32–50.

Foucault, M. (1984b) 'Politics and ethics: an interview', in P. Rabinow (ed.) *The Foucault Reader*, New York: Pantheon.

Foucault, M. (1984c) 'Space, knowledge and power', in P. Rabinow (ed.) *The Foucault Reader*, Harmondsworth: Penguin, pp. 239–256.

Foucault, M. (1984d) 'Le Retour de la morale', in *Les Nouvelles*, 28 June–5 July: 36–41.

Foucault, M. (1986) *The History of Sexuality*, vol. 3, *The Care of the Self*, London: Penguin.

Foucault, M. (1988a) 'Critical theory/intellectual history', in L. Kritzman (ed.) *Michel Foucault: Politics, Philosophy, Culture*, New York: Routledge, pp. 17–46.

Foucault, M. (1988b) 'The ethic of care for the self as a practice of freedom', in J. Bernauer and D. Rasmussen (eds) *The Final Foucault*, Cambridge, MA: The MIT Press.

Foucault, M. (1990 [1978]) *The History of Sexuality*, vol. 1, *An Introduction*, New York: Vintage.

Foucault, M. (1991a) 'Governmentality', in G. Burchell, C. Gordon and P. Miller (eds) *The Foucault Effect: Essays in Governmentality*, London: Harvester Wheatsheaf, pp. 87–104.

Foucault, M. (1991b) 'Questions of method', in G. Burchell, C. Gordon and P. Miller (eds) *The Foucault Effect: Essays in Governmentality*, London: Harvester Wheatsheaf, pp. 73–86.

Franzway, S., Court, D. and Connell, R. (1989) *Staking a Claim: Feminism, Bureaucracy and the State*, Sydney: Allen & Unwin.

Fraser, N. (1989) *Unruly Practices: Power, Discourse, and Gender in Contemporary Social Theory*, Cambridge: Polity Press.

Freestone, R. (1995) 'Women in the Australian town planning movement, 1900–1950', *Planning Perspectives*, 10: 259–277.

Friedmann, J. (1959) 'Introduction', *International Social Science Journal* 11(3): 327–339.

Friedmann, J. (1973) *Retracking America: A Theory of Transactive Planning*, Garden City, New York: Double Day Anchor.

Friedmann, J. (1987) *Planning in the Public Domain*, Princeton, NJ: Princeton University Press.

Friedmann, J. (1989) 'The dialectic of reason', *International Journal of Urban and Regional Research* 13(2): 217–236.

Friedmann, J. (1991) 'Toward a non-Euclidean mode of planning', *Journal of the American Planning Association* Autumn: 482–485.

Friedmann, J. (1994) 'The utility of non-Euclidean planning', *Journal of the American Planning Association* Summer: 377–379.

Friedmann, J. (1996) 'The core curriculum in planning revisited', *Journal of Planning Education and Research* 15: 89–104.

Friedmann, J. (1997) 'Planning theory revisited', Nijmegen Academic Lecture. University of Nijmegen, 29 May.

Friedmann, J. and Douglass, M. (1998) 'Editors' introduction', in M. Douglass and J. Friedmann (eds) *Cities for Citizens. Planning and the Rise of Civil Society in a Global Age*, Chichester: Wiley, pp. 1–6.

Friedmann, J. and Lehrer, U. (1998) 'Urban policy responses to foreign in-migration: the case of Frankfurt-am-Main', in M. Douglass and J. Friedmann (eds) *Cities for Citizens: Planning and the Rise of Civil Society in a Global Age*, Chichester: Wiley, pp. 67–90.

Friend, J.K. and Jessop, W.N. (1969) *Local Government and Strategic Choice*, Oxford: Pergamon Press.

Friend, J.K., Power, J. and Yewlett, C.J.L. (1974) *Public Planning and the Intercorporate Dimension*, London: Tavistock Institute.

Gambetta, D. (1998) ' "Claro!" An essay on discursive machismo', in J. Elster (ed.) *Deliberative Democracy*, Cambridge: Cambridge University Press, pp. 19–43.

Gamson, W. (1995) *The Strategy of Social Protest,* Homewood, IL: Dorse Press.

Garmanikow, E. (ed.) (1978) 'Women and the city', special issue of *International Journal of Urban and Regional Research* 2/3.

Gibson, K. and Watson, S. (1995) 'Postmodern politics and planning: a postscript', in S. Watson and K. Gibson (eds) *Postmodern Cities and Spaces*, Oxford: Blackwell.

Giddens, A. (1984) *The Constitution of Society*, Cambridge: Polity Press.

Giddens, A. (1985) 'Reason without revolution? Habermas's *Theorie des Kommunikativen Handelns*', in R.J. Bernstein (ed.) *Habermas and Modernity*, Cambridge: Polity Press, in association with Basil Blackwell, London, pp. 95–121.

Giddens, A. (1990) *Consequences of Modernity*, Cambridge: Polity Press.

Giddens, A. (1998) *The Third Way*, Cambridge: Polity Press.

Giddens, A. (2000) *The Third Way and Its Critics*, Cambridge: Polity Press.

Gleeson, B. (2000) 'Reflexive modernization: the re-enlightenment of planning?', *International Planning Studies* 5(1): 117–135.

Goffman, E. (1959) *The Presentation of Self in Everyday Society*, Harmondsworth: Penguin.

Goldstein, H.A. (1984) 'Planning as argumentation', *Environment and Planning B: Planning and Design* 11(3): 297–312.

Goodchild, B. (1990) 'Planning and the modern/postmodern debate', *Town Planning Review* 61(2): 119–137.

Gordon, P. and Richardson, H. (1997) 'Are compact cities a desirable planning goal?', *Journal of the American Planning Association* Winter: 95–103.

Gottdiener, M. (1995) *Postmodern Semiotics: Material Culture and the Forms of Postmodern Life,* Oxford: Blackwell.

Graham, S. and Healey, P. (1999) 'Relational concepts of space and place: issues for planning theory and practice', *European Planning Studies* 7(5): 623–646.

Grant, J. (1994a) *The Drama of Democracy: Contention and Dispute in Community Planning*, Toronto: University of Toronto Press.

Grant, J. (1994b) 'On some public uses of planning "Theory" ', *Town Planning Review* 65(1): 59–76.

Grant, M. (1999) 'Planning as a learned profession', *Plans and Planners* 1: 21–26.

Gray, J. (1993) *Beyond the New Right: Markets, Government and the Common Environment*, London: Routledge.

Greed, C. (1994) *Women and Planning: Creating Gendered Spaces*, London: Routledge.

Gregson, N. and Rose, G. (2000) 'Taking Butler elsewhere: performativities, spatialities and subjectivities', *Environment and Planning D: Society and Space* 18: 433–452.

Grosz, E. (1995) *Space, Time, and Perversion*, New York: Routledge.

Guhathakurtu, S. (1999) 'Urban modelling and contemporary planning theory: is there a common ground?', *Journal of Planning Education and Research* 18(4): 281–292.

Gutmann, A. and Thompson, D. (1996) *Democracy and Disagreement*, Cambridge, MA: Harvard University Press.

Gutmann, A. and Thompson, D. (2000) 'Why deliberative democracy is different', *Social Philosophy and Policy* 17(1): 161–180.

Haber, H.F. (1994) *Beyond Postmodern Politics: Lyotard, Rorty, Foucault*, London: Routledge.

Habermas, J. (1979) *Communication and the Evolution of Society*, London: Heinemann.

Habermas, J. (1981) 'Modernity versus postmodernity', *New German Critique* Winter(22): 3–13.

Habermas, J. (1983) *The Theory of Communicative Action*, vol. 1, Cambridge, MA: The MIT Press.

Habermas, J. (1984) *The Theory of Communicative Action*, vol. 1, *Reason and the Rationalization of Society*, trans. T. McCarthy, Boston: Beacon Press.

Habermas, J. (1985) 'Questions and counterquestions', in R.J. Bernstein (ed.) *Habermas and Modernity*, Cambridge, MA: The MIT Press.

Habermas, J. (1987a) *The Theory of Communicative Action*, vol. 2, *Lifeworld and System: A Critique of Functionalist Reason*, trans. T. McCarthy, Boston: Beacon Press.

Habermas, J. (1987b) *The Philosophical Discourse of Modernity*, Cambridge: Polity Press.

Habermas, J. (1990) *Moral Consciousness and Communicative Action*. Cambridge, MA: The MIT Press.

Habermas, J. (1992a) 'Further reflections on the public sphere', in C. Calhoun (ed.) *Habermas and the Public Sphere*, Cambridge, MA: The MIT Press.

Habermas, J. (1995) *Die Normalität einer Berliner Republic*, Frankfurt: Suhrkamp.

Habermas, J. (1996a) *Between Facts and Norms,* Cambridge: Polity Press.

Habermas, J. (1996b) *Between Facts and Norms: Contributions to a Discourse Theory of Law and Democracy*, Cambridge, MA: The MIT Press.

Habermas, J. (1996c) *Die Einbeziehung des Anderen: Studien zur politischen Theorie*, Frankfurt: Suhrkamp.

Habermas, J. (1998) *The Inclusion of the Other,* Cambridge: Polity Press.

Habermas, J. (undated) *On the Relationship of Politics, Law and Morality*, Frankfurt: University of Frankfurt, Department of Philosophy.

Hage, G. (1998) *White Nation: Fantasies of White Supremacy in a Multicultural Society*, Sydney: Pluto Press.

Hague, C. (1991) 'A review of planning theory in Britain', *Town Planning Review* 62(3): 295–310.

Hague, C. (1995a) 'Introductory texts on urban and regional planning: a review article', *Town Planning Review* 66(2): 207–212.

Hague, C. (1995b) 'No more heroes any more?', *Planning Week* 20 July: 19.

Hague, C. (1996) 'Transforming planning: transforming the planners', paper presented at the 50th Anniversary conference, University of Newcastle, 25–27 October.

Hall, P. (1983) 'The Anglo-American connection: rival rationalities in planning theory and practice, 1955–1980', *Environment and Planning B: Planning and Design* 10: 41–46.

Hall, P. (1999) *Sustainable Cities or Town Cramming?*, London: Town and Country Planning Association.

Harper, T.L. and Stein, S.M. (1993) 'Normative ethical theory: Is it relevant to contemporary planning theory?', *Plan Canada*, September: 6–12.

Harper, T.L. and Stein, S.M. (1995a) 'Out of the postmodern abyss: preserving the rationale for liberal planning', *Journal of Planning Education and Research*, 14: 233–244.

Harper, T.L. and Stein, S.M. (1995b) 'Contemporary procedural ethical theory and planning theory', in S. Hendler (ed.) *Planning Ethics: A Reader in Planning Theory, Practice and Education*, New Jersey: Center for Urban Policy Research, pp. 49–65.

Harris, N. (1997) 'Orienting oneself to practice: a comment on Alexander', *Environment and Planning B: Planning and Design* 24(6): 799–801.

Harris, N. (1999) 'Working away from home: the import of philosophical understanding in the development of planning theory', *Journal of Planning Education and Research* 19(4): 101–105.

Harrison, A. (1977) *Economics and Land Use Planning*, London: Croom Helm.

Harrison, P. (1995) ' "The terrifying landscape of postmodernism": some pitfalls for planning education in South Africa', paper presented at the Toward and Beyond 2000: The Future of Planning and Planning Education conference, East London, June.

Harrison, P. (1996) 'Postmodernism confronts planning: some thoughts on an appropriate response', *Town and Regional Planning* 40: 26–34.

Harrison, P.J. (1998) 'Re-imagining planning: an engagement with postmodernism and pragmatism', unpublished PhD thesis, University of Natal, Durban, South Africa.

Hartsock, N. (1990) 'Foucault on power: a theory for women?' in L. Nicholson (ed.) *Feminism/Postmodernism*, New York: Routledge, pp. 157–175.

Harvey, D. (1987) 'Three myths in search of a reality in urban studies', *Environment and Planning D* 5: 367–376.

Harvey, D. (1989a) *The Condition of Postmodernity: An Enquiry into the Origins of Cultural Change*, Oxford: Blackwell.

Harvey, D. (1989b) 'From managerialism to entrepreneurialism: the transformation in urban governance in late capitalism', *Geografiska Annaler* 71B(1): 3–17.

Harvey, D. (1990) 'Looking backwards on postmodernism in A.C. Papadakis (ed.) *Postmodernism on Trial: Profile No. 88*, London: Academy Editions.

Harvey, D. (1992) 'Social justice, postmodernism and the city', *International Journal of Urban and Regional Research* 16(4): 588–601.

Harvey, D. (1993a) 'Class relations, social justice and the politics of difference', in J. Squires (ed.) *Principled Positions: Postmodernism and the Rediscovery of Value*, London: Lawrence & Wishart Limited.

Harvey, D. (1993b) 'From space to place and back again: reflections on the condition of postmodernity', in J. Bird *et al.* (eds) *Mapping the Futures: Local Cultures, Global Change*, London: Routledge.

Harvey, D. (1996) *Justice, Nature and the Geography of Difference*, Oxford: Blackwell Publishers.

Hayek, F.A. (1944) *The Road to Serfdom*, London: Routledge.

Hayek, F.A (1948a) *Individualism and Economic Order*, Chicago: Chicago University Press.

Hayek, F.A. (1948b) 'Individualism: true and false', in F.A. Hayek (ed.) *Individualism and Economic Order*, Chicago: Chicago University Press, pp. 1–32.

Hayek, F.A. (1948c) 'Economics and knowledge', in F.A. Hayek (ed.) *Individualism and Economic Order*, Chicago: Chicago University Press, pp. 33–56.

Hayek, F.A (1948d) 'The meaning of competition', in F.A. Hayek (ed.) *Individualism and Economic Order*, Chicago: Chicago University Press, pp. 92–106.

Hayek, F.A. (1952) *The Sensory Order*, Chicago: Chicago University Press.

Hayek, F.A. (1957) *The Counter-Revolution of Science*, London: Routledge.

Hayek, F.A. (1960) *The Constitution of Liberty*, London: Routledge.

Hayek, F.A. (1973) *Rules and Order*, Chicago: Chicago University Press.

Hayek, F.A. (1978) 'Competition as a discovery procedure', in *New Studies in Politics, Economics and the History of Ideas*, London: Routledge.

Hayek F.A. (1988) *The Fatal Conceit: The Errors of Socialism*, London: Routledge.

Healey, P. (1983) ' "Rational method" as a mode of policy formation and implementation in land-use policy', *Environment and Planning B: Planning and Design* 10(1): 19–39.

Healey, P. (1991) 'The content of planning education programmes: some comments from recent British experience', *Environment and Planning B: Planning and Design* 18(2): 177–189.

Healey, P. (1992a) 'Planning through debate: the communicative turn in planning theory', *Town Planning Review* 63(2): 143–162.

Healey, P. (1992b) 'A planner's day: knowledge and action in communicative practice', *Journal of the American Planning Association* 58, 9–20

Healey, P. (1992c) 'An institutional model of the development process', *Journal of Property Research* 9(1): 33–44.

Healey, P. (1993a) 'The communicative work of development plans', *Environment and Planning* 20: 83–104.

Healey, P. (1993b) 'Planning through debate: the communicative turn in planning theory', in F. Fischer and J. Forester (eds) *The Argumentative Turn in Policy Analysis and Planning*, London: UCL Press Ltd, pp. 233–253.

Healey, P. (1996a) 'The communicative turn in planning theory and its implications for spatial strategy formation', *Environment and Planning B: Planning and Design* 23(2): 217–234.

Healey, P. (1996b) Personal communication to Philip Allmendinger and Mark Tewdwr-Jones, dated 16 December 1996, Centre for Research in European Urban Environments, Department of Town and Country Planning, University of Newcastle, Newcastle (unpublished).

Healey, P. (1996c) 'Collaborative planning in a stakeholder society', paper presented at the 50th Anniversary conference, University of Newcastle, Newcastle, 25–27 October.

Healey, P. (1996d) 'The communicative work of development plans', in S. Mandelbaum, L. Mazza and R. Burchell (eds) *Explorations in Planning Theory*, New Brunswick: Center for Urban Policy Research.

Healey, P. (1997a) *Collaborative Planning: Shaping Places in Fragmented Societies*, Basingstoke: Macmillan.

Healey, P. (1997b) 'Introduction', *Planning Theory* 17: 10–12.

Healey, P. (1997c) 'Situating communicative practices: moving beyond urban political economy', *Planning Theory* 17: 65–82.

Healey, P. (1998) 'Collaborative planning in a stakeholder society', *Town Planning Review* 69(1): 1–21.

Healey P. (1999a) 'Institutionalist analysis, communicative planning and shaping places', *Journal of Planning Education and Research* 19: 111–121.

Healey, P. (1999b) 'Deconstructing communicative planning theory: a reply to Tewdwr-Jones and Allmendinger', *Environment and Planning A* 31(6): 1129–1135.

Healey, P. (2000) 'Planning theory and urban and regional dynamics: a comment on Yiftachel and Huxley', *International Journal of Urban and Regional Research* 24(4): 917–921.

Healey, P. and Barrett, S.M. (1990) 'Structure and agency in land and property development processes', *Urban Studies* 37(1): 89–104.

Healey, P., Cameron, S., Davoudi, S., Graham, S. and Mandani-Pour, A. (eds) (1995) *Managing Cities: The New Urban Context*, Chichester: John Wiley.

Healey, P., Doak, A., McNamara, P. and Elson, M. (1988) *Land Use Planning and the Mediation of Urban Change: The British Planning System in Practice*, Cambridge: Cambridge University Press.

Healey, P. and Hillier, J. (1996) 'Communicative micropolitics: a story of claims and discourses', *International Planning Studies* 1(2): 165–184.

Healey, P., Khakee, A., Motte, A. and Needham, B. (eds) (1997) *Making Strategic Spatial Plans: Innovation in Europe*, London: UCL.

Healey, P., McDougall, G. and Thomas, M.J. (1982) 'Theoretical debates in planning', in P. Healey, G. McDougall and M.J. Thomas (eds) *Planning Theory: Prospects for the 1980s*, Oxford: Pergamon Press.

Healey, P. and Underwood, J. (1978) 'Professional ideals and planning practice', *Progress in Planning* 9(2): 73–127.

Hemmens, G.C. (1980) 'New directions in planning theory: introduction', *Journal of the American Planning Association* 46(3): 259–260.

Hemmens, G. (1992) 'The postmodernists are coming, the postmodernists are coming', *Planning*, July: 20–21.

Hemmens, G. and Stiftel, B. (1980) 'Sources for the renewal of planning theory', *Journal of the American Planning Association*, 46: 341–345.

Hesse, M. (1980) *Revolutions and Reconstructions in the Philosophy of Science*, Bloomington: University of Indiana Press.

Higgins, M. and Allmendinger, P. (1999) 'The changing nature of public planning practice under the New Right: the legacies and implications of privatization', *Planning Practice and Research* 14(1): 39–67.

Hillier, J. (1993) 'To boldly go where no planners have ever . . .', *Environment and Planning D: Society and Space* 11(1): 89–113.

Hillier, J. (1995) 'Discursive democracy in action', in R. Domanski and T. Marszal (eds) *Planning and Socioeconomic Development*, Lodz: University Press, pp. 75–100.

Hillier, J. (1996a) 'Cultural values, social justice', paper presented at the 50th Anniversary Conference, Department of Town and Country Planning, University of Newcastle, Newcastle, 25–27 October.

Hillier, J. (1996b) 'Deconstructing the discourse of planning', in S.J. Mandelbaum, L. Mazza and R.W. Burchell (eds) *Explorations in Planning Theory*, New Jersey: Center for Urban Policy Research, pp. 289–298.

Hillier, J. (1998a) 'Beyond confused noise: ideas toward communicative procedural justice', *Journal of Planning Education and Research* 18: 14–24.

Hillier J. (1998b) 'Representation, identity, and the communicative shaping of place', in A. Light and J. Smith (eds) *The Production of Public Space*, Maryland: Rowman & Littlefield, pp. 207–232.

Hillier, J. (2000) 'Going round the back? Complex networks and informal associational action in local planning processes', *Environment and Planning A* 32: 33–54.

Hillier J. and van Looij, T. (1997) 'Who speaks for the poor?', *International Planning Studies* 2(1): 7–25.

Hirschman, A. (1970) *Exit, Voice and Loyalty*, Cambridge, MA: Harvard University Press.

Hoch, C. (1984) 'Doing good and being right – the pragmatic connection in planning theory', *American Planning Association Journal* 4(1): 335–345.

Hoch, C. (1992) 'The paradox of power in planning practice', *Journal of Planning Education and Research* 12: 206–215.

Hoch, C. (1994) *What Planners Do*, Chicago: Planners Press.

Hoch, C. (1996) 'A pragmatic inquiry about planning and power', in S. Mandelbaum, L. Mazza and R. Burchell (eds) *Explorations in Planning Theory*, New Brunswick: Center for Urban Policy Research.

Hoch, C. (1997a) 'Planning theorists taking an interpretive turn need not travel on the political economy highway', *Planning Theory* 17: 13–37.

Hoch, C. (1997b) 'A reply', *Planning Theory* 17: 83–85.

Hollinger, R. (1994) *Postmodernism and the Social Sciences: A Thematic Approach*, Thousand Oaks, CA: Sage Publications.

Hooper, A. (1982) 'Methodological monism or critical dualism? Reflections on Andreas Faludi's planning theory', *Built Environment* 8: 247–248.

Hooper, B. (1998) 'The poem of male desires: female bodies, modernity, and "Paris, Capital of the Nineteenth Century" ', in L. Sandercock (ed.) *Making the Invisible Visible: A*

Multicultural Planning History, Berkeley, CA: University of California Press, pp. 227–254.

Howe, E. (1994) *Acting on Ethics in City Planning*, New York: Rutgers State University of New York.

Howe, E. and Kaufman, J. (1979) 'The ethics of contemporary American planners', *Journal of the American Planning Association* 45(3): 243–255.

Howe, E. and Kaufman, J. (1981) 'The values of contemporary American Planners', *Journal of the American Planning Association* 47(3): 266–278.

Hudson, B. (1979) 'Comparative and current planning theories: counterparts and contradictions', *Journal of the American Planning Association* 45(4): 387–398.

Hunter, A. and Staggenborg, S. (1988) 'Local communities and organised action', in C. Milofsky (ed.) *Community Organisations*, Oxford: Oxford University Press, pp. 243–276.

Huxley, M. (1994a) 'Planning as a framework of power: utilitarian reform, Enlightenment logic and the control of urban space', in S. Ferber, C. Healy and C. McAuliffe (eds) *Beasts of Suburbia: Reinterpreting Cultures in Australian Suburbs*, Melbourne: Melbourne University Press, pp. 94–110.

Huxley, M. (1994b) 'Space, knowledge, power and gender', in L. Johnson (ed.) *Suburban Dreaming: An Interdisciplinary Approach to Australian Cities*, Geelong: Deakin University Press, pp. 181–192.

Huxley, M. (1996) 'Regulating spaces of production and reproduction in the city', in K. Gibson, M. Huxley, J. Cameron, L. Costello, R. Fincher, J. Jacobs, N. Jamieson, L. Johnson and M. Pulvirenti (eds) *Restructuring Difference: Social Polarisation and the City*, AHURI Working Paper 6, Melbourne: Australian Housing and Urban Research Institute, pp. 93–102.

Huxley, M. (1997) 'The "hidden injuries" of regulation: land-use/environmental/social control', paper presented at the Environmental Justice, Global Ethics for the 21st Century conference, University of Melbourne, 1–3 October.

Huxley, M. (1998a) 'The limits to communicative planning: a contribution to the critique of actually existing practice', paper presented to Planning Theory conference, Oxford, April.

Huxley, M. (1998b) 'If planning is anything, maybe it's geography', *Australian Planner* 36(3): 128–133.

Huxley, M. and Yiftachel O. (1998) 'New paradigm or old myopia? Unsettling the communicative turn in planning theory', paper presented at Planning Theory conference, Oxford: Oxford Brookes University, April.

Huxley, M. and Yiftachel, O. (2000) 'New paradigm or old myopia? Unsettling the communicative turn in planning theory', *Journal of Planning Education and Research* 19: 333–342.

Hwang, S.W. (1996) 'The implications of the nonlinear paradigm for integrated environmental design and management', *Journal of Planning Literature* 11: 167–187.

Innes, J. (1992) 'Group processes and the social construction of growth management: the case of Florida, Vermont and New Jersey', *Journal of the American Planning Association* 58: 275–278.

Innes, J. (1995) 'Planning theory's emerging paradigm: communicative action and interactive practice', *Journal of Planning Education and Research* 14(3): 183–190.

Innes, J. (1996) 'Planning through consensus building: a new view of comprehensive planning ideal', *Journal of the American Planning Association* Autumn: 460–472.

Innes, J. (1998a) 'Challenge and creativity in postmodern planning', *Town Planning Review* 69(2): v–ix.

Innes, J. (1998b) 'Information in communicative planning', *Journal of the American Planning Association* Winter: 52–63.

Innes, J. (1999a) 'Evaluating consensus building', in L. Susskind, S. McKearnan and J. Thomas-Larmer (eds) *The Consensus-Building Handbook*, Thousand Oaks, CA: Sage, pp. 631–675.

Innes, J. (1999b) 'Planning strategies in conflict: the case of the Metropolitan Transportation Commission', paper presented at the Association of European Schools of Planning conference, Bergen, July.

Innes, J. and Booher, D. (1998) 'Network power and collaborative planning: strategy for the informational age', paper presented at the Association of Collegiate Schools of Planning conference, Pasadena, November.

Innes, J. and Booher, D. (1999a) 'Consensus building and complex adaptive systems', *APA Journal* 65(4): 412–423.

Innes, J. and Booher, D. (1999b) 'Consensus building as role playing and bricolage: toward a theory of collaborative planning', *APA Journal* 65(4): 9–26.

Jacobs, J. (1961) *The Death and Life of Great American Cities*, Harmondsworth: Penguin Books Ltd.

Jacobs, J.M. and Fincher, R. (1998) 'Introduction', in R. Fincher and J.M. Jacobs (eds) *Cities of Difference*, New York: The Guilford Press.

Jacobs, M. (1992) *The Green Economy*, London: Pluto Press.

Jameson, F. (1984) 'Postmodernism, or the cultural logic of late capitalism', *New Left Review* 146: 53–92.

Jencks, C. (1986) *What Is Postmodernism?*, London: Academy Editions.

Joas, H. (1991) 'The unhappy marriage of hermeneutics and functionalism', in A. Honneth and H. Joas (eds) *Communicative Action*, Cambridge: Polity Press.

Joas, H. (1998) 'The inspiration of pragmatism: some personal remarks', in M. Dickstein (ed.) *The Revival of Pragmatism: New Essays on Social Thought, Law and Culture*, Durham, NC and London: Duke University Press.

Kaufman, J. and Escuin, M. (1996) 'A comparative study of Dutch, Spanish and American planner attitudes', paper presented at ACSP/AESOP Joint Congress, Toronto, October.

Kellner, D. (1988) 'Postmodernism as social theory', *Theory, Culture and Society* 5: 239–269.

Kellner, D. (1989) *Jean Baudrillard: From Marxism to Postmodernism and Beyond*, Cambridge: Polity Press.

Kemp, R. (1982) 'Critical planning theory – review and critique', in P. Healey, G. McDougall and M.J. Thomas (eds) *Planning Theory: Prospects for the 1980s*, Oxford: Pergamon, pp. 59–67.

Kemp, R. (1985) 'Planning, public hearings, and the politics of discourse', in J. Forester (ed.) *Critical Theory and Public Life*, Cambridge, MA and London: The MIT Press, pp. 177–201.

Kincheloe, J.L. and MacLaren, P.L. (1998) 'Rethinking critical theory and qualitative research', in N.K. Denzin and Y.S. Lincoln (eds) *The Landscape of Qualitative Research: Theories and Issues*, London: Sage, pp. 260–299.

Kirzner, I. (1985) *Discovery and the Capitalist Process*, Chicago: Chicago University Press.

Kirzner, I. (1992) *The Meaning of Market Process*, London: Routledge.

Kirzner, I. (1997) 'Entrepreneurial discovery and the competitive discovery process: an Austrian approach', *Journal of Economic Literature* 35: 66–85.

Kitchen, T. (1997) *People, Politics, Policies and Plans: The City Planning Process in Contemporary Britain*, London: Paul Chapman.

Kloppenberg, J. (1998) 'Pragmatism: an old name for some new ways of thinking', in M. Dickstein (ed.) *The Revival of Pragmatism: New Essays on Social Thought, Law and Culture,* Durham, NC and London: Duke University Press.

Koczanowicz, L. (1999) 'The choice of tradition and the tradition of choice: Habermas' and Rorty's interpretation of pragmatism', in *Philosophy and Social Criticism* 25(1): 55–70.

Krumholz, N. (1982) 'A retrospective view of equity planning', *Journal of the American Planning Association* 48(2): 163–183.

Krumholz, N. (1994) 'Dilemmas of equity planning: a personal memoir', *Planning Theory* 10/11: 45–56.

Kuhn, T. (1970) *The Structure of Scientific Revolutions*, Chicago: Chicago University Press.

Laclau, E. (1996a) *Emancipation(s)*, London: Verso.

Laclau, E. (1996b) 'Deconstruction, pragmatism, hegemony', in C. Mouffe (ed.) *Deconstruction and Pragmatism*, London and New York: Routledge.

Laclau, E. (1997) 'Subject of politics, politics of the subject', in R. Bontekoe and M. Stepaniants (eds) *Justice and Democracy*, Honolulu: University of Hawaii Press, pp. 363–379.

Laclau, E. and Mouffe, C. (1985) *Hegemony and Socialist Strategy: Towards a Radical Democratic Politics*, London: Verso Books.

Lakatos, I. (1978) *The Methodology of Scientific Research Programmes*, Cambridge: Cambridge University Press.

Lapintie, K. (1998) 'Analysing and evaluating argumentation in planning', *Environment and Planning B: Planning and Design* 25(2): 187–204.

Latour, B. (1987) *Science in Action*, Cambridge, MA: Harvard University Press.

Lauria, M. (1997) 'Communicating in a vacuum: will anyone hear?', *Planning Theory* 17: 40–42.

Lauria, M. and Soll, M.J. (1996) 'Communicative action, power, and misinformation in a site selection process', *Journal of Planning Education and Research* 15: 199–211.

Lauria, M. and Whelan, R. (1995) 'Planning theory and political economy: the need for reintegration', *Planning Theory* 14: 8–13.

Lavoie, D. (1985) *Rivalry and Central Planning*, New York: Cambridge University Press.

Lax D. and Sebenius, J. (1986) *The Manager as Negotiator*, New York: Free Press.

Lee, K. (1993) *Compass and Gyroscope: Integrating Science and Politics for the Environment*, Washington, DC: Island Press.

Leontidou, L. (1993) 'Postmodernism and the city: Mediterranean versions', *Urban Studies* 30(6): 920–965.

Leontidou, L. (1996) 'Alternatives to modernism in (southern) urban theory: exploring in-between spaces', *International Journal of Urban and Regional Research* 20(2): 178–195.

Lewi, H. and Wickham, G. (1996) 'Modern urban government: a Foucaultian perspective', *Urban Policy and Research* 14(1): 51–64.

Lewis, B. (1998) 'Postmodernism and literature', in S. Sim (ed.) *The Icon Critical Dictionary of Postmodern Thought*, London: Icon Books.

Lewis, R. (ed.) (1992) *Rethinking the Environment*, London: Adam Smith Institute.

Lim, G.C. (1986) 'Toward a synthesis of contemporary planning theories', *Journal of Planning Education and Research* 5(2): 75–85.

Lindblom, C. (1959) 'The science of muddling through', *Public Administration Review* 19: 79–88.

Lodge, D. (1977) 'Modernism, anti-modernism and postmodernism', inaugural lecture delivered at the University of Birmingham, 2 December.

Long, M. (1982) *Moral Regime and Model Institutions: Precursors of Town Planning in Early Victorian England*, Department of Civic Design Working Paper 20, Liverpool: University of Liverpool.

Longino, H. (1990) *Science as Social Knowledge*, Princeton, NJ: Princeton University Press.

Low, N. (1991) *Planning, Politics and the State: Political Foundations of Planning Thought*, London: Unwin Hyman.

Luhmann, N. (1982) *The Differentiation of Society*, New York: Columbia University Press.

Lyon, D. (1993) 'An electronic panopticon? A sociological critique of surveillance theory', *Sociological Review* 41(4): 653–678.

Lyotard, J.-F. (1984) *The Postmodern Condition*, Manchester: Manchester University Press.

Mabin, A. (1995) 'On the problems and prospects of overcoming segregation and fragmentation in southern Africa's cities in the postmodern era', in S. Watson and K. Gibson (eds) *Postmodern Cities and Spaces*, Oxford: Blackwell, pp. 187–198.

McAdam, D. (1996) 'Conceptual origins, current problems, future directions', in D. McAdam, J. McCarthy and M. Zald (eds) *Comparative Perspectives on Social Movements*, Cambridge: Cambridge University Press, pp. 23–40.

McAdam, D., McCarthy, J. and Zald, M. (eds) (1996) *Comparative Perspectives on Social Movements*, Cambridge: Cambridge University Press.

McArdle, J. (1999) *Community Development in the Market Economy*, Melbourne: Vista.

McCarthy, T. (1981) *The Critical Theory of Jürgen Habermas*, Cambridge, MA: The MIT Press.

McCarthy, T. (1991) 'Complexity and democracy: or seducements of systems theory', in A. Honneth and H. Joas (eds) *Communicative Action*, Cambridge: Polity Press.

Macedo, S. (ed.) (1999) *Deliberative Politics*, Oxford: Oxford University Press.

Machiavelli, N. (1984) *The Prince*, Harmondsworth: Penguin.

McKean, M. and Ostrom, E. (1995) 'Common property regimes in the forest: just a relic from the past?', *Unaslyva* 46: 3–15.

McLoughlin, J.B. (1994) 'Centre of periphery? Town planning and spatial political economy', *Environment and Planning A* 26: 1111–1122.

McNay, L. (1992) *Foucault and Feminism: Power, Gender and the Self*, Cambridge: Polity Press.

McNay, L. (1994) *Foucault: A Critical Introduction*, Cambridge: Polity Press.

Madsen, D. (1995) *Postmodernism: A Bibliography, 1926–1994*, Amsterdam: Rodopi.

Mahowald, M. (1997) 'What classical American philosophers missed: Jane Addams, critical pragmatism and cultural feminism', *The Journal of Value Inquiry* 31: 39–54.

Maloney, W., Jordan, G. and McLaughlin, A. (1994) 'Interest groups and public policy: the insider/outsider model revisited', *Journal of Public Policy* 14(1): 17–38.

Mandelbaum, S.J. (1990) 'Reading plans', *Journal of the American Planning Association* Summer: 350–356.

Mandelbaum, S.J. (1991) 'Telling stories', *Journal of Planning Education and Research* 10(3): 209–214.

Mandelbaum, S.J. (1993) 'Reading old plans', *Journal of Policy History* 5(1): 189–198.

Mandelbaum, S.J. (1996) 'The talk of the community', in S. Mandelbaum, L. Mazza and R. Burchell (eds) *Explorations in Planning Theory*, New Jersey: Center for Urban Policy Research.

Mandelbaum, S.J., Mazza, L. and Burchell, R.W. (eds) (1996) *Explorations in Planning Theory*, New Jersey: Center for Urban Policy Research.

Mansbridge, J. (1992) 'A deliberative theory of interest representation', in M. Petracca (ed.) *The Politics of Interests*, Boulder: Westview Press, pp. 32–57.

Mansbridge, J. (1995) 'A deliberative perspective on neocorporatism', in E. Wright (ed.) *Associations and Democracy*, London: Verso, pp. 133–147.

Marcuse, P. (1976) 'Professional ethics and beyond: values in planning', *Journal of the American Institute of Planners* 42: 264–294.

Marks, J. (1995) 'A new image of thought', in *Michel Foucault: j'accuse: New Formations* 25: 66–76.

Marquand, D. (1996) 'Moralists and hedonists', in D. Marquand and A. Seldon (eds) *The Ideas that Shaped Post-War Britain*, London: Harper-Collins.

Massey, D. (1994) *Space, Place and Gender*, Minneapolis: University of Minnesota Press.

Matless, D. (1998) *Landscape and Englishness*, London: Reaktion Books.

Melucci, A. (1988) 'Social movements and the democratisation of everyday life', in J. Keane (ed.) *Civil Society and the State*, London: Verso, pp. 245–260.

Melucci, A. (1989) *Nomads of the Present*, London: Radius.

Melucci, A. (1996) *Challenging Codes*, Cambridge: Cambridge University Press.

Miller, J. (1993) *The Passion of Michel Foucault*, New York: Simon and Schuster.

Milofsky, C. (ed.) (1987) *Community Organisations*, New York: Oxford University Press.

Moore-Milroy, B. (1989) 'Constructing and deconstructing plausibility', *Environment and Planning D* 7(3): 313–326.

Moore-Milroy, B. (1991) 'Into postmodern weightlessness', *Journal of Planning Education and Research* 10(3): 181–187.

Moore-Milroy, B. (2000) 'Cracks, light, energy', in K. Miranne and A. Young (eds) *Gendering the City: Women, Boundaries, and Visions of Urban Life*, Lanham, MD: Rowman and Littlefield, pp. 209–217.

Morone, J. (1990) *The Democratic Wish*, New York: Basic Books.

Morrow, R.A. and Brown, D.D. (1994) *Critical Theory and Methodology, Contemporary Social Theory*, vol. 3, London: Sage.

Mouffe, C. (1992) *Dimensions of Radical Democracy*, London: Verso.

Mouffe, C. (1993) *The Return of the Political*, London: Verso.

Mouffe, C. (1996) 'Deconstruction, pragmatism and the politics of democracy', in C. Mouffe (ed.) *Deconstruction and Pragmatism*, London: Routledge, pp. 1–12.

Mouffe, C. (1997) 'Democratic identity and pluralist politics', in R. Bontekoe and M. Stepaniants (eds) *Justice and Democracy*, Honolulu: University of Hawaii Press, pp. 381–393.

Mouffe, C. (1998) 'Blairism: Thatcher's final victory', *CSD Bulletin* 6(1): 11–13.

Mouffe, C. (1999) 'Deliberative democracy or agonistic pluralism?', *Social Research* 66(3): 745–758.

Mulgan, G. (1997) *Connexity*, London: Chatto & Windus.

Muller, J. (1998) 'Paradigms and planning practice: conceptual and contextual considerations', *International Planning Studies* 3(3): 287–302.

Murdoch, J., Abram, S. and Marsden, T. (1998) 'Modalities of planning: a reflection on the persuasive powers of the development plan', *Town Planning Review* 70(2): 191–212.

Meyerson, M. and Banfield, E. (1955) *Politics, Planning and the Public Interest*, New York: Free Press.

Myerson, G. and Rydin, Y. (1994) 'Environment and planning: a tale of the mundane and the sublime', *Environment and Planning D* 12: 437–452.

Nelson, R. (1977) *Zoning and Property Rights*, Cambridge, MA: Harvard University Press.

Neuman, M. (1998) 'Planning, governing and the image of the city', *Journal of Planning Education and Research* 18: 61–71.

Nietzsche, F. (1954) *Twilight of the Idols*, New York: Penguin (1968 edition).

Nietzsche, F. (1966) *Beyond Good and Evil*, New York: Vintage Books.

Norris, C. (1985) *The Contest of Faculties: Philosophy and Theory after Deconstruction*, London: Methuen.

O'Driscoll, G. and Rizzo, M. (1985) *The Economics of Time and Ignorance*, New York and Oxford: Basil Blackwell.

O'Neill, John. (1995) *The Poverty of Postmodernism*, New York: Routledge.

Oranje, M. (1995) 'Postmodern world, modern/postmodern South Africa: in search of a rationale, role and methodology for planning', paper presented at the Toward and Beyond 2000: The Future of Planning and Planning Education conference, East London, June.

Oranje M. (1996) 'Modernising South Africa and its forgotten people under postmodern conditions', paper presented at the 50th Anniversary Conference, University of Newcastle, Newcastle, 25–27 October.

Oranje, M. (1997) 'The language game of South African urban and regional planning: a cognitive mapping from the past into the future', unpublished PhD thesis, University of Pretoria, Pretoria, South Africa.

Oranje, M. (1999) 'Using South African frames on land use, roads and transport planning and "development" as a counter-frame to the paradigm-based/framed approach to planning and "planning change" ', paper presented at the 'Planning Futures' conference, University of Sheffield, 29–31 March.

Ostrom, C. (1992) *Crafting Institutions for Self-governing Irrigation Systems*, San Francisco: ICS Press.

Ostrom, E. (1990) *Governing the Commons*, Cambridge: Cambridge University Press.

Outhwaite, W. (1994) *Habermas: A Critical Introduction*, Oxford: Polity Press in association with Blackwell Publishers.

Painter, J. and Goodwin, M. (1995) 'Local governance and concrete research: investigating the uneven development of regulation', *Economy and Society* 24: 334–356.

Paris, C. (ed.) (1982) *Critical Readings in Planning Theory*, Oxford: Pergamon.

Parker, M. (1993) 'Life after Jean-François', in J. Hassard and M. Parker (eds) *Postmodernism and Organizations*, London: Sage.

Parker, D. and Stacey, R. (1994) *Chaos, Management and Economics: The Implications of Non-Linear Thinking*, London: Institute of Economic Affairs.

Parton, J. (1869) 'Log-rolling at Washington', *Atlantic* 24 (Sep.): 361–378.

Pearce, D. (1989) *Blueprint for a Green Economy*, London: Earthscan.

Pennington, M. (1997) 'Budgets, bureaucrats and the containment of urban England', *Environmental Politics* 6(4): 76–107.

Pennington, M. (1999) 'Free market environmentalism and the limits of land use planning', *Journal of Environmental Policy and Planning* 1(1): 43–59.

Pennington, M. (2000) *Planning and the Political Market: Public Choice and the Politics of Government Failure*, London: Athlone Press.

Perkin, H. (1987) *The Rise of Professional Society: England since 1880*, London and New York: Routledge.

Petracca, M. (ed.) (1992) *The Politics of Interests*, Boulder, CO: Westview Press.

Phelps, N.A. and Tewdwr-Jones, M. (2000) 'Scratching the surface of collaborative and associative governance: identifying the diversity of social action in institutional capacity building', *Environment and Planning A* 32(1): 111–130.

Pihlstron, S. (1998) 'Peirce vs James: Susan Haack on old and new pragmatism', *The Philosophical Forum* XXIX(2): 66–89.

Pigou, A.C. (1920) *The Economics of Welfare*, London: Macmillan.

Pile, S. and Rose, G. (1992) 'All or nothing: politics and critique in the modernism-postmodernism debate', *Environment and Planning D* 10: 123–136.

Poulton, M.C. (1991) 'The case for a positive theory of planning. Part 1: What is wrong with planning theory?', *Environment and Planning B: Planning and Design* 18(2): 225–232.

Poxon, J. (2001) 'Shaping the planning profession of the future: the role of planning education', *Environment and Planning B: Planning and Design* 28(4): 563–580.

Pruitt, D. (1991) 'Strategic choice in negotiation', in W. Breslin and J. Rubin (eds) *Negotiation Theory and Practice*, Program on Negotiation, Cambridge, MA: Harvard Law School, pp. 27–46.

Putnam, H. (1998) 'Pragmatism and realism', in M. Dickstein (ed.) *The Revival of Pragmatism: New Essays on Social Thought, Law and Culture*, Durham, NC and London: Duke University Press.

Rabinow, P. (ed.) (1984) *The Foucault Reader*, London: Penguin Books.

Rabinow, P. (1989) *French Modern: Norms and Forms of the Social Environment*, Chicago: The University of Chicago Press.

Rabinow, P. (1994) 'Modern and counter-modern: ethos and epoch in Heidegger and Foucault', in G. Gutting (ed.) *The Cambridge Companion to Foucault*, Cambridge: Cambridge University Press, pp. 197–214.

Rajchman, J. (1988) 'Habermas's complaint', *New German Critique* 45: 163–191.

Ravetz, J. (1999) 'Citizen participation for integrated assessment: new pathways in complex systems', *International Journal of the Environment and Pollution* 11(3): 331–350.

Reade, E. (1987) *British Town and Country Planning*, Milton Keynes: Open University Press.

Reiger, K. (1985) *The Disenchantment of the Home: Modernising the Australian Family, 1880–1940*, Melbourne: Oxford University Press.

Rein, M. and Schön, D. (1993) 'Reframing policy discourse', in F. Fischer and J. Forester (eds) *The Argumentative Turn in Policy Analysis and Planning*, London: UCL Press.

Reuter, W. (1997) 'Power and discourse in planning', *Planning Theory* 18: 132–141.

Rhodes, R. and Marsh, D. (1992) 'Policy networks in British politics', in D. Marsh and R. Rhodes (eds) *Policy Networks in British Government*, Oxford: Clarendon Press, pp. 1–26.

Richardson, H. (1995) 'Beyond the good and the right: towards a constructive ethical pragmatism', *Philosophy and Public Affairs* 24(2): 108–141.

Richardson, J. and Jordan, A. (1979) *Governing Under Pressure*, Cambridge: Martin Robertson.

Richardson, T. (1996) 'Foucauldian discourse: power and truth in urban and regional policy making', *European Planning Studies* 4(3): 279–292.

Richardson, T. (1997) 'The Trans-European Transport Network: environmental policy integration in the EU', *European Urban and Regional Studies* 4(4): 333–346.

Richardson, T. (forthcoming) 'Before the pendulum swings again: grounding the new transport realism', *Environmental Politics*.

Robinson, J. (1990) ' "A perfect system of control?" State power and "native locations" in South Africa', *Environment and Planning D: Society and Space* 8: 135–162.

Robinson, J. (2000) 'Power as friendship: spatiality, femininity and "noisy surveillance" ', in C. Philo, P. Routledge and J. Sharp (eds) *Entanglements of Power*, London: Routledge, pp. 67–93.

Rorty, R. (1982) *Consequences of Pragmatism*, Minneapolis: University of Minnesota Press.

Rorty, R. (1989) *Contingency, Irony and Solidarity*, Cambridge: Cambridge University Press.

Rorty, R. (1991) *Objectivism, Relativism and Truth: Philosophical Papers*, vol. 1, Cambridge: Cambridge University Press.

Rose, N. (1999) *Powers of Freedom: Reframing Political Thought*, Cambridge: Cambridge University Press.

Rosenau, P.M. (1992) *Post-modernism and the Social Sciences: Insights, Inroads and Intrusions*, Princeton: Princeton University Press.

Rosenfeld, M. (1998) 'Pragmatism, pluralism and legal interpretation: Posner and Rorty's justice without metaphysics meets hate speech', in M. Dickstein (ed.) *The Revival of Pragmatism: New Essays on Social Thought, Law and Culture*, Durham, NC and London: Duke University Press.

Routledge, P. (1997) 'The imagineering of resistance: Pollock Free State and the practice of postmodern politics', *Transactions of the Institute of British Geographers* NS 22: 359–376.

Roweis, S. (1983) 'Urban planning as professional mediation of territorial politics', *Environment and Planning D: Society and Space* 1: 139–162.

Rubin, J. (1991) 'Some wise and mistaken assumptions about conflict and negotiation', in W. Breslin and J. Rubin (eds) *Negotiation Theory and Practice*, Program on Negotiation, Cambridge, MA: Harvard Law School, pp. 3–12.

Sabatier, P. (1987) 'Knowledge, policy-oriented learning and policy change', *Knowledge* 8(4): 649–687.

Sager, T. (1990) *Communicate or Calculate: Planning Theory and Social Science Concepts in a Contingency Perspective*, Dissertation 11, Nordic Institute for Studies in Urban and Regional Planning.

Sager, T. (1994) *Communicative Planning Theory*, Aldershot: Ashgate.

Samuels, A. (1993) *The Political Psyche*, London: Routledge.

Sancar, F.H. (1994) 'Paradigms of postmodernity and implications for planning and the design review process', *Environment and Behaviour* 26(3): 3–37.

Sandercock, L. (1995) 'Voices from the Borderlands: a meditation on a metaphor', *Journal of Planning Education and Research* 14: 77–88.

Sandercock, L. (1997) 'The planner tamed: preparing planners for the twenty-first century', *Australian Planner* 34(2): 90–95.

Sandercock, L. (ed.) (1998a) *Making the Invisible Visible: A Multicultural Planning History*, Berkeley, CA: University of California Press.

Sandercock, L. (1998b) 'The death of modernist planning: radical praxis for a postmodern age', in M. Douglass and J. Friedmann (eds) *Cities for Citizens: Planning and the Rise of Civil Society in a Global Age*, Chichester: John Wiley & Sons Ltd.

Sandercock, L. (1998c) *Towards Cosmopolis*, London: John Wiley.

Savage, M. and Witz, A. (eds) (1992) *Gender and Bureaucracy*, Oxford: Blackwell.

Sawicki, J. (1991) *Disciplining Foucault: Feminism, Power and the Body*, New York: Routledge.

Sayer, A. (1994) 'Cultural studies and "the economy, stupid"', *Environment and Planning D* 12: 635–637.

Sayer, A. and Storper, M. (1997) 'Ethics unbound: for a normative turn in social theory', *Environment and Planning D: Society and Space* 15: 1–17.

Scheffler, I. (1974) *Four Pragmatists: A Critical Introduction to Peirce, James, Mead, and Dewey*, London: Routledge and Kegan Paul.

Schmidtz, D. (1994) 'Market failure?', *Critical Review* 7: 525–537.

Schön, D. (1983) *The Reflective Practitioner*, New York: Basic Books.

Schön, D. and Rein, M. (1994) *Frame Reflection: Towards the Resolution of Intractable Policy Controversies*, New York: Basic Books.

Scott, A.J. and Roweis, S.T. (1977) 'Urban planning in theory and practice: a reappraisal', *Environment and Planning A* 9: 1097–1119.

Seigfried, C. (1996) *Pragmatism and Feminism: Reweaving the Social Fabric*, Chicago: University of Chicago Press.

Sennett, R. (1973) *The Uses of Disorder*, Harmondsworth: Pelican Books.

Shackle, G. (1972) *Epistemics and Economics*, Cambridge: Cambridge University Press.

Shapiro, I. (1999) 'Enough of deliberation: politics is about interests and power', in S. Macedo (ed.) *Deliberative Politics*, Oxford: Oxford University Press, pp. 28–38.

Sharp, L. and Richardson, T. (1999) ' "Using Foucault" – reflections on discourse analytics in planning and environmental policy research', paper presented at the 'Planning Futures' conference, University of Sheffield, 29–31 March.

Shearmur, J. (1996) *Hayek and After: Classical Liberalism as a Research Programme*, London: Routledge.

Shiffer, M.J. (1992) 'Towards a collaborative planning system', *Environment and Planning B: Planning and Design* 19(6): 709–722.

Short, J.R. (1993) 'The "myth" of postmodernism', *Tijdschrift voor Econ. en Soc. Geografie* 84(3): 169–171.

Shotter, J. (1993) *Conversational Realities: Constructing Life Through Language*, London: Sage.

Sibley, D. (1998) 'Problematising exclusion: reflections on space, difference and knowledge', *International Planning Studies* 3(1): 93–100.

Silver, C. (1991) 'The racial origins of zoning: southern cities from 1910–40', *Planning Perspectives* 6: 189–205.

Sim, S. (ed.) (1998) *The Icon Critical Dictionary of Postmodern Thought*, Cambridge: Icon Books.

Simon, D. (1998) 'Rethinking (post)modernism, postcolonialism, and posttraditionalism: South-North perspectives', *Environment and Planning D* 16: 219–245.

Simon, J. (1995) *Foucault and the Political*, London: Routledge.

Simonsen, K. (1990) 'Planning on postmodern conditions', *Acta Sociologica* 33: 51–62.

Smith, L.G., Nell, C. and Prystupa, M. (1997) 'The converging dynamics of interest representation in resources management', *Environmental Management* 21(2): 139–146.

Soderstrom, O. (1996) 'Paper cities: visual thinking in urban planning', *Ecumene* 3(3): 249–279.

Soja, E. (1997) 'Planning in/for postmodernity', in G. Benko and V. Strohmayer (eds) *Space and Social Theory: Interpreting Modernity and Postmodernity*, Oxford: Blackwell.

Stallybrass, P. and White, A. (1986) *The Politics and Poetics of Transgression*, London: Methuen.

Steele, D.R. (1992) *From Marx to Mises*, La Salle, IL: Open Court.

Sudjic, D. (1993) *The 100-Mile City*, London: Flamingo.

Susskind, L McKearnan, S. and Thomas-Larmer, J. (eds) (1999) *The Consensus-Building Handbook: A Comprehensive Guide to Reaching Agreement*, Thousand Oaks, CA: Sage.

Taylor, N. (1980) 'Planning theory and the philosophy of planning', *Urban Studies* 17: 159–168.

Taylor, N. (1998) *Urban Planning Theory Since 1945*, London: Sage.

Taylor, N. (1999) 'Anglo-American town planning theory since 1945: three significant developments but no paradigm shifts', *Planning Perspectives* 14(4): 327–345.

Tett, A. and Wolfe, J.M. (1991) 'Discourse analysis and city plans', *Journal of Planning Education and Research* 10(3): 209–214.

Tewdwr-Jones, M. (1995) 'Development control and the legitimacy of planning decisions', *Town Planning Review* 66(2): 163–181.

Tewdwr-Jones, M. (1996) 'Reflective planning theorising and professional protectionism', *Town Planning Review* 67(2): 235–247.

Tewdwr-Jones, M. (1999) 'Reasserting town planning: challenging the image and representation of the planning profession', in P. Allmendinger and M. Chapman (eds) *Planning Beyond 2000*, Chichester: John Wiley & Sons, pp. 123–149.

Tewdwr-Jones, M. and Allmendinger, P. (1998) 'Deconstructing communicative rationality: a critique of Habermasian collaborative planning', *Environment and Planning A* 30: 1975–1989.

Tewdwr-Jones, M. and Harris, N. (1998) 'The New Right's commodification of planning control', in P. Allmendinger and H. Thomas (eds) *Urban Planning and the British New Right*, London: Routledge.

Tewdwr-Jones, M. and Thomas, H. (1998) 'Collaborative action in local plan-making: planners' perceptions of "planning through debate" ', *Environment and Planning B: Planning and Design* 25(1): 127–144.

Thayer, H.S. (1968) *Meaning and Action: A Critical History of Pragmatism*, Bobbs-Merrill: New York.

Thayer, H.S. (1982) 'Introduction', in H.S. Thayer (ed.) *Pragmatism: The Classic Writings*, Indianapolis: Hackett Publishing Company.

Thayer, H.S (1985) 'John Dewey', in M.G. Singer (ed.) *American Philosophy*, Cambridge: Cambridge University Press.

Thomas, H. (ed.) (1994) *Values and Planning*, Aldershot: Avebury.

Thomas, H. (1996) 'Public participation in planning', in M. Tewdwr-Jones (ed.) *British Planning Policy in Transition*, London: UCL Press.

Thomas, H. and Healey, P. (eds) *Dilemmas of Planning Practice: Ethics, Legitimacy and the Validation of Knowledge*, Aldershot: Avebury.

Thomas, M.J. (1982) 'The procedural planning theory of A. Faludi', in C. Paris (ed.) *Critical Readings in Planning Theory*, Oxford: Pergamon Press.

Thompson, J. and Tuden, A. (1959) 'Strategies, structures and processes of organisational decision', in J. Thompson and A. Tuden (eds) *Comparative Studies in Administration*, Pittsburgh: University of Pittsburgh Press.

Thornley, A. (1991) *Urban Planning Under Thatcherism*, London: Routledge.

Thornley, A. (1993) *Urban Planning Under Thatcherism: The Challenge of the Market*, 2nd edn, London: Routledge.

Throgmorton, J.A. (1992) 'Planning as persuasive storytelling about the future: negotiating an electric power rate settlement in Illinois', *Journal of Planning Education and Research* 12: 17–31.

Throgmorton, J. (2000) 'Practising as a skilled voice-in-the-flow', paper presented at Habitus 2000 Conference, Perth, September.

Tilly, C. (1975) 'Revolutions and collective violence', in F. Greenstein and N. Polsby (eds) *Handbook of Political Science*, vol. 3, Reading, MA: Addison-Wesley.

Topalov, C. (1990) 'From the "social question" to "urban problems": reformers and the working classes at the turn of the twentieth century', *International Social Science Forum* 125: 319–336.

Topalov, C. (1993) 'The city as *terra incognita*: Charles Booth's poverty survey and the people of London, 1886–1891', *Planning Perspectives* 8: 395–425.

Turner, D.K., Pearce, D. and Bateman, I. (1994) *Environmental Economics: An Elementary Introduction*, Brighton: Harvester.

Underwood, G. (ed.) (1996) *Implicit Cognition*, New York: Oxford University Press.

Underwood, G. and Bright, J.E.H. (1996) 'Cognition with and without awareness', in G. Underwood (ed.) *Implicit Cognition*, Oxford: Oxford University Press.

Underwood, J. (1980) *Town Planners in Search of a Role*, Bristol: School of Advanced Urban Studies Occasional Paper, University of Bristol.

Urban Task Force (1999) *Towards an Urban Renaissance*, Final Report of the Urban Task Force chaired by Lord Rogers of Riverside, London: E and FN Spon.

Valk, A.J. van der (1989) 'Amsterdam in aanleg: planvorming en dagelijks handelen 1850–1900', *Planologische Studies* 8, Amsterdam: Planologisch en Demografisch Instituut, Universiteit van Amsterdam.

Varian, H. (1994) 'Markets for Public Goods?', *Critical Review* 7(4): 539–556.

Verma, N. (1996) 'Pragmatic rationality and planning theory', *Journal of Planning Education and Research* 16: 5–14.

Voogd, H. and Woltjer, J. (1999) 'The communicative ideology in spatial planning: some critical reflections based on the Dutch experience', *Environment and Planning B: Planning and Design* 26(6): 835–854.

Wachs, M. (1985) *Ethics in Planning*, New York: State University of New Jersey.

Wachs, M. (1989) 'When planners lie with numbers', *Journal of the American Planning Association* 55(4): 476–479.

Walker, R. (1994) 'Social movements/world politics', *Millennium* 23(3): 669.

Walkowitz, J. (1992) *City of Dreadful Delight: Narratives of Sexual Danger in Late Victorian London*, London: Virago.

Wallas, G. (1926) *The Art of Thought*, New York: Franklin Watts.

Walzer, M. (1999) 'Deliberation, and what else?', in S. Macedo (ed.) *Deliberative Politics*, Oxford: Oxford University Press, pp. 58–69.

Ward, S.C. (1996) *Reconfiguring Truth: Postmodernism, Science Studies, and the Search for a New Model of Knowledge*, London: Rowman & Littlefield Publishers, Inc.

Warren, R., Warren, S., Nunn, S. and Warren, C. (1998) 'The future of the future in planning: appropriating cyberpunk visions of the city', *Journal of Planning Education and Research* 18: 49–60.

Watson, S. (1990) *Playing the State: Australian Feminist Interventions*, London: Verso.

Watson, S. (1996) 'Spaces of the "Other": planning for cultural diversity in Western Sydney', in K. Darian-Smith, L. Gunner and S. Nuttall (eds) *Text, Theory, Space: Land, Literature and History in South Africa and Australia*, London: Routledge.

Watson, S. and Gibson, K. (eds) (1995) *Postmodern Cities and Spaces*, Oxford: Blackwell.

Weber, E. (1998) *Pluralism by the Rules*, Washington, DC: Georgetown University Press.

Weedon, C. (1997) *Feminist Practice and Poststructuralist Theory*, 2nd edn, Oxford: Blackwell.

West, C. (1993) *Keeping Faith: Philosophy and Race in America*, New York and London: Routledge.

West, W.A. (1969) *Private Capital for New Towns*, Occasional Paper 28, London: Institute of Economic Affairs.

Westman, C. (1996) 'David Ray Griffin and constructive postmodern communalism', in T.W. Tilley (ed.) *Postmodern Theologies: The Challenge of Religious Diversity*, New York: Orbis Books.

White, S.K. (1988) *The Recent Work of Jürgen Habermas: Reason, Justice and Modernity*, Cambridge: Cambridge University Press.

Wickham, G. (1991) 'Theorising Sociology in the face of postmodernism', *Australian and New Zealand Journal of Sociology* 27(3): 351–368.

Wilson, E. (1991) *The Sphinx in the City: Urban Life, the Control of Disorder, and Women*, London: Virago.

Wilson, G. (1990) *Interest Groups*, Oxford: Blackwell.

Wilson, T.D. and Stone, J.I. (1985) 'Limitation of self knowledge: More on telling more than we can know', *Review of Personality and Social Psychology* 6: 167–193.

Wirka, S. (1998) '*City Planning for Girls*: exploring the ambiguous nature of women's planning history', in L. Sandercock (ed.) *Making the Invisible Visible: A Multicultural Planning History*, Berkeley, CA: University of California Press, pp. 150–162.

Wittgenstein, L. (1958) *Philosophical Investigations*, Oxford: Blackwell.

Wolfe, A. (1998) 'The missing pragmatic revival in American social science', in M. Dickstein (ed) *The Revival of Pragmatism: New Essays on Social Thought, Law and Culture*, Durham, NC and London: Duke University Press.

Wolin, S. (1996) 'Fugitive democracy', in S. Benhabib (ed.) *Democracy and Difference*, Princeton, NJ: Princeton University Press, pp. 31–45.

Wong, C. (1997) 'Old wine in a new bottle? Planning methods and techniques in the 1990s', unpublished working paper, University of Manchester.

Yiftachel, O. (1992) *Planning a Mixed Region in Israel: The Political Geography of Arab–Jewish Relations in the Galilee*, Avebury: Gower Publishing.

Yiftachel, O. (1995a) 'Planning as control: policy and resistance in a deeply divided society', *Progress in Planning* 44: 115–184.

Yiftachel, O. (1995b) 'The dark side of modernism: planning as control of an ethnic minority', in S. Watson and K. Gibson (eds) *Postmodern Cities and Spaces*, Oxford: Blackwell, pp. 216–242.

Yiftachel, O. (1996) 'Regional policy and ethnic relations: Arabs and Jews in the Galilee, in Y. Gradus and G. Liposhitz (eds), *The Mosaic of Israeli Geography*, Beer Sheva: The Negev Center for Regional Development, Ben-Gurion University of the Negev, pp. 237–247.

Yiftachel, O. (1998) 'Planning and social control: exploring the dark side', *Journal of Planning Literature*, 12: 395–406.

Yiftachel, O. and Huxley, M. (2000) 'Debating dominance and relevance: notes on the "communicative turn" in planning theory', *International Journal of Urban and Regional Research*, 24(4): 907–913.

Young, I. (1995) 'Social groups in associative democracy', in E. Wright (ed.) *Associations and Democracy*, London: Verso, pp. 207–213.

Young, I. (1997) 'Asymmetrical reciprocity: on moral respect, wonder and enlarged thought', *Constellation* 3(3): 340–363.

Young, I.M. (1993) 'Together in difference: Transforming the logic of group political conflict', in J. Squires (ed.) *Principled Positions: Postmodernism and the Rediscovery of Value*, London: Lawrence & Wishart Limited.

Young, T.R. (1991) 'Chaos and social change: metaphysics of the postmodern', *The Social Science Journal* 28(3): 289–305.

Index